HIGHER EDUCATION FOR DEMOCRACY

Experiments in Progressive Pedagogy at Goddard College

EDITED BY
Steven A. Schapiro

PETER LANG
New York · Washington, D.C./Baltimore · Boston · Bern
Frankfurt am Main · Berlin · Brussels · Vienna · Canterbury

LIBRARY OF CONGRESS CATALOGING-IN-PUBLICATION DATA

Higher education for democracy: experiments in progressive
pedagogy at Goddard College / edited by Steven A. Schapiro.
p. cm. — (Higher ed; vol. 1)
Includes bibliographical references and index.
1. Goddard College. 2. Progressive education—United States.
3. Democracy—Study and teaching (Higher)—United States. I. Title.
II. Series: Higher ed (New York, N.Y.); vol. 1.
LD2001.G452.S33   378.743'4—DC21   98-30466
ISBN 0-8204-4107-4
ISSN 1523-9551

DIE DEUTSCHE BIBLIOTHEK-CIP-EINHEITSAUFNAHME

Higher education for democracy: experiments
in progressive pedagogy at Goddard College / ed. by Steven A. Schapiro.
–New York; Washington, D.C./Baltimore; Boston; Bern;
Frankfurt am Main; Berlin; Brussels; Vienna; Canterbury: Lang.
(Higher ed; Vol. 1)
ISBN 0-8204-4107-4

Cover design by Nona Reuter

The paper in this book meets the guidelines for permanence and durability
of the Committee on Production Guidelines for Book Longevity
of the Council of Library Resources.

© 1999 Peter Lang Publishing, Inc., New York

Printed in the United States of America

This book is dedicated to those at Goddard College—students, staff, and faculty—who have worked so hard to keep alive the democratic spirit in education.

ACKNOWLEDGMENTS

This book has grown out of many years of conversations at Goddard College, where faculty, students and staff are engaged in an ongoing experiment about how best to engage in educational practices that are based, as the college's mission statement asserts, "on the principles of progressive education and the ideals of democracy." While most of us have been far too busy teaching to take as much time out as we'd like to reflect on what we have been learning from those experiments, this book has developed out of efforts to do just that, and to share those reflections and learnings with others. I want to thank, first of all, my students who, during my fourteen years of teaching at Goddard, have constantly inspired me and challenged me to practice what I preach. I would also like to thank all of my faculty and staff colleagues, from whose thinking about education I continue to learn. In particular, I want to thank my colleagues represented in this book, who accepted my invitation to put down on paper some of those insights that we share in our faculty meetings and at the lunch table.

I would also like to thank the members of the Institute for Democracy in Education, the North Dakota Study Group, and the Folk and People's Education Association of America who have welcomed me into their conversations and inspired me with their work; Jill Mattuck Tarule at the College of Education at the University of Vermont for her hospitality during a sabbatical leave when I began work on this volume; and several colleagues who gave me helpful feedback on early drafts of some of what follows: Maxine Greene, Carl Glickman, Katherine Jelly, Ken Bergstrom, Richard Schramm, Kathleen Kesson, Shelley Vermilya, Eduardo Aquino, Gus and Geraldine Lyn-Piluso, and Nora Mitchell. I would also like to express my appreciation to the members of my men's group—Tom, Greg, Peter, Richard, and Ken—for their support and encouragement. Katherine Jelly, my spouse, has taught me more than anyone else about the respect and mutuality that true democracy requires, and she has done so much to help me find the time and the energy that I needed to finish this project. My sons—Joshua and Eli—have continued to remind me, in their own ways, that democratic education begins at home. Their approach to life gives me much hope for the future. While this book would not be what it is without the contributions of all of those named above, the responsibility and blame for any shortcomings remain mine.

I would like to acknowledge the following for their permission to reprint the copyrighted poems that are quoted in Nora Mitchell's chapter, "But I Don't Read Poetry: Relearning to Read Literature": Mark Doty, "Brilliance," from *My Alexandria,* copyright 1993 by Mark Doty, used with the permission of the University of Illinois Press; W.C. Williams, "To a Poor Old Woman," from *Selected Poems*, copyright 1985, used by permission of New Directions Publishing Company; James Wright, "The Jewel," from *Above the River: The*

Complete Poems, copyright 1990 by Anne Wright, Wesleyan University Press, by permission of University Press of New England. I would also like to thank: Alexia Camberas and Jeff Tonn for permission to print their poems, and Kristin Lougheed for permission to reproduce her drawing in that same chapter; the following for permission to quote from their unpublished memoirs written as part of their work at Goddard College and included in Shelley Vermilya's chapter, "Writing Our Lives": Allison Bluj, David Boyce, Yolanda Brown, Claudia Conlan, Marisa Durden, April Faye, Kathleen Hope, Chanda Martin, Chris Remick, Terry Stoecker, Lisa Townsend; and Goddard colleagues Caryn Goldberg, Ralph Lutts, and Cherry Muhanji for use of their quotations included in Vermilya's chapter.

Steven A. Schapiro
Montpelier, Vermont

CONTENTS

Part 3: Conclusion

Part One

Introduction

ONE

Higher Education for Democracy:
Renewing the Mission of Progressive Education

Steven A. Schapiro

The purpose of this book is to serve as a source of ideas and inspiration for those interested in how higher education can, in theory and in practice, support the development of a more democratic society, both through its own practices and through the support it can and must provide for the movement toward more democratic practices in our K-12 schools. Building on the legacy of the progressive education movement of the '30s and '40s, which held education for democracy to be one of its central tenets, the book explores: the enduring principles and practices of that earlier movement; the new challenges facing democracy to which our schools and colleges must respond; and some new principles and practices that are now being developed as the historical legacy of progressive education is brought up to date. The concept of "education for democracy" can once again bring together, in new ways, the progressive goals of fostering individual development within democratic communities.

The book uses as its basis the historical legacy and current experiments being conducted at Goddard College in Plainfield, Vermont, which was founded over 60 years ago to put into practice at the post-secondary level the democratic and progressive educational philosophy of John Dewey, William Heard Kilpatrick, and others with whom they worked. For those who are attempting to teach in more progressive and democratic ways, there is much to learn from in the history of that experiment, and in the current innovations being developed today.

When Goddard College was founded, at the core of its mission, in the words of its president, Royce "Tim" Pitkin, was the preparation of students "to assume the responsibilities of membership in a democratic society" (in Benson and Adams, 1987, 59). Those responsibilities were defined in response to the challenges to democracy that our society was confronting at that time, economic depression at home and a rising tide of fascism abroad. The central question that this book addresses is what should a renewed education for democracy consist of, both at Goddard and elsewhere, if it is to respond to the different set of challenges facing us today.

That same year (1938) in which the new Goddard College received its charter, Boyd Bode, an Ohio State University professor with whom Tim Pitkin studied at a special summer program at Yale in 1931, published a book titled *Progressive Education at the Crossroads*. In that book Bode joined a chorus of other progressive educators who, during the mid-late 1930s, were attempting to bring together under the banner of "education for democracy" the two diverging strands of the progressive education movement: the child-centered strand, which had come to characterize the movement during the '10s and '20s and that looked to freedom, self-direction, and the flowering of personality and individuality as its defining elements; and the social reconstructionist strand, which, in response first to the problems of industrialism brought on during the first part of this century, and again and more forcefully in response to the economic and social problems of the great depression, called on the schools, in George Counts' words, to "dare [to] build a new social order" (Counts, 1932). Counts and other social reconstructionists of the time indicted the Progressive Education Association's alleged ties to the upper middle class and its philosophy of extreme individualism, and called on the group to align itself more with the needs of the working class and to work for the creation of a classless society and collectivist economic system.

In using the concept of education for democracy as an overarching concept that could weave these two strands together, Bode and his like-minded colleagues, including W.H. Kilpatrick (a protégé of John Dewey and one of Pitkin's professors at Teachers College, Columbia, who chaired the planning meeting at which the new Goddard College plan was developed) maintained that progressive education needed to become "an avowed exponent of a democratic philosophy of education," (Bode, 1932, 122) arguing essentially that progressive education was based on the democratic ideal of the full individual development of each person in her unique personality, and that such a development could occur best in a particular kind of society and community, a participatory democratic community. In their view, progressive education therefore needed to base its programs on a vision of that sort of social order. Or, as Kilpatrick put it in the first edition of the new journal, *Frontiers of Democracy*, to "accept democracy both as end and as means" (in Bowers, 1969, 176). While some of the more radical reconstructionists had, as noted above, been calling on the schools to help create a socialist economy along the lines of those in the Soviet Union in order to deal with the economic problems exacerbated by the Depression, Bode and others argued for democratic processes that might or might not lead to a particular outcome, maintaining that schools should help students learn how to identify social problems and develop their own solutions; to ask their own questions and come to their own conclusions. As Kilpatrick put it, "we need not a planned society, but a planning society" (1933, 172).

The rise of fascism in Europe at this time, and the subsequent outbreak of WW II , also helped bring to the fore the question of the meaning of American democracy and of what the schools and colleges could do to defend it and extend it. During this period, from the mid '30s to the late '40s, education for democracy came to be more and more identified with the role of the schools in general and of the progressive education movement in particular. In 1939, for example, the American Federation of Teachers adopted as their slogan, "Education for Democracy: Democracy in Education." The 1938, 1939, and 1940 editions of the yearbook of the John Dewey Society, collections of essays by major thinkers in the field, were titled *Democracy and the Curriculum, Educational Freedom and Democracy*, and *Teachers for Democracy*. The October 31, 1938 cover of *Time* magazine featured Frederick Redefer (executive director of the Progressive Education Association), with the accompanying lead article concluding that "the first principle and religion of Progressive Education is Democracy, and their biggest question, how to achieve it."

It was in this context that the new plan for Goddard was developed and put into practice. While other progressive colleges, such as Bard, Sarah Lawrence, and Bennington were created in the late '20s or early '30s, and grew more out of the child-centered movement, emphasizing individuality and the expression of the creative personality, Goddard grew out of the intense social and political ferment of the Depression years, and out of a blend of the social reconstuctionist and child-centered approaches. Goddard's emphasis on education for democracy was clearly reflected in the college's plan to include: self-directed study and self-evaluation (recognizing the uniqueness of each personality); work program (emphasizing the dignity of manual labor and the need for everyone in a community to do his share); community government (modeled after the Vermont town meeting and embodying a participatory approach to democracy); and social action projects (within the College and within the larger community). These elements of the Goddard curriculum enabled the college to address what Pitkin saw as the need for "colleges to contribute to the building of a democratic society" by helping students to "learn the techniques of social action" and find ways to "devote themselves to the reconstruction of society" (in Benson and Adams, 1987, 59).

The outbreak of WWII made Goddard's democratic mission even more central. Again in Pitkin's words:

> As Goddard was getting up on its feet so to speak, the world was in the chaos of World War II. After 300 years of steady progress, democracy was on the defensive and fascism was in the ascendancy.....there was no assurance that democracy would survive....Military power alone could not save it. The only power that could save it was spiritual power. *The college had to function to cultivate this spiritual power* [emphasis mine]. Neglect of this function in an emergency is treason. Unless the masses of people believe in democracy and are loyal to its principles, unless they have the will and the spirit and the understanding to make democracy work, the battle is lost (in Benson and Adams, 1987, 62).

This emphasis on education for democracy and the democratic spirit was clearly not meant in narrow political terms, but was based on Dewey's conception of democracy as a moral and ethical ideal. In his seminal 1888 article, "The Ethics of Democracy," Dewey drew on James Russel Lowell's thesis that "democracy, in a word, is a social, that is to say, an ethical conception, and upon its ethical significance is based its significance as governmental" (in Dewey, 1881, 18), and went on to say in his own words, "Democracy and the one, the ultimate ethical ideal of humanity are to my mind, synonymous. The ideal of democracy, the ideal of liberty, equality, fraternity represents a society in which the distinction between the spiritual and the secular has ceased (1888, 28). Years later, in his 1916 book *Democracy and Education*, he defined this ideal as follows:

> A democracy is more than a form of government; it is primarily a form of associated living, of conjoint communicated experience.... It is the name of a way of life of free and enriching communion in which free social inquiry is indissolubly wedded to the art of full and moving communication....(1916, 81)

This view of democracy began with the individual: "Democracy means that personality is the first, final reality....Personality is the one thing of permanent and abiding worth, and...in every human being there lies personality..." (Dewey, 1888, 22), but it was only through participation in community life that personality and individuality could be realized. As Robert Westbrook explains in his recent book, *John Dewey and American Democracy*, this conception of democracy made Dewey throughout his life our society's

> most important advocate of participatory democracy; that is, of the belief that democracy as an ethical ideal calls upon men and women to build communities in which the necessary opportunities and resources are available for every individual to realize fully his or her particular capacities and powers through participation in political, social, and cultural life. (Westbrook, 1991, xiv-xv)

Defined in this way, democracy must be thought of not as something that has already been achieved, but as an ideal that we are always striving to reach, an unrealized project that we must continually struggle to complete. In that respect, it is both "a vision of an ideal society, and a process by which this vision can be pursued" (Goodman, 1992, 1).

In our continuing struggle to fulfill and extend the democratic ideal, I believe that the concept of democratic education (democracy in education and education for democracy) can still provide the unifying and overarching focus that progressive education needs, both at Goddard and elsewhere. In bringing together the personal and the political, individual development and community development, this vision for democracy can potentially reconcile and weave together the strands of progressive education that are still at times being pulled in different directions; the student-centered strand with its emphasis on self-directed learning, personal growth, and self-actualization; and the social reconstructionist strand, with its renewed emphasis on education for social change, and more recent focus on helping individuals and groups to overcome the effects of oppression based on issues of gender, race, and other aspects of social identity. But our conceptualization of the means and ends of democratic education must be redefined and brought up to date. As Dewey and Childs said in 1933 in the *Educational Frontier*, written during that first crossroads for progressive education, our "social and educational theories and conceptions must be developed with definite reference to the needs and issues which mark and divide our domestic, economic, and political life in the generation of which we are a part" (in Kilpatrick, 1933, 36). If the earlier progressive education movement in general and the specific program and plan for a school for living and an education for democracy of the Goddard College of the late '30s and '40s grew out of the context, problems, and issues of that time, we must then ask the question: what should be the key elements of an education for democracy that responds to the context and challenges of this generation?

This question is being asked once again with the same fervor as it was in the '30s and '40s. A review of library catalogues shows that for the first time since then, the topic of democracy and education has again become a major theme in educational literature, with numerous titles on the topic published in the last few years. Just last year, conferences of two of the major professional organizations for educators, the Association for Supervision and Curriculum Develop-ment and the Association for Teacher Educators, focused on the theme of democracy and education. The Annenberg Foundation for school reform has just launched a new initiative organizing a network of democratic schools, and the Institute for Democracy and Education has for the past ten years published a new journal called *Democracy and Education*. A recurring theme in all of these writings and initiatives is the need to reclaim democracy as the central purpose of schooling in this society, transcending the need to outdo the foreign competition or prepare students for the needs of the workplace and appealing to larger purposes than vocationalism and narrow self-interest.

While it is beyond the scope of this introduction to delve deeply into any of the issues and trends currently confronting us and contributing to this re-emphasis on the relationship between democracy and education, some of these issues can be identified as follows:

- the end of the cold war, which has deprived the country of an adversary against which to define itself and led many people to look more critically at the shortcomings of democracy in America;
- the growing power of multinational corporations and multimedia conglo-merates;
- the continuing decline of voting rates, of participation in civic associations, and of a sense of community in our towns, cities, and suburbs;
- an increasing awareness of how oppression around issues of race, gender, class, sexual orientation, and so on, deprive so many of their full develop-ment and humanity and of the opportunity to be fully equal participants in American society;
- the growing influence of post-modernism and post-structuralism, which has

brought an increasing awareness of how our forms of reason and knowledge are embedded in personal biography, social history, and group relations, leading in turn to extreme skepticism about any truth claims and about any common values or principles, and to an emphasis on the particularities of individual and group identity as opposed to an emphasis on what we have in common;

- the emphasis in our culture on extreme individualism, on self-interest and on rights, with much less attention to common interests and to mutual responsibilities;

- the increasing multiculturalism of American society, the increasing globalization of our world economies, and the increasing realization of a global interdependence.

These developments create both challenges and opportunities for the future of American democracy, with the potential for an increase in liberty and equality for many, but with a potential as well for increased fragmentation, alienation, and isolation. They pose new challenges and raise new questions about how to educate for democracy in response, questions such as the following:

- How can we help students to acquire the skills, attitudes, dispositions, and knowledge they will need in order to be active and responsible democratic citizens, able both to: (1) participate in democratic deliberation, discourse, and decision-making, and also (2) examine critically and when necessary reconstruct our economic, political, and social institutions?

- How can we create democratic learning communities which recognize and affirm the diversity of all of our members; that is, how can we remove the impediments and assure that all can participate with equal voice and equal access to power?

- How can we affirm and develop each student's individual and particular identity while also helping each of them to develop a commitment to the common good?

- How can we help students to work for social, political, and environmental reconstruction, as they define such terms, without falling into the traps of dogmatism, political elitism, and sectarianism; that is, how can we help them to become both committed and searching?

- How can we affirm new epistemologies and new ways of constructing meaning, while maintaining a common discourse and common standards of scholarship?

In order to respond to these challenges and find answers to these questions, progressive higher education must re-emphasize and build on the elements that we have inherited, such as: the freedom to engage in self-directed learning, the collaborative learning process of the group study, the dignity of manual work, the lessons to be learned from cooperative living and democratic decision-making in the small community, and the process of identifying and solving shared social problems. But we must add to those elements a commitment to the principles I will describe below, and we must be intentional and deliberate in applying them. It is not enough to hope that if students are given the freedom to follow their own interests and run their own communities, the desired competencies, awareness, and knowledge will automatically develop. We need to teach to our aims; to help our students not only to become empowered but also to be enabled; to help them to not only find their voices but also learn how to use those voices in constructive and responsible ways.

I believe that a renewed democratic education for our times, education for liberty, equality, and community, must be characterized by a commitment to the following principles of democratic education that have been developed and articulated over the course of the past quarter century.

- *critical pedagogy*: which helps students to identify and critically analyze the gap between our vision of a more just and democratic society, and our present reality; and to engage in collaborative struggle with others to transform that reality; education that, to quote Giroux and Maclaren, engages students in both "a discourse of critique and a project of possibility." (in Goodman, 1992, xii)
- *feminist pedagogy*: which is based in an ethic of care, concern, and mutual responsibility, and which helps students to make connections between the personal and the political, between themselves and others, and between their experience and their construction of knowledge; an approach that helps people become more aware of the individual and social construction of our gender identities and of our individual and collective power to deconstruct and then reconstruct those identities and the social norms and structures that support them.
- *multicultural pedagogy*: which helps us to recognize and affirm our cultural and racial differences, that accepts and nurtures multiple ways of knowing; that helps us to constructively engage with "others" and with "otherness," and that helps us to see that the path to true community comes through conflict and an embracing of our differences, not through attempting to make those conflicts and those differences disappear.
- *participatory democracy*: which is a form of democracy that, following Dewey, engages us all as active participants in the civic and community life of our schools, our cities, and our neighborhoods; a "strong democracy," in Barber's terms (1984), that supplements but does not replace representative democracy, and as an educational principle, calls for the participation of students and teachers in curriculum planning, in mutual evaluation, and in school governance and that calls for the active participation of our schools and colleges (and therefore of our teachers and students) in the lives of our communities; a form of democracy that must be supported by new forms of *civic education* which can help students to learn the democratic arts of listening, collaborating, deliberating, and decision-making; and the tools and techniques of civil discourse and public problem-solving.

In applying these four principles or approaches, it can be useful to think in terms of the components of an educational program that they should address, components that can be conceptualized as: instructional practice (the process of teaching and learning); curricular content (what people are learning about);

organizational structure and policies (how decisions are made and who makes them); interpersonal dynamics (how people relate to one another) (Goodman, 1992). Education for democracy in these times must find a way to address each of the above principles in each of these areas.

From Practice to Theory

The chapters that follow include essays written by (current or former) Goddard faculty describing either: a specific educational experiment/experience and what they learned from it or a general teaching approach or structure and their learnings about that. Each chapter includes in different forms a discussion of: the aims or goals of the specific experiment/experience/structure/process (what people were trying to accomplish or learn, what problem they were trying to solve); a narrative or description of the experiment/experience/structure/process (what happened); and reflections on and learnings from that experiment (implications for theory, and for future practice, unresolved questions). Through this process of analysis and reflection we have been able to move from questions, to experience, to new theory and new questions drawn from the lessons of practice.

These chapters are preceded by a preface to that section which describes more fully the context—the Goddard College of the 1990s—in which these experiments were carried out, and the principles and democratic practices that provide a common foundation for all of Goddard's educational programs. The specific chapters in this "practice to theory" section of this volume can each be described briefly as follows.

In *Knowledge, Authority, and Dialogue: Teaching as an Emancipatory Relationship*, Gus and Geraldine Lyn-Piluso reflect on their experience team-teaching a course on "Ecology and the Politics of Meaning" and on their long-distance mentoring work with individual students, and explore topics such as: problematizing knowledge claims in the classroom, teacher as facilitator/authority, teaching as dialogue, and the problems and process of liberatory teaching with adult students.

In *A Pedagogy of Reciprocity: Interdisciplinary Art Education at Goddard*, Eduardo Aquino describes how Goddard's student-centered, dialogical, and naturally interdisciplinary approach to learning and teaching with adult students, and in particular a new MA program in interdisciplinary art, provide an opportunity to move beyond the traditional constraints of institutionalized art education and provide art students with support for their natural creative process and for a new democratization of art-making and meaning making. By implication, he also describes how such an approach can be used with students in other fields of study, with similar results.

In my chapter, *Toward a Pedagogy of the "Oppressor": A Freirian Approach to Anti-Sexist Education for Men*, I draw on principles and practices from human relations training, Freirian education for critical consciousness, and anti-oppression education to describe the key dimensions of an integrated pedagogy for men's consciousness-raising that I have developed in my teaching at Goddard and elsewhere. This pedagogy, which can be adapted for use with members of both dominant and subordinant groups, was developed in response to the following questions or problems: How can we engage men in the study of gender issues and of men and masculinity in ways that can help them to critically examine traditional gender roles and structures and to consider alternatives, without having them feel attacked and threatened in ways that lead to defensiveness and resistance? How in general can we help people to grow and change in regard to issues of oppression, without subjecting them to coercion, indoctrination, or other forms of political correctness? How can we do these things in a student-centered way that at once raises issues of social justice and also involves learners in genuine inquiry and collaborative construction of knowledge in regard to issues of real and meaningful concern?

In *Writing for Our Lives: The Power of Memoir for Marginalized Students,* Shelley Vermilya draws on her work as a mentor/advisor in the college's undergraduate external degree program, to explore how autobiographical writing, within the context of the program's self-directed learning, dialogical relationship with a faculty mentor, and strong community of learners, has the potential to lead to empowering results for members of socially marginalized groups. In this chapter, which she wrote in collaboration with some of her colleagues and students, Vermilya explains both the means and the ends of what she calls this "identity pedagogy."

In *But I Don't Read Poetry: Relearning to Read Literature,* Nora Mitchell draws on her teaching experiments in Goddard's resident undergraduate program, and on the work of Kolb and Rosenblatt to describe an emerging approach to teaching literature that begins with each student's experience, not with an analysis of texts. By the time students reach college or graduate school, they have developed habits of and assumptions about reading. In the classroom, they treat books as sources of information, or as intricately wrought puzzles with a correct solution. In contrast, reading a poem or a novel can productively be framed as a form of experiential learning. Through intersections between reader-response and experiential learning theories, new approaches to teaching literature are developed.

In *Investigating Spiritual Experience: Progressive Pedagogy and the Non-Rational,* Kathleen Kesson explores how Goddard's democratization of the curriculum can raise a number of perplexing epistemological and pedagogical issues that can challenge some of the tenets of progressivism. For example, the interests of many of our students lie outside the canon of mainstream knowledge (e.g. alternative healing, mysticism, queer theory, transpersonal psychology, deep ecology). Ways of knowing as well as content areas are contested: students sometimes scorn logic in favor of intuition, eschew scientific method, and resist theorizing experience. Beneath the surface of a potentially emancipatory curriculum, however, lurk the ghosts of our collective academic past; and questions of rigor, intellectual integrity, the limits of interdisciplinarity, and the problem of standards are ever-present. This chapter explores, through a case study of a small group of students studying Wicca, how the author dealt with some of these complex issues, and how she negotiates the overlapping, but sometimes contradictory terrains of progressivism and postmodernism, pointing the way toward the principles of a postmodern spiritual pedagogy, a progressive approach to the study of nonrational experience.

In *Between Individual and Society: An Essential Dialectic in Progressive Teaching and Learning*, Katherine Jelly uses her description and analysis of the goals, teaching and learning processes, topics of inquiry, and learning outcomes of two group studies, "The Self and Others: Unraveling Human Relations" and "Alternatives in Education in Theory and Practice," to explore the interaction between individual and social aims, processes, and outcomes, and to discuss the profound and necessary relationship between individual development and social reconstruction. In so doing, she provides detailed examples of a democratic curriculum negotiation process and of successful ways to integrate individual and social concerns within the progressive classroom.

In *Learning to Teach as We Were Not Taught: Democratic Teacher Education at Goddard College,* Ken Bergstrom describes how learners' experience with Goddard's democratic pedagogy of self-directed learning, dialogic communication, and authentic assessment, with an emphasis on the importance of teacher self-knowledge, can help prospective teachers learn to teach as they were not taught in their own K-12 experience. Drawing on the seven domains of teaching that form the core of Goddard's teacher education program and on the author's experience working with students in Goddard's teacher education program and illustrated with anecdotes and vignettes of the author's work with students in that program, this chapter discusses a conscious reconstruction of this preparation program around students' self-exploration of personal resistance and the moral aspect of the call to teach, and a determination to model good practice and collegiality to help produce a cadre of teachers who integrate their practice into their lives.

In *Democratic Education: Judy and the Dance,* Carl Glickman discusses what he learned in his year as a visiting faculty member at Goddard, how he and his colleagues are applying those learnings in their work at the University of Georgia, and what small progressive colleges and large research universities can learn from each other in tightening the connection between pedagogy, schooling, and democracy.

In the final chapter in this practice to theory section, *Extending Democracy from Classroom to Schoolhouse: Studying Democratic Governance at Goddard College*, Richard Schramm looks at the benefits of placing higher educational activities within a democratic college and the elements that need to be in place for a school to be operated democratically. The chapter highlights the importance of the organizational structures that support democratic governance and, using Goddard College as a case study, suggests ways in which a college's governance system, from board of trustees on down, can be organized more democratically. It also reports how the "Task Force" model used to carry out this study enhanced group learning and supports a faculty role of partner with students, rather than a role of directive teacher or passive resource person.

The *conclusion* synthesizes the lessons of practice drawn from these experiences, while also articulating some of the challenges, questions, and contradictions that we at Goddard and other democratic educators around the country still need to resolve. It is my hope that this book will help us both to recognize the strengths of what we are already doing and to develop the focus and commitment to address those shortcomings. It is in a recognition of where we fall short, of where we are uncertain, and where we are confused, that we have the potential for growth. We need to have both the courage to act on our convictions and the courage to face and confront our doubts and our conflicts.

Some 40 years ago, at a meeting marking the demise of the Progressive Education Association as a separate organization, Boyd Bode said:

> If democracy is here to stay, then the spirit of progressive education can never become obsolete. We may discard the name...but we can never surrender the vision which it has tried to bring us. (in Graham, 1967, 145)

That vision has in fact continued to thrive and develop, but not without a struggle. It is up to people at places like Goddard, and the other schools and colleges across the country where teachers are committed to these ideals, to keep that vision, and that democratic spirit in education, alive.

14 *Introduction*

References

Barber, B. 1984. *Strong Democracy: Participatory Politics for a New Age.* Berkeley: University of California Press.

———.1992. *An Aristocracy of Everyone: The Politics of Education and the Future of America.* New York: Ballantine Books.

Benson, A.G. and F. Adams. 1987. *To Know for Real: Royce S. Pitkin and Goddard College.* Adamant, Vermont: Adamant Press.

Beyer, L.E. and D.P. Liston. 1996. *Curriculum in Conflict: Social Visions, Educational Agendas, and Progressive School Reform.* New York: Teachers College Press.

Bode, B. 1938. *Progressive Education at the Crossroads.* New York: Arno Press.

Bowers, C.A. 1969. *The Progressive Educator and the Depression: The Radical Years.* New York: Random House.

Bunch, C. and S. Pollack, S. eds. 1983. *Learning Our Way: Essays in Feminist Education.* Trumansburg, New York: The Crossing Press.

Counts, G. 1932. *Dare the School Build a New Social Order?* New York: Arno Press.

Dewey, J. 1888. *The Ethics of Democracy.* Ann Arbor: Andrews and Co.

———1916. *Democracy and education.* New York: Free Press..

Goodman, J. 1992. *Elementary Schooling for Critical Democracy.* Albany, New York: SUNY Press.

Graham, P.A. 1967 *Progressive Education from Arcady to Academe: A History of the Progressive Education Association, 1919–1955.* New York: Teachers College Press.

hooks, b. 1994. *Teaching to Transgress: Education as the Practice of Freedom.* New York: Routledge.

Kilpatrick, W.H., ed. 1933. *The Educational Frontier.* New York: The Century Co.

Lappe, F.M. and P.M. Dubois.1994. *The Quickening of America.* San Francisco: Jossey-Bass.

Mclaren, P. and C. Sleeter, eds. 1995. *Multicultural Education, Critical Pedagogy, and the Politics of Difference.* Albany, New York: SUNY Press.

Shor, I. 1992 *Empowering Education: Critical Teaching for Social Change.* Chicago: University of Chicago Press.

Soder, R. ed.1996. *Democracy, Education, and the Schools.* San Francisco: Jossey-Bass.

Westbrook, R.W. 1991. *John Dewey and American Democracy.* Ithaca, New York: Cornell University Press.

Part Two

From Practice to Theory:

Learning from New Experiments

in Progressive Pedagogy

The Context: Goddard College[*]

Goddard is a small college in rural Vermont for plain living and hard thinking. Founded in 1938 as successor to Goddard seminary, a respected secondary school in Barre, Vermont, dating back to 1863, Goddard is recognized for innovation in education. Its mission is to advance the theory and practice of learning by undertaking new experiments based upon the ideals of democracy and on the principles of progressive education first asserted by John Dewey. At Goddard, students are regarded as unique individuals who will take charge of their learning and collaborate with other students, staff, and faculty to build a strong community. Goddard encourages students to become creative, passionate, lifelong learners, working and living with an earnest concern for others and for the welfare of the Earth.

—From the Goddard College Mission Statement

The College was chartered by the State of Vermont in March of 1938 as "an institution of learning for secondary and higher education." Its aims included making work necessary to the maintenance and operation of the College part of its curriculum, and providing educational opportunities for adults. Both are important aspects of the Goddard College of 1998.

The College was planned to be small, so that students, faculty, and staff would know one another and work together in the manner of a Vermont village (combining "rugged individualism" with neighborly cooperation). The few remaining facilities of Goddard Seminary and Junior College were transferred to the new Goddard campus on the Greatwood Farms Estate in nearby Plainfield in 1938.

The College was to apply the principles and practices of "progressive education," eschewing lectures for inquiry and problem-solving based as much as possible in practical experience. Its curriculum would place the arts and the philosophy and practice of education on the same level as the more usual liberal arts and sciences. The college would also be "experimental," and its first major experiment was to substitute "evaluations" written by students and the faculty with whom they had worked for letter or number grades.

The founding president, Dr. Royce S. Pitkin, consulted many other Vermonters, including Senators Ralph Flanders and George Aiken and writer/educator Dorothy Canfield Fisher in the planning of the new college. Of great importance was a non-Vermonter, William Heard Kilpatrick of Columbia University's Teachers College, who had helped many institutions bring the educational ideas of John Dewey to vital life.

The Goddard of 1999 includes a small residential undergraduate program

---

[*] This overview of the College, printed here in italics, is adapted from a recent report to the New England Association of Schools and Colleges, 5th Year Report, 1997.

(some 200 young men and women students) with a liberal arts curriculum leading to the Bachelor of Arts degree, and a variety of low-residency mentored-study programs for adult learners, enrolling over 380 students in six separate programs leading to the BA, MA, and MFA degrees.

Goddard's original aim to serve adult students was met in the 1950s and 1960s through a series of summer and winter conferences on topics related to education and to Vermont's social needs and problems. In 1963 Goddard began a major experiment, initiating a study format that would spread nationwide: its Adult Degree Program. Students came to the campus for week-long (originally two-week) "residencies," during which they took intensive short courses and planned semester-long independent study, to be carried out at home, with "Packets" of work-in-progress mailed to their faculty study-supervisors every three or four weeks and returned with comments by the faculty. The program led to the BA degree; later the model was adapted to graduate study, with current programs leading to the Goddard MA in Liberal Arts Studies, in Psychology, in Education, in Social Ecology, and in Health Studies, and to the MFA in Writing and in Interdisciplinary Arts. Today this "Adult Off-Campus population" makes up a major part of Goddard's total enrollment.

The residential undergraduate program (now called the Campus Program) has evolved from the Goddard of 1938, with the curriculum changing from year to year in response to the needs of students and the changing social context. The Progressive Education philosophy calls for an evolving curriculum of group studies designed and implemented by faculty to meet what they discover to be the felt needs of students, and there is significant faculty-supervised individual study. As in many progressive institutions, studies in the Arts (literary, visual, performing) enroll many students. So do studies in Education and in the Environmental Sciences. The Physical Sciences and the Social Studies enroll smaller numbers Faculty at Goddard do not see their role as transmitting their knowledge to students, but rather as facilitating learning that involves hands-on experience and problem-solving, and through group discussions of material read or written, or of works in the visual and performing arts. Eight hours per week of Work Program, through which students contribute to the upkeep, maintenance, and functioning of the College, are a required part of the curriculum. Students participate in college governance through weekly student-life committee meetings in which they govern their own student affairs, periodic, usually monthly community meetings, and membership on virtually all College committees, including the Board of Trustees. Upper level students in the Campus Program have the option of taking field semesters away from campus, communicating at least every few weeks with their faculty mentors on campus as they carry on their studies and experiential learning activities anywhere in the world.

The Foundation: Democratic Practices in Education

The specific programs and practices at Goddard continue to evolve in response to the changing needs of our learners and of the society of which they are a part, but the new experiments described in the chapters that follow are based on a shared set of beliefs about teaching and learning and the practices that flow from those beliefs. All Goddard programs share a common set of *democratic practices*, which can be described as follows:

Student-centered learning: For learning to be most real, meaningful, and significant, it must begin with needs, questions, and purposes of individual learners, not with those of teachers and professors; just as political and social democracy must begin with the needs and concerns of individual members of society, not with the needs of rulers and governments.

Problem-focused learning: Learning should focus not on other people's predetermined answers, but on engaging students in the active search for solutions to classroom, community, and global problems. This inquiry-based process can make learning more meaningful and significant while helping students learn to become effective problem-solvers.

Integrative learning: Both the aims and the means of education should involve an integration of thought, action, and feeling, each of which is an integral element of the learning process and of the development of the whole person. Goddard's degree criteria therefore include an equal emphasis on the functions of knowing, doing, and being.

Teachers as facilitators: The primary role of the teacher is defined not as an expert or dispenser of information, but as a facilitator of learning, as someone who helps to plan and facilitate experiences through which people can learn as they construct knowledge for themselves, both individually and collaboratively. In this process, teachers enter into dialogue with their students and help students to dialogue with each other, not in an effort to convince one another of the truth, but, as Paolo Freire so aptly put it, "as a democratic relationship, dialogue is the opportunity available to me to open up to the thinking of others." Teachers also help students to reflect on and learn from the experiences that they have, both in and out of the classroom, following Dewey's premise that learning is the reconstruction of experience.

Negotiated curriculum: The content and process of learning is not predetermined by teachers and administrators, but negotiated between each individual learner and his or her faculty advisor/mentor (in independent study – on or off-campus) or between teachers and groups of learners involved in a collaborative group study. Teachers and students together plan studies that can help students to reach their learning goals while also developing the competencies needed to meet the college's degree criteria.

Study plans and learning contracts: Through this negotiated curriculum process, teachers and students (either 1-1 or in groups of students and a facilitator/teacher) develop and agree on a study plan or learning contract that defines the goals and methods of study and means of evaluation and assessment. Implementing the first two principles noted above, students initiate their learning goals and negotiate with their teachers the goals, activities, and outcomes upon which they will be evaluated.

Authentic Assessment: There are no grades or tests, and therefore no competition between students for the highest ratings. Rather, evaluations of students, which are written in narrative form both by the students themselves and their teachers, are based on: their completion of the agreed-upon study plan or learning contract; a narrative description of what they have learned through fulfilling that plan; and their progress toward reaching their own learning goals and meeting the college's degree criteria. Undergraduate students also participate every three semesters in periodic reviews of their learning progress, in which they develop portfolios that contain products of their learning and that demonstrate their fulfillment of specific learning competencies.

Work program/community service: Based on democratic ideals about the dignity of all forms of labor and the importance of each member of a community contributing to its upkeep, the Goddard program expects students to contribute to the running and maintenance of the College and/or to do service in the local community.

These basic beliefs and practices provide the foundational structure in which the recent experiments described in the chapters that follow have been carried out, either in the residential campus program, or in one of the low-residency off-campus programs, or in a combination of the two. Where relevant, the particular context is described more fully.

TWO

Knowledge, Authority, and Dialogue: Teaching as an Emancipatory Relationship

Geraldine and Gus Lyn-Piluso

Our exploration began with an argument. After seven years as colleagues in the teacher education program at Goddard College, we could not agree on why we did the things we did. Whenever we tried to have a thoughtful conversation about our teaching we inevitably ended up bickering. "That's not what progressive education is about," one of us would say. "Well," the counter would fly back, "you've obviously misread Dewey . . ." Given that we live together, this presented a poignant problem. Struggling with questions about authority, autonomy, the political nature of education, and our epistemological assumptions —while trying to prepare dinner—did not work well for us. We could not, for the sake of domestic tranquility, allow this to continue, and we called a truce.

What follows is the fruit of a consciously more cordial dialogue that ensued after a much-needed rest. It is a record of some recent encounters with these questions: a self-examining, dialectical narrative. We offer it here in this form in the hope that it will be more useful than a systemic prescription, will spark more dialogue, and will maybe even spark an argument or two.

Problematizing Knowledge Claims in the Classroom

When the idea of liberation, is carried into the classroom it must, above all things, be useful. We've found that in practice it often means the collective formulation of questions that would never have been asked before—that could not have been asked, because assumptions (ours and our students') had been too firmly held. These are the questions of radical sweep and depth that are familiar to critical educators. For instance, pedagogical theorist Elizabeth Minnich has cautioned that an authentic feminist scholarship must be a system of knowledge that contests dominant systems in form as well as content. Feminist education, she has advised, should not be regarded as an "add-on," but instead should challenge more traditional pedagogies while aspiring to transform students.

Minnich's simple but challenging counsel reminds us of our own struggles, for our work at Goddard demands that we—with our students—continually invent a new form of education. Such creative work requires thoughtful and determined interrogation of more established means; that is, we begin by questioning methods, ideologies, and selves. As our narrative should illustrate, the challenging of assumptions is ongoing, and has absolute terminus.

For instance, we may begin by asking: how does a purportedly liberatory curriculum (feminist or otherwise) end up exemplifying a dominant worldview? More to the point, how is any given curriculum socially constructed? How do we as critical educators remain cognizant of this subtle construction when we are "doing" critical pedagogy? How do we, in the words of Roger Simon, "hold open for assessment those practices which generate one's claim to knowledge"? (Simon 1992, 16). How can we inform our "new" knowledge claims with the thoughts and experiences of those who have been rendered voiceless? How can we be sure that our "new" curriculum is not just a "further unfolding of all that has gone before"? (Minnich 1990, 12).

If we are to understand knowledge claims as by definition having limited meaning, how can we remain open and flexible and yet take a principled stand? Here is our dilemma: we reject the universality of knowledge claims—yet we have solid and presumably sound political beliefs. How do we justify this, or even explain it? For example, a woman student who has been denied a political voice openly denounces homosexuality. As critical educators, is it appropriate for us to argue against her opinion and run the risk of victimizing her further from our position of "power"? What do we do if and when our values are thought of as oppressive by others? That is, how do we establish a process of affirming our ethical limits? (Simon 1992, 16).

At the beginning of a recent course that we co-facilitated on "Ecology and the Politics of Education," we asked participants to share what they hoped to learn from the class. Geraldine then wrote their responses on flip chart paper so that we could refer back to them as needed.

Janice, who is an undergraduate student who works as a teacher's aide in a fifth-grade classroom and is also a single mother, wanted to become "better able to handle questions like 'what is the world going to be like when I grow up?' and 'why do people pollute?'" She went on to say that the children she teaches "are worried that the world is polluted and is not going to be cleaned up by the time they grow up. Quite frankly, I'm worried too. All I hear about is deforestation, the ozone layer, acid rain. It's all a mess. We have to do something instead of leaving it for the next generation."

Janice continued to say that in a number of situations she felt powerless over her ability to help her own children. She married quite young, leaving her father's home for her husband's. When her children were born, she began to realize that there was a conflict between what she wanted for her children and what her husband wanted. She found little support in her town and church community, but was able to take part in an in-service course at the school, where she began to risk saying what she felt. She explained she was "shocked" when she realized that people there didn't automatically think she was crazy. One of the teachers with whom she shared her ideas eventually suggested Goddard to her, and since enrolling, Janice has spent a good deal of time articulating beliefs about children, education, and herself. "I also want to feel comfortable telling people about my ideas," she says.

Hearing Janice tell the group that she wanted to help children understand, and that she wanted to have the power to influence their lives in a positive way, made good sense to us. It seemed at the time to be the focus of her study at Goddard. As best as we could understand, her mission at Goddard was to find support for and to understand her desire to create change. In doing so, she has obviously struggled with her feelings. She had spent much of her life in an atmosphere where there had been little emphasis on her feelings; and seemingly as a result, she did not commonly develop personal opinions about issues but instead waited to see what others thought. It was interesting, then, to trace the theme of helplessness in Janice's introductory statement. As group facilitator during that initial moment, Gus struggled to assist the process so that this theme was not lost to her.

Of course, one of the struggles in running such a group is to help ensure that everyone's concerns or issues are addressed. When Tony spoke, we recognized we were in one of those delicate situations teachers must negotiate with tact. Unlike Janice, Tony did not have a problem expressing himself or letting the group know just what he felt. Although Gus wasn't sure at the time, he suspected that Tony was capable of monopolizing group time. As a critical teacher, Gus needed to determine how much support Janice required and how much intervention was needed to ensure smooth group functioning.

Was Janice again about to be victimized by a dominating man? Was the mere fact that Tony was a man enough to allow us to pin him as the oppressor? We didn't know much about his background. Who was he? Had he led a privileged life, with college tuition paid for by some rich relative? Or was he a working-class child, himself struggling to understand the world and his place in it? Would our feelings about the way he monopolized class time change if we found out that he was gay? An oppressor/oppressed dichotomy clearly wouldn't work here. It was easier for Geraldine to identify with Janice. Yes, Geraldine is a "white" professor (at least in appearance), but she too had grown up as a woman overpowered by patriarchal social forms. She could empathize with Janice—but what about Tony? Was it Geraldine's responsibility to empathize with him? Was it possible? For Gus, on the other hand, Tony's behavior was comfortable. He was clear, to the point, and passionate.

Surely it was different for Tony to speak in the class than it was for Janice. As a man he'd received assurances all his life that he was a member of a dominant group. Like Gus, his voice had power simply because he was a man—a power rooted in the experience of those who control the creation of meaning. As a man his thoughts and actions were braced by a tradition of power that demands consent by limiting the possibilities of interpreting the world. In this sense, patriarchy acts as player, referee, and rule maker. As players, men benefit from their own interpretations of the rules that they themselves have created. Tony's voice was common and recognizable. It seemed to speak with a "common sense" that made it comfortable.

As a woman and a member of a marginalized group, on the other hand, Janice exposed herself to a barrage of attacks every time she spoke from a genuinely personal perspective. Simply because it was not rooted in male experience and in male "common" sense, her voice or standpoint was tacitly assumed to lack validity—the result, perhaps, of an illogical (nonmale) thought process. It was unstated but evident: her experience and self were not valued and were not to be taken seriously.

As critical educators, however, this was precisely why we felt she should be taken seriously. The mere fact that she spoke from a "different" place made—makes—her and her experiences potentially subversive. She offered the group the gift of seeing the world from another side: from her point of view. Every time Janice or someone like her speaks, we are offered a window on the world of a marginalized group. As teachers we must guarantee her the space to speak. We also need to be sure that she is safe from the attack that subversive utterances will elicit.

All this took place at the very beginning of a course on transformative education; already, it seemed, we were about to change directions. We could have ignored this tension and moved to some prescribed "fifteen principles of transformative education," but instead we opted to engage in transformative education by using this sudden turn of events as the focal point of our conversation. Once the remainder of the group had stated what they wanted from the course, and all eyes had turned to Gus as the facilitator, he solicited from the students a general sense of the direction they wished to take:

> Before we move to developing the agenda, how can I help facilitate this process so that everyone's point of view is heard? One thing that I'm aware of is that we are products of a hierarchical society and that some of us have learned that our point of view is not welcome or in fact, understood. If we take kids, for example, we know that they learn from experience that they are not going to be listened to and so they often don't bother saying anything.

At this point Geraldine interjected:

> the same goes for women. Speaking out for women means taking a big risk. What can we do to help make sure that we all feel safe to say whatever it is we want and need to say?

What was going on here? What were we doing? Although we weren't completely aware of it at the time, we both knew that we didn't want to leave this potentially hot issue unexamined. Based on past experiences, we had good reason. A few years prior to giving this course, we were part of a conference workshop on "challenging the global economic order" where the facilitator expressed her concern that special care needed to be given to ensure that the non-Americans in the group felt free to speak their minds. Some of the Americans in the group felt that there wasn't a need to give "special privileges." The resulting discussion lasted three hours. The facilitator was trying to raise the issue of a potential cultural bias against non-American points of view. This proved to be a hot topic even within the group of activists who had gathered for the conference. Perhaps this was what has been called "naming the moment." As a critical educator she was trying to generate a discussion, hoping to help us understand the social and political forces at work at that given time and place— forces which inevitably influenced any discussion of the world economic order.

This is what we were trying to do with our class. Of course it happened too suddenly for us to have been entirely sure of our actions, but we now feel that the questions we raised led to a form of conjunctural analysis, whereby our group had the opportunity to develop awareness of the social forces that made Janice, for example, feel the way she did about herself, her world, and her ability to change things. As Judith Williamson (1981) has pointed out, education is ultimately about providing an environment in which the questioning of commonly unchallenged assumptions is allowed to take place. As she says, "the more I have taught in further education, the more I think it hardly matters, in a way, what you teach as long as it leads to this questioning, which itself is a prerequisite for social change" (16).

Williamson argues for a "cultural relativism" whereby the powers that have helped to shape our selves are not relegated to the realm of certainty, but are seen as socially created political forces with specific and prescribed missions. In fact, she contends that the college experience can be deemed successful if and when students leave with a radical sensibility that calls even one's own language and thought into question. When we asked the group to examine the tension between the socializing forces that treat men and women differently, we raised the possibility that perhaps special accommodations might be required to ensure that all voices had been given the opportunity to be heard. We also suggested that what we as a society generally consider universal truth may in fact be politically motivated, serving the interests of some over others. In other words, we assisted in a politically charged dialogue. The turn of the conversation forced the group members to take a stand, to consider taking a stand, or at least to become aware that they were not engaged in a neutral process:

Sam: I don't get it . . . We're all equal.
Deirdre: You think so?
Sam: I mean here, at Goddard, not the world.
Deirdre: That's so easy for you to say. I mean, no matter where you go you are a man—the city, some conservative little town or a place like Goddard. I don't see it that way. I have to be careful, assertive, and scared no matter where I go. Did you hear that there was an attack here a few months ago? You might not think it's a big deal and you probably don't think it is for me but it is.
Sam: Well, with all due respect, I just don't see how you could say you feel threatened.
Deirdre: Phhhhh? . . .
Sam: Here . . . you're surrounded by like-minded people. As far as I can see there isn't anything to worry about. People here care for each other. It's not as

though you should feel worried . . . about. There is . . . support here . . . we should be . . .

Deirdre: (Silent.)

Sam: I remember last night there were --

Deirdre: Wait! I really think you're missing something here. I'm telling you that I do feel threatened, that I am scared, and that women do feel this more than men. I get so pissed off when guys don't hear that!

Hannah: I agree with Deirdre. She is speaking from her experience and I don't think that any man here can really understand. It's really scary sometimes to be a woman.

Deirdre (to Hannah): Thanks . . .

Silence . . .

Tony: Maybe this is a good time to break and cool off.

Geraldine: This may be a good time to have a break but I'm also wondering if it might diffuse the tension. I'm not sure that's a good thing. Maybe we need to struggle with this some more.

Critical Pedagogy and Classroom Discussion: Teacher as Facilitator

At this point, we were well past the halfway mark of the first session and already we were challenging—or at least raising questions about—capitalism, consumerism, and patriarchy. As the discussion continued and became more heated, we struggled with our roles as facilitators and educators who sought to pose problems for exploration. We realized that the issues that we raised often led the discussion. Why should this be so?

Indeed, a teacher's role is political. We acknowledge this, but should we not try to avoid introducing issues or allowing our own thinking to fuel the discussion? Are we not subject to the same hegemonic forces that influence the students? How do we know that in our desire to help liberate by calling basic assumptions into question, we're not—as Minnich warned—replacing one old (male-centered) tree of knowledge with another that is equally capable of developing oppressive tendencies?

As we asked ourselves questions like these, we came to avoid thinking in terms of replacing existing knowledge claims with new and improved ones. Instead, we now think of evolving knowledge by making connections and discoveries. Our work has become a joint effort to reveal the power base that underlies common perspectives, the mandatory myths of dichotomies, and the often gendered antimonies of dualistic thinking. However, in an attempt to reveal the absurdity of certainty, we are also becoming aware of the need to avoid the "slippery slope of relativism" (Minnich 1990, 166).

Here again, we return to the distinction between what Simon (1992) calls epistemological and ethical limits. Although we need to avoid thinking in terms of absolute truths, our work usually provides us with an opportunity to foster democratic decision making and in turn, diversity and social justice.

Minnich has warned that a position like Sam's—that group members should "agree to disagree"—is not a relativistic stance but is in fact a stubborn posturing—and anchoring—of unquestioning, socially constructed values. For our part, affirming ethical limits certainly involves reasoning that is based on values and morality, but we do so with the implicit understanding of a multiplicity of social and political possibilities. Sam's "red jelly bean for me, green jelly bean for you" approach, on the other hand, excludes the possibility of providing one half of each color for each or even a melting and mixing of colors. As long as he can have his red jelly bean, he is assured his lot.

We knew (sort of) at the time that the tension was good and therefore we tried to keep the group from taking a break. Geraldine attempted to as Minnich (1990) has phrased it "open them to the challenge of exploring a rich complexity of differences understood from the beginning as being in transactional relation to each other" (167). The group, however, decided that it was best to take the break at that point and "carry on after." Of course, after the break the nature of the discussion changed and the intensity was lost. Had we failed? We couldn't very well demand that we press ahead. We realize that cultural forces are omnipresent and extremely powerful, despite the fact that we are often—as in this case (critical teachers included)—unaware of their workings. We are, as the saying goes, like fish unaware of the very water in which we swim.

What was our goal here? Was it simply to allow the group a safe environment in which to explore issues experientially? Was it the radicalization of consciousness? According to Freire, education either acts to preserve existing social relationships, or it acts to expose their true nature. Surely the unreasoned, passive absorption into experiential event is inadequate. Without critical questioning we run the risk of unwittingly consenting to structures, actions, and intellectual frameworks that institutionalize hierarchical social forms and often deny our own humanity.

Here, Gramsci's notion of hegemony seems helpful. The political might of the state cannot compare in reach to the structuralized process of acquiescing consent. Whenever we're with students, whether in a class environment or individually, we encounter not only an individual or group of individuals, but a system of alliances that is instituted to protect the dominant order and create mass consent. Hegemony, according to Raymond Williams's eloquent interpretation of Gramsci, is a "lived system of meanings and values, not simply an ideology, a sense of reality beyond which it is, for most people, difficult to move, a lived dominance and subordination, internalized" (Holub 1991, 104). Individuals find themselves alienated from the social, political, and economic systems that govern their lives; they are able to identify neither their role within society nor the oppression that they experience. They lack both self- and political awareness—without which recognition of hierarchy and injustice is not possible. The result is that imported or extraneous thoughts live in the minds of individuals, thoughts that masquerade as their own. As the anarcho-individualist Max Stirner put it,"man, your head is haunted; you have wheels in your head" (Stirner 1963, 342).

This dehumanized social reality demands that individuals remain unaware of the historical forces that have acted upon them, and it leaves them powerless against an unacknowledged and unchallenged historical tide. Swimming against this tide—overcoming it—requires the development of critical insights into one's existence, and the elimination of what Freire refers to as the culture of silence. Simply experiencing one another, or the moment, will not help to confront and expose injustice unless it is accompanied by critical social inquiry. It's necessary to keep in mind that critical pedagogy, as we understand it, is based on a dissonance between present reality and a counterhegemonic vision. Liberatory pedagogy—which is, in the end, a call to action—works by simultaneously provoking a critique and a vision of what ought to be.

The former requires the type of dialogic process we have referred to—but what about the latter? The development of a vision—or announcement—of the way life ought to be might best be achieved through the affirming, empathetic, democratic educational experience itself. As people familiar with this experience find themselves relating in ways that were previously foreign to them, they discover a politically powerful social form. They have the opportunity to experience the world from an adversarial place: a counterhegemony, an engagement with the potentiality of society.

Although we've argued back and forth on this, it seems that for us this experimentation with vision ought to make use of the teachings of humanistic educators. Although they clearly neglect the need to demythologize popular awareness through dialectically describing the reality behind the myths (failing to emphasize, for example, the inherent contradictions of capitalism and the manipulative forces of our schools and other institutions), they do offer some very practical insights into the creation of healthy, nonalienating relationships and social environments. Carl Rogers (1969) in particular provides a useful analysis of the educational and "therapeutic" potential of interpersonal relations. For Rogers, the relationship is the vehicle toward achieving authentic understanding of the self, without which the ability to empathize with others—and indeed with one's own plight—is not possible. Self is related to other, and self-understanding, awareness, and authenticity are the precursors to changes in behavior.

For us, then, the goal of progressive education is to create the awareness of what is and what ought to be. Striking a balance is what we find most difficult. It would be relatively easy to function completely along humanistic lines. If the group feels they need a break, then that's what they need. There is no reason to question their need. On the other hand, it would also be easy to engage in some type of militant critical pedagogy or guerrilla education, whereby the task would be to act as radical shit-disturbers; calling everything into question, challenging assumptions, never worrying about picking up the pieces.

The group's desire for a break at the height of the tension tested our ability to strike that balance. By pushing a little more, Geraldine may have been able to help expose the ideological assumptions implicit in the discussion. However, she may also have reinforced their comfort with hierarchy by playing her power-wielding professorial hand. Even at a progressive college like Goddard, it is very difficult, if not impossible, to eliminate the top-down relationship between teacher and student. As much as we try, as good as our intentions may be, the teacher still—in the end—has the power to sign or not to sign evaluations. As facilitators we unveil our own politics by revealing our goals, desires, and persuasive techniques; for if the power of hegemony lies in its ability to masquerade its tactics and render people unaware of their own manipulation, education needs to make us aware not only of the wheels in our heads, but also of the tools and processes which may, despite a degree of acknowledged complicity, dismantle these wheels.

Although we never completely returned to the gender issue, at least not with the same degree of passion and tension, we—all of us—profited from that discussion. It forced us to begin to recognize that in the classroom a multiplicity of cultural and historical forces operated quietly and almost unobserved. The group eventually labeled these forces as "baggage." Later in the week the group began to make some interesting connections between our interactions and our baggage. During a small-group activity, for instance, one group actually cut out shapes of baggage and recorded on them what they felt they were "lugging around." Some of the baggage read: "the right to inexpensive commodities, showers every day, comfortable cars, paper towels, meat"; "as a man I'm not afraid to walk downtown at night, therefore nobody is"; "we're all equally to blame for pollution"; "unemployment = laziness"; "technology will fix things"; "when I teach I'm being objective"; "this course would be about recycling."

Some of these assumptions were challenged by the group. One of the assigned readings, for instance, was Janet Beihl's "Ecofeminism and Deep Ecology: Unresolvable Conflict?" (1989). While discussing this article, a question arose: "Who is to blame for the environmental crisis?" Beihl argues it is irresponsible and in fact an attack on feminism when deep ecologists prescribe "selflessness for women and ask them to 'think like a mountain'"(26). After having been historically denied the power to make change, denied even their own selfhood, women cannot afford to relinquish the personal autonomy and political momentum they are only now developing. When, Beihl argues, deep ecologists call for a radical shift in consciousness that allies itself with an almost mystical perception of "nature," the impetus for a feminist consciousness is destroyed.

Beihl's position has profound implications for the who-is-to-blame question. She argues that the popularized notion of "man" as nature's greatest enemy is dangerous, since it denies the multiplicity of hierarchical relations and systems of dominance. How could a mother of five in southern India, who toils every day to feed her children, be responsible for the depletion of the ozone? Is there not a difference between her and Lee Iacocca?

The questions raised by Beihl's article prompted a number of small-group discussions, some of which spilled into the lunch break. Later, Gus asked the group to write an autobiographical piece reflecting on how this issue might inform everyday life. Hannah in particular had a rather difficult emotional response worth noting. She wrote:

> So here I am at home with a composter running full steam, I refuse to buy over-packaged food and I drive my kids crazy getting them to turn off all the lights—now I find out that I should have been worrying about myself—about who I am as a woman. I should have been asking myself why I put up with all the shit that's handed to me every day by my co-workers, my husband and my church. Shit. I didn't even let my kid use a straw the other day. Why am I taking on the weight of the world? What about the company that makes the straws? They're making money out of this—I'm not.

She was not able to "finish." Her response was very personal and emotional. She felt angry, abused, and fooled. Some group members shared Hannah's feelings and were intellectually and emotionally supportive. Others sided with the deep ecologists, feeling that we cannot escape our responsibility regardless of the extent to which we are responsible for the degradation of the earth. We had started to discuss this issue in small groups but it eventually and spontaneously broke out into a heated full-group encounter. After some interesting and often intense moments, Geraldine had the opportunity to offer her opinion for Beihl's social ecology position. She was passionate and forceful. Like that of the other members of the group, Geraldine's intent was to say what she felt, to elicit some response to her position. She had been making similar statements throughout the course but something about what she said at this point was different. It seemed to deflate the intensity of the discussion. Why did this happen? What was it about Geraldine's statement? Or was it she? After much discussion and thought on this we are left feeling that it had little to do with the statement, but rather with the fact that it was made by someone who had "authority."

This is terribly troubling, since we both do everything we can to avoid a "power over" relationship with students. Is this proof that egalitarian relationships between students and teachers are impossible (at least within accredited, degree-granting institutions)? What does this episode tell us about freedom, equality, and the authority of expertise?

Critical Pedagogy and Classroom Discussion: Teacher as Authority

In our struggle to come to terms with this, we turned to Mikhail Bakunin's (1972) concept of the "authority of expertise." Bakunin's primary concern is freedom—which, to him, refers to the full development of human and social potentials. As an anarchist, he rejects the authority of the state, even if it is the state's intention to preserve individual freedom. Freedom cannot be "purely formal" and "conceded, measured and regulated by the state" (160). Likewise, he rejects all externally imposed restrictions, whether by the authority of the state or of God. He does, however, argue for the authority of expertise. For example, although he rejects the authority of the scientist, he accepts that of science itself. It is not the authority of the scientific truth that he rejects, but those who claim sole access to it. Experts, Bakunin (1972) argues, should be consulted, as long as one's individual autonomy is not lost; but their position should always be subjected to one's own reason. "I do not content myself with consulting a single authority in any special branch; I consult several; I compare their opinions, and choose that which seems to me the soundest" (Bakunin1970, 32). This leaves ample opportunity for a teacher's expertise. Whereas critical pedagogy speaks to teachers, and asks that they remain constantly aware of the politics of their position, Bakunin warns the students to be aware.

When Geraldine positioned herself with Beihl and Hannah, among others, she was identified with her role as a professor. She inadvertently played the scientist preaching the science, leaving little room for interpretation. A too-familiar sentiment intruded: if the teacher said it, it must be true. Is it possible to overcome this all-but-automatic reaction? Would this problem have been avoided if we had been more successful in developing a method of teaching that is more congruent with our vision? How much did Geraldine's fiery passion influence our group's acquiescence? If she had been calmer would this have happened? To what extent should teachers temper their emotional responses?

Unfortunately, Gus did not take the opportunity to ask the group to discuss what had happened. He didn't become aware of this until much later when we had the time to think, reflect, and discuss. We were later able to ask a few students what their thoughts were on this. Although Anne did not feel that Geraldine's statement had anything to do with the change in the nature of the discussion, Hannah and Janice did. Hannah was worried that it would have seemed as though she was riding on the teacher's coattails. "I calmed down because I didn't want everyone to think that I was saying, 'Ha, ha. I'm right, the teacher agrees with me.'" For Janice, it was time to listen since everyone had already "had their say." She felt that because "everyone was all fired up and had been talking for so long that it was time to hear your (Geraldine's) opinion. After all, you prepared the course, so you know where we should go. I wanted to hear what you felt about deep ecology and women."

Janice's response was most intriguing. Why did she want to hear from Geraldine? This led us to wonder about the extent to which Janice's response had to do with pleasing and being pleased by Geraldine. Janice has, in the past, gone out of her way to tell Geraldine how much she appreciates her work and how glad she is that she has her as an advisor. After examining some of the correspondence between her and Geraldine, we realize that over the past year Geraldine has given her similar messages. In a letter responding to a paper Janice prepared on television, violence, and childhood aggression, Geraldine wrote, "I read your paper this morning . . . The image of Big Bird beating up on the poor Ninja Turtle is hilarious. You're such fun!" To what extent does the relationship feed off this mutual admiration?

Simon's (1995) controversial work on the eros of pedagogy might be an interesting way to try to make sense of this. If Geraldine's work with Janice is an "act of love" and perhaps "structured by (her) desire to arouse and instruct" (12), Janice's desire for Geraldine's personal, complimentary response to her work may in fact be an attempt (although she was not conscious of it at the time) to imbue her teaching with the power and seduction of emotional contact. We are, for instance, often surprised by the extent to which teaching can bring a sense of satisfaction. In fact, the act of teaching has the potential for profound egocentric satisfaction. We use the term egocentric because although there is clearly a sharing of self, the motivation is a narcissistic desire to project one's intellect and persona onto another and thereby create an externalized object for admiration. It feels good to know that Janice likes Geraldine's teaching and indeed that she likes her. It's also gratifying to know that Janice is there "for" her teacher. She provides a safe "love object" who will not ridicule or abandon her advisor and acts as a partner in intellectual explorations. Although it is much too onerous a task to explore this issue further here, it does illustrate the complexities of teacher-student dynamics. Geraldine's passionate statement in the group may have meant different things to different people, and perhaps for Janice it had something to do with the nature of her relationship with her teacher, but what's clear is that we can escape neither politics nor psychology while teaching, and must therefore be vigilant in confronting the complexities of social forces and providing the opportunity for analysis.

Teaching as Dialogue: Building Emancipatory Relationships

We have tried over the past year to identify characteristics of our dialogue with students that play an integral role in developing critical consciousness and inspiring purposeful social action. We have also tried to identify some of the ways in which our work has evolved. Our work with students is characterized by a commitment to building what we hope are emancipatory relationships. We put a great deal of effort into connecting with students so that we—both teachers and students—experience a degree of freedom to maneuver within the academic institution. This requires a certain amount of mutual security, prompted by the sense that the student-teacher relationship is open, straightforward, and free of personal attacks. We have found that the degree to which we are successful in developing this type of relationship depends on our ability to express our feelings and articulate our positions clearly and honestly.

However, the more we adopt the role of traditional teacher, concentrating more rigorously on content and our own versions of knowledge, the less we are able to create a genuine dialogue with students. The classroom focus shifts from the student's experiences, thoughts, and practices to a struggle with power. Rather than reading their relationship to the world, the emphasis changes to reading us as teachers: "What does Geraldine want me to study?" "Does Gus want me to write three or four essays?" "Is this what she wants me to write?" "Will he think this is enough—how many pages does he want?"

When we aspire to be aboveboard in our dialogue with students this preoccupation with us as "authorities" is diminished. The cards, so to speak, are on the table, and at the request of either party we can sit, examine them, make changes, or argue about them. The emancipatory potential of this type of relationship is twofold. It challenges conventional assumptions about the student-teacher relationship and emphasizes classroom dynamics from the student's standpoint. In so doing it suggests possibilities of other, more egalitarian relationships. Of course, this endeavor requires patience and vigilance because most students are lifelong veterans of educational hierarchies where success necessitates pleasing the teacher. Often our students are teachers themselves and find themselves—intentionally or not—dealing with their students in a hierarchical way.

Our struggle to develop this type of relationship seems to intensify after students have attended their first residency and have submitted their first packets of written material. The following are some excerpts from cover letters from first packets:

From Susan:
Being a student is harder than I imagined. There is so much work. I spend a lot of time worrying about whether I am putting enough into this. I get the feeling you're not as worried about this as I am but I want you to tell me if I'm doing enough. This packet has just over 23 pages. Is this average? I hope it is satisfactory . . .
From Paula:
Please accept this knowing that I realize that there is more depth in the subject and have created a work that only touches the surface. I am confident that I will, however, fulfill criteria . . . I do welcome your help in this new process I am undertaking. Please let me know if this packet demonstrates that I'll be able to carry on. I haven't been a student for a long time and wonder if I can do this. I'm afraid my fifty years are really starting to show.

Our role as the arbiter of the educational process is a theme clearly apparent in these first communications. These students are unsure of our expectations and ask us to tell them. They know that the Goddard process is different and that they are responsible for the development of their study plan, but they still seem confused. Typically, students ask each other about the length and content of their submissions. They are concerned with assimilating. They are troubled by the ambiguity of the process and turn to us for structure. The nature of our responses in such situations will have profound implications for the development of an emancipatory relationship. It would be easy to tell Susan that her twenty-three pages is either enough or not. Indeed, considering our collective educational history, this response would be welcome. The responsibility and power would rest with the teacher and the student would be left to carry out various tasks. However, we have found that unilaterally relinquishing this culturally sanctioned power is not in the best interest of the relationship. Simply saying, "It's up to you, Susan. Whatever you like is fine" may produce an almost euphoric response by providing a taste of freedom, but it doesn't allow for an adequate analysis of the forces that have made this an issue in the first place.

Often this becomes the first generative theme of the dialogic process. In a sense our hope is to use the teacher-student relationship to examine hierarchy and power in general. Our responses communicate a message that says, "This is a complicated question that we should think seriously about together. I often struggle with this and would like to think it through together with you."

The following are excerpts from Gus's dialogue with Susan.

> It is difficult adjusting to all this work, isn't it? I have found that part of the struggle is creating a style that feels comfortable. How do you feel about the amount of work you produced? How did the work of putting these twenty-three pages together impact on you? I always struggle with the amount question. Students often raise this question about their work but I also worry that my responses are not enough. Do you have any ideas on resolving this? Is it resolvable? Maybe we can develop some sort of ratio where an advisor is responsible for a one-page response for every ten pages a student submits. I guess this is pretty silly but I really do want to deal with this. I don't want you to think that I am ignoring this issue. How do you handle this type of issue with your third graders? I was volunteering at my daughter's school the other day and one child asked me if her drawing was nice. Wow! What a question! It may be a common question but it is, I think, pretty complicated . . .
> Susan's response:
> You sure don't make life easy, do you? You asked me so many questions and brought up such complicated issues that I spent most of my time thinking about "how much work is enough" and neglected my work. Maybe there isn't an answer to this question . . .
> From Susan at the end of the semester:
> I find I don't worry about the technical things anymore—expectations, length. Now I just think, write, think, write . . . I have written a paper discussing how teacher expectations are perceived by children.

In this type of exchange, the teacher is not required to deliver curriculum content; instead, academic structure engenders curriculum. The curriculum, in turn, is scrutinized in a close reading and analysis: together, student and teacher discuss issues of power, control, authority, epistemology, and autonomy. Posing the how-much-is-enough issue as a problem for serious investigation allows for the possibility of exposing contradictions implicit in the Goddard process, or indeed—and perhaps more so—in all educational structures. Often for the first time, students are able to recognize the socially constructed nature of related regulations and the processes that develop such regulations.

Equally important, by referring to his own role in the process, the potential for exposing Gus's own subjectivity and all its attendant contradictions was heightened. As was determined, for instance, in the study by Britzman and her colleagues (1991), the players in the educational arena are not "autonomous transcendental individuals" (151). Both Susan and Gus came to this exchange carrying the weight of a multiplicity of cultural forces. Their subjectivities should also be included for unpacking, and "must serve as the place of departure in critical practices" (152). The point of departure must, however, be a relationship built on trust and mutual respect. Consistently raising questions about reified, established procedures obligates rendering oneself vulnerable to criticism—which is justifiable only within the confines of a safe and secure relationship.

Teachers as Radical Intellectuals

When we precipitate this type of confrontation we release students from their traditional passive role. Instead, it is necessary that they think and act not as information processors but as creators of meaning. In this respect, we have found Gramsci's notion of the intellectual rather useful. According to Gramsci, we are able to actively participate in our own development only if we have a clear sense of possibilities and are free from the blinding impact of hegemonic rule. This requires an understanding of the historical circumstances of our existence and ideally leads to an awareness of our ability to act as players in social affairs, and thereby become participants in the drama of history.

This, in effect, is Gramsci's organic intellectual. That is, one who knows his or her history, is aware of the present, and acts to change the future. Gramsci distinguishes this type of intellectual activity from that of the traditional intellectual. In the latter group he refers to individuals who act as clerks of a particular profession, in much the same way as Bakunin's scientist administers the affairs of science. Their power is derived from their expertise and social position; whereas the authority of the organic intellectual emerges from class struggle.

The power of traditional intellectuals, as clerks of their profession, is secured by the world they represent. Teachers clearly run the risk of playing this role. David Purpel (1989) argues that teachers, as a rule, have neglected to speak out against the cultural and political forces that work against the development of critical consciousness. Instead, they endorse the limits set by their profession and accept this framework as reasonable, perhaps needing adjustment from time to time, and have failed to reflect seriously on its inadequacies. A related explanation speaks more clearly to the basic fear in our profession, a fear that produces our prodigious docility and passivity. What one hears regularly from many professionals in response to the pitiful working conditions for teachers is the belief that "we" should not seriously rock the boat lest "they" react in anger and retribution. This is the employer-employee, master-slave mentality in which we are reminded of our place and our powerlessness, are urged to count our blessings, and are warned about the consequences of protest. We are a profession that has, to a very large degree, internalized the oppressors' consciousness (107).

In other words, the profession of teaching—as it now stands—is not motivated by a desire to change, but to serve. In their assessment of the political dynamics at work in the institutionalized school environment, Aronowitz and Giroux (Purpel 1989) portray a milieu that is antagonistic to radical intellectual activity and is characterized by a "tendency to reduce teachers to either high-level clerks implementing the orders of others within the school bureaucracy or to specialized technicians" (103). Questions about which textbooks to order, proper classroom behavior management, grading systems, and other such concerns divert attention and ensure that vital social issues are avoided.

Such familiar discussions turn teachers into secular priests who are concerned more with where to begin circulating the collection plate than with serious discussion about eliminating poverty. By and large, our profession is diligent in its desire to fulfill its designated role. However, by encouraging a dialogue in which students are confronted with issues of oppression, the radical possibility of organic intellectual activity in the classroom is more likely to be realized. When we are able to do this we act as intellectuals whose "function is essentially an organizational and educative one" (Morgan 1987, 303). As Morgan points out, Gramsci's "concept of working-class adult education was that of an essentially critical, self-conscious and revolutionary activity" (306). Radical teaching for us, then, means leaving no stone unturned until the hegemonic mechanisms that work to "manufacture consent" are fully exposed. In this we recognize that our role is to work in solidarity with students who themselves act as intellectuals who are attempting to bring meaning to their lives.

Shoshana Felman (1994) echoes Gramsci when she argues that meaning is dependent on the ability to act as one's own advisor. In our work we are—at the same time—teachers and learners; and thereby we provide a model, and hopefully an environment in which students can play this dual role as well. Felman associates the analysand/analysis roles with the student/teacher roles, suggesting that "the most radical, perhaps the most far reaching insights psychoanalysis can give us into pedagogy" (37) is the need for students to be their own teachers. According to Felman, the analysand becomes the analyst when he or she develops the awareness that the psychoanalytic process is an ongoing struggle.

Gramsci—who was writing from prison with little access to Freud's work, and at a time when psychoanalysis was relatively new—made a similar connection. James Joll (1979) has written that the "central point of all Gramsci's philosophy" can be found in his prison letters dealing with his wife's psychological illness. Emotional health is possible, "if one succeeds in thinking 'historically', dialectically, and identifying one's own task with intellectual dispassionateness. [I]n this sense. . . one can and therefore one must be one's own doctor" (89). Patient, student, and worker share the need to develop themselves as intellectuals.

How then do we act as radical intellectuals? What sorts of questions do we ask? The following are excerpts from a set of lesson plans developed by Hafeezah, a kindergarten teacher living and working in Saudi Arabia who has described herself as a "dedicated Muslim . . . with proud traditional values."

Children will learn . . .
. . .the blue veins that carry dirty blood can usually be seen; especially when doctors take a blood test . . .
. . .doctors are nice, gentle men. They are our friends.

Geraldine's response . . .
I'm very interested in some of the terms you use in describing your curriculum. How do you think the children might perceive the concept of "dirty blood"? Can you share your thoughts on how you came to settle on using this term? Although I haven't studied this much myself, it seems to me that the concept of blood has powerful connotations for many people. What are your thoughts on this?
I wonder why you chose to specify that doctors are men? Was this a conscious decision? Are there any women doctors in Saudi Arabia? Are they all gentle? I know that a lot of early childhood educators in Canada are trying to promote the idea that women can be doctors, astronauts, etc....How do you feel about this? You might be interested in reading...

In these examples, Geraldine resorts to asking a lot of questions, but there is a fine line between inspiring organic intellectual activity and intellectual aggression. Often it's difficult to be aware of how much to push. It is interesting that when Geraldine mentioned Hafeezah's work to a group of teacher educators, many were rather critical of Hafeezah's work until they found out something of her background. At first, they felt that the dirty blood issue was intolerable from a graduate student who was already working in the field. They identified the curriculum as teacher-directed and overwhelming for children who require a play-based educational experience. However, the knowledge that this lesson plan was designed by a Muslim woman from overseas changed the nature of the discussion. Culture became a focal point as did Hafeezah as a person. Clearly this response raises many questions. Is it a teacher's responsibility to know the social and political setting from which a student comes to the educational process? How is it possible to account for the complexities of human experiences? Should our expectations of students change based on their culture? Should a student who, for example, grew up in a culture with a rich oral tradition not be required to express ideas in writing?

Posing such questions can aid in the development of sociopolitical awareness provided that such problem-posing takes place within a reflective relationship between teacher and student. If teacher and student are to be comrades in a struggle to understand the historical circumstances of their existence, they must engage in common reflection. Indeed, the theme of reflection appears repeatedly in our work with students. It allows students to step back and examine their own experiences and histories in light of new learnings. Histories can be recorded—in written or other form—and shared with peers and advisors. Our role in this process has been to first encourage students to struggle for as much detail as possible without worrying about analysis. The point, initially, is to collect and make available.

One student recorded her grandfather's account of the McKinley assassination in Buffalo because, she says, as a child she had heard the story "over and over and it terrified me to know that it happened in my hometown with my own grandfather right there." Another wrote about his first experience as a student teacher fifteen years earlier: "I was not given any room to manoeuvre. They told me what to do, what to teach and that's what I did . . ." Once these records are available students may then simultaneously attach meaning and feelings to them. Such knowledge has been identified by David Hunt (1991) as "experienced knowledge." Hunt (7) argues for an "inside-out" approach to theory development. By beginning with herself as a researcher and her life as the research subject, one student wrote that she had "always thought of menopause as a biological process. I never thought I would think of it as a political, feminist issue. Interviewing my mother and aunts really helped me to see what a profound experience it is for women in our society."

Such a process seems to engender learnings far beyond those of any prescribed curriculum, textbook, learning outcome, or formal examinations. When they look inward with questions about self and education, students find themselves dealing with the most elusive personal and political themes that seem to originate in the tangle where culture, family, and history converge. In a sense, it helps make things real and brings clarity to what are often difficult abstractions. One such example occurred with Patrick, a student who was quite comfortable with abstract theory. In addition to specific comments concerning content and structure which normally form the basis of responses to graduate theses, Gus encouraged Patrick to reflect on how his experiences had influenced his writing. The following is an excerpt of Gus's response:

> I'd also like to encourage you to consider how you fit into this thesis or should I say how the thesis fits into you. Let me explain. Right now you are spending a great deal of time in front of your computer writing this thesis. But who is this person sitting there typing? How did you get to be the way you are? Why are these issues your issues? Can you speak to some of the cultural experiences that have created this thesis? I guess I should also ask how this is relevant to your work. Is it? What good might come out of the type of thinking I am asking you to do?

This was followed by a long, complicated, and rather exhausting dialogue that inspired Patrick to reflect on his experiences. He commented that "I can hardly believe that this is me. I do that shit (manual labor) every day but it's still unbelievable. I see my work with a different set of eyes now." The next installment of his thesis dealt with theory from the inside out. It began:

> I sit here in front of my word processor after eight hours on the assembly line. Somehow I'm supposed to pretend that I'm a writer, a student, a thinker. Three hours ago I was being hollered at by the shop foreman for rearranging my workspace. He yelled and screamed about productivity but now I'm a scholar. Like hell . . .

In addition to this new introductory statement, reflection motivated Patrick to restructure his entire thesis to include his "own working experience." He was confronted with the reality of what it means to be a laborer. In his own words, he was "trapped by the sounds, sights, and smells of my daily toil." The connections that students make between the experiences they are reflecting on and their present lives, thoughts, and studies often serve as the precursors to social action. As he later said, he thought that he "knew all about this stuff." He had read Marx "inside-out" but didn't realize that he was hoping to escape the misery of wage labor through education. Now he chose to confront his work situation head-on.

Toward a New Epistemology

If we are to move in the direction of a new epistemology, a new means to understand the creation and use of knowledge, reflection needs to become a common element of educational activity. In his call for a new way of creating meaning, William Doll (1993) attempts to overcome the knower/known dualism that reduces students to "spectators" of objective truths. This at best is a discovery model in which the task is to find, uncover, and decode the secret messages recorded by elite intellectuals. Instead, Doll argues for an "interactive and dialogic" theory of knowledge, which "emphasizes knowledge creation not discovery, negotiation not verification" (126). He calls for a dialectical involvement, a process in which both knower and known are subjects requiring unraveling and engagement with each other. In Doll's words,

> a curriculum that emphasizes culture and its role in our building of organizing frames, incorporates private and public reflection on what we do, why we do and who we are. At the practical level, journal writing and storytelling can play important roles in such a curriculum (127).

The encouragement and space to reflect provided Patrick with an opportunity to create a clear and satisfactory portrait of his situation. He used it to frame his inquiry, his intellectual journey. As an organic intellectual he created knowledge from his experiences, from his private space. He engaged in a very personalized moral reasoning that reinterprets language, culture, politics.

As we try to develop some understanding of our teaching we realize the magnitude of the task. We found dialogue, reflection, and critical theories to be extremely helpful. More specifically, this self-exploration exercise has reminded us that "looking inward" in order to understand the world is wise. We have, in the past neglected this and have become aware that theory without reflection as a counterbalance increases the potential to become alienated from the teaching process. For example, as we struggle to understand postmodern thought, we are forced to adapt ourselves to its style and to adopt its language. The more proficient we become at this, the more it becomes our style; in turn, we run the risk of becoming more inaccessible to students. At present, we worry about its elitism just as we worry about the potential for feminist scholarship becoming an elite system of knowledge accessible only to a privileged few.

Certainly we need the language and structures that academic critical theories offer, but we also need to remind ourselves that we—as teachers—are important. Like our students, we need to create a record of what we do, of who we are and where we come from, in order to make sense of our work and its implications. We need to share our own reflections with our students and ally ourselves with them in thinking about (and rethinking) education, teaching, and critical theories, and the equally important struggle to create change.

Endnotes

1. Goddard College's off-campus teacher education program requires attendance at residencies followed by academic study and field experience. Students attend courses and workshops at residencies and, together with their faculty advisor and peer group, develop their study plans. Students apply theory to practice in varied practicum situations in their home communities. Academic progress is documented, demonstrated, and monitored through a series of packets submitted to the faculty advisor. Content, form, and structure are varied because the study plan is designed to meet the specific needs of students.

References

Bakunin, M. 1970. *God and the State.* New York: Dover Publications.

Beihl, J. 1989. "Ecofeminism and Deep Ecology: Unresolvable Conflict?" *The Anarchist Papers.* Montreal: Black Rose Books.

Berman, Paul. 1972. ed. *Quotations from the Anarchists.* New York: Praeger Publications.

Britzman, D., K.A. Santiago-Valles, G.M. Jiminez-Munoz, and L.M. Lamash. 1991. "Dusting Off the Erasures: Race, Gender and the Problem of Pedagogy.". *Education and Society* 9 (1-2): 145–166.

Doll, W.E. Jr. 1993. *A Post-Modern Perspective on Curriculum.* New York: Teachers College Press.

Ellsworth, E. 1989. "Why Doesn't This Feel Empowering? Working Through the Repressive Myths of Critical Pedagogy," *Harvard Educational Review,* 59(3): 297–324.

Felman, S. 1993 "Psychoanalysis and Education: Teaching Terminable and Interminable," *Yale French Studies.* 12(3): 21-44.

Freire, P. 1981. *Pedagogy of the Oppressed.* New York: Continuum.

Holub, R. 1992. *Antonio Gramsci: Beyond Marxism and Postmodernism.* London: Routledge.

Joll, J. 1979. *Gramsci.* Glasgow: William Collins Sons and Co. Ltd.

Minnich, E. 1990. *Transforming Knowledge.* Philadelphia: Temple University Press.

Morgan, W.J. 1987. "The Pedagogical Politics of Antonio Gramsci— Pessimism of the Intellect, Optimism of the Will," *International Journal of Lifelong Education.* 6(4): 295–308.

Purpel, D. 1989. *The Moral and Spiritual Crisis in Education: A Curriculum for Justice and Compassion in Education.* Granby, Massachusetts: Bergin and Garvey.

Rogers, C. 1969. *Freedom to Learn.* Columbus, Ohio: Charles E. Merrill.

Simon, R. 1995. "Face to Face with Alterity: Postmodern Jewish Identity and the Eros of Pedagogy." In *Pedagogy: The Questions of Impersonation,* edited by Jane Gallop. Bloomington, Indiana: University of Indiana Press.

Simon, R. 1992. *Teaching Against the Grain.* Toronto: OISE Press.

Stirner, M. 1963. *The Ego and His Own.* Trans. Steven T. Byington. New York: Libertarian Book Club.

Williamson, J. 1981. "How Does Girl Number Twenty Understand Ideology?" *Screen Education.* 4(40): 80–87.

THREE

A Pedagogy of Reciprocity: Interdisciplinary Art Education at Goddard

Eduardo Aquino

Many people are aware that the system isn't working, that it's time to move on and to revise the destructive myths that guide us. Our entire cultural philosophy and its narrowness of concern are under intense scrutiny.

—Suzi Gablik

The Artist at the Center

As an artist and educator I have always questioned the theories and practices in place in art schools, how relevant they are for art students and art teachers, and how they relate to the world outside the academy. Disciplinary tradition plays such a strong role in defining art practices inside art departments that it frequently sets the parameters of the potential creative vision of both students and educators. Why do art schools insist on curricular and pedagogical strategies that are often archaic and do not respond to present sensibilities? How are new educational and art theories and new technological advances effectively helping the learning process in the arts? As Gablik indicates, students are telling us: "The system isn't working." As one of the responses to the present situation I will introduce here the conceptual and pedagogical experimentation taking place at this moment at Goddard College in relation to the learning process in the creative arts; an attempt to propose a case study of education in the arts that is consistent with the days in which we are living.

The students I tend to work with at Goddard have at least one of their interests closely related to art making, but not exclusively connected to the arts. For example, recently I had the opportunity to work with a juggler who was deeply engaged with astrophysics. At Goddard this is not uncommon. A broader research interest is not an occurrence only at this college, but ·it is an increasing pattern observed among students. As a reflection of the information revolution and the constant changes observed in the economy, politics, and in our social landscape, art students are usually not engaged in art exclusively; their curiosity invites a whole new world into their learning process, making them look at art as a possible venue for research. It is not rare to see art students expanding their horizons through their commitment to the exploration of issues related to politics, sexuality, education, ecology, science, literature, sociology, philosophy, history, etc. The art students that I tend to work with always have their eyes set on horizons that extend beyond artistic practice. They look forward to expanding their artistic visions through the exploration of other disciplines as well. For an educator this circumstance of our time seems to be the ideal for personal growth: as I relate my own teaching with a new student's learning goal I am, in fact, increasing my own knowledge frontiers. I am bound to engage in the students' learning process and curiosity and also expand my own cultural experience. Traditional institutions not only reinforce a strict focus on the teacher's discipline, but also reflect (through no demand on self-examination, and through focusing only on disciplines) a teacher's identity in terms of race, class, and gender. This is an invitation to be critical about each one's reality beyond the predictable tenets of exclusive art education, which is generally based on a single particular interest of the teacher, whether it be film, theater, engraving, sculpture, or another. My role in this process is not to determine the direction of their creative process, but to facilitate the students as they map their own multiple interests into conceptual frameworks that make sense for them and, consequently, for their immediate communities and future audiences.

The serenity that helps me to face this challenge comes from the deficiency of creative openness that I experienced in my own formal artistic education and from my own spontaneous, self-taught logic of interdisciplinarity. It was, I believe, architecture and not art school that nurtured the first intuitive interdisciplinary understanding of my creative process. Before then, I had abandoned all attempts to have any formal artistic education and had become a self-taught artist. Just as architecture resides in a typical interdisciplinary territory, where specific knowledge about geography, history, landscape, physics, and the environment go hand in hand with specialized knowledge on aesthetics, philosophy, social issues, economy, and engineering, the interconnection between the disciplines during my time at architecture school was left to the discretion of each individual student. Being an artist and an architect facilitated my understanding of the intertwining relationships among disciplines and the integrity that raises from that interdependence through the image of the body, the building, and the city. Within my own artistic practice the creative process can be characterized by or compared to the complexity of the conceptual, material, organizational, and functional relationships within the body. By extension, the city serves these same functions as a place where society proposes to organize itself as a consistent "body." So it doesn't amaze me when a student presents a program of studies that usually doesn't have an apparent theoretical logic attached to it. The student's previous life experience always reflects a strong reasoning that naturally associates those interests, even if those disciplines are as disparate as astrophysics and juggling. It is personal experience, desire, and vision that validate and condition a possible learning structure, and not any preconceived methodological knowledge that is superimposed upon the student's learning. Creating an open context for their investigation, allowing the students to find meaning within their own interests, and building a solid learning framework to make the student's desire possible remains one of the main educational goals at Goddard.

Interdisciplinarity, in this case, becomes a natural pedagogical strategy in creating this open field of exploration and discovery. If in art making the artist remains at the center of the creative process, why aren't art students given the same liberties in their learning environment? Is it possible to place the student at the center of the learning process, using interdisciplinary pedagogical strategies to create the necessary space for exploration? The student-centered approach that allows and encourages the most creative associations of different learning interests is the natural response to the aspirations they always bring to us, if not the only consistent way to respond to the learning expectations of students. Creative freedom and free association are essential for any creative endeavor, and at Goddard we have in place a pedagogy that integrally supports an open base for artistic creation. These are some of the issues I want to discuss here using our present experience at Goddard College.

Democracy and the Education of the Artist

A significant transformation has happened in the education of artists during the past one hundred years or so. At the dawn of this century, moved by a new poetic, creative energy, new technological possibilities, and new philosophies inspired by innovative ideas, the fine arts academy initiated a process of change that would reorient art production toward new genres and unleash new exploratory possibilities in the creative arts. There was a suggestion, then, that art could imply an image of democracy by way of the creative process through the idea of self-realization within a social structure. However, the specialization that developed after World War II, guided by the need to rebuild Europe using North American industrial prowess, gave rise to a curricular structure in the arts that is typically and contradictorily disciplinary, and stands in contrast to the visionary artistic innovation observed at the beginning of the century. It is worth mentioning that art programs were initiated in the university system at this same time, just after the war. Such a disciplinary imposition within arts education remains as the standard pedagogical method until the present day. It has removed, paradoxically, the possibilities of creative expansion in the academic context. Even if there is a significant increase in interest and opportunities for arts education today, the academic system resists reinventing itself in order to respond consistently to the present demands from art students. The system instead supports the institutional status quo.

There is an increasing interest in the arts, amidst so many difficulties and adversities in a changing world, where the phenomena of globalization and mass media culture produced by multinational corporations seem to support the interests of the big economic and political powers and divert energy away from a genuine democratic world order. Despite the overpowering corporate influence in the definition of our cultural landscape, today there are art education opportunities without precedent: from children's curricula in K–12 programs all the way through university terminal degrees and continuing education for adults.[1] Museums, art galleries, television, theaters, artists' cooperatives, art festivals, symposia, and the Internet are tapping into the existing cultural networks and technologies of mass communication, furthering the exposure of the arts to wider and wider audiences.

In times of economic and political instability there is a tendency to return to values that are removed from patterns of consumption. This was demonstrated during the excessive 1980s, when many people sought a return to more social, spiritual, or poetic meaning in their lives. The overall concern with the environment and its survival has also triggered a new consciousness, and artists are responding to these concerns as well. Despite the adversities and instabilities today, art remains as a significant element in people's lives. However, inside the parameters of art making today there is the constant dichotomy that separates the professionalization of art production (which invariably brings about a close relationship to mass media consumption) and the democratization of art making. While, for some individuals, art seems to be an effective response to everyday questions, the institutionalization of art reduces the possibility of self-realization to just a few by confining art making within a framework of specialization, commercialization, and privilege.

Why do art departments rely heavily on tradition, and less so on experimentation and exploration? Art making, as art education, is directly related to the comprehension of our society, and art is somehow the artist's individual response to society's need for understanding, expression, articulation, communication, and change. A permanent investigation of the relationship between artist and society leads to a questioning of the confined system of the art world and the limited networks of support that govern and distribute cultural products. It would be demagogic here to say that artists have something more important to say, or something better to contribute. Instead, in a democratic society, the opportunity of expression and cultural contribution should not be given only to a few artists, but to all individuals who participate in society's progress. As Royce "Tim" Pitkin, Goddard's founding president said: "We treated the visual arts as a vital part of living, not as something separate from the ordinary person. Even students with no particular talent could gain a new awareness of beauty in nature and in things created by man" (Adams and Benson 1987, 142).

It would be also redundant, if not foolish, to say that art can change the supposed democratic mechanism that impels the most important political decisions and the creation of new laws. Nevertheless, in the face of a reality that is rapidly collapsing through the imbalance of the environment, the uncontrolled, impulsive political and military threat, and the increasing instability of urban life caused by industrial and demographic growth, art can be still viewed as a resource for personal and collective release, repose, and celebration, as well as an instrument for consciousness raising. Art's role is to question assumptions and to provide a reflective surface for critical assessment of issues of personal and collective concern. To understand society, in the case of art making, is a task that requires constant exploration and experimentation because the times lived now were never experienced before.

But the art academy is not prepared yet to teach experimentation, because experimentation cannot be confined in a locked set of principles to be directly applied to art making. Specialization was the answer to art education within the academy because technique and discipline are knowledge models that can be clearly framed and systematized within the postwar consumerist mentality, and therefore can be easily "taught," but not put into experimentation. In art making, the conflict between specialization, professionalization, and credibility is opposed to innovation and creativity. Techniques and disciplinary knowledge should be an integral part of the learning process, and not a ruler of an educational structure. It is in this contradiction that art departments, and all art institutions for that matter, are caught up. The problem resides in the lack of experience or knowledge about how to teach in an experimental and exploratory environment.[2]

The increasing access to art appreciation and art making enables art to be more present in everyday life. The model of specialization in the arts, a result of the capitalist ideal for industrial supremacy, is exclusive in character, because technique is valued above concept, design, and process. Art, as a result, is a distant phenomenon from everyday life, and it is consumed by a specialized audience almost exclusively through art institutions, which, therefore, control its content, production, and distribution.

As a consequence, the old, discipline-bound, specialized beaux-arts system prevails as a general principle in the determination of art programs in the academy, even with the continuing deconstruction of the modernist model initiated by Dada and Surrealism. The artists connected with both these movements challenged the way art was conceived and institutionalized by subverting the parameters of modernism. Their challenge was reinforced in the 1960s and 1970s by the feminist, gay rights, black power, antiwar, and civil rights movements. These challenges to hegemony generated art manifestations such as happenings, videoart, agitpop, conceptual art, street art, land art, pop art, and performance art as mediums of critical resistance and political activism.

Yet today most art programs are still defined by specific disciplines such as film, sculpture, painting, drawing, crafts, ceramics, photography, theater, etc., in a time when art practitioners, performers, and even students are constantly subverting discipline or medium boundaries to find expressions that convey their visions to the world through all sorts of material and conceptual weavings that are intended to approximate themselves to end-of-century aesthetic perceptions and social-political patterns of growth and change.[3]

If art today is no one's land to the disappointment of some critics of the Clement Greenberg school,[4] for artists it is a time of opening, exploration, and more opportunity, a time when the dominance of single dogmas are fading from the art history's canon. Postmodernism attempted to deconstruct some myths of the modernist paradigm, but the lesson after the storm is that history is here to inform a process, and history's continuity is more resistant than any single theory that may seek to shift art's orientation. If there are no major canons of art history to narrowly guide artistic production today, the most important gain from recent history is that assumptions cannot continue to be made in favor of a few privileged artists, and that aesthetic and social value are, to good effect, in constant critical scrutiny.

Such psychological and cultural conditions are propitious for the freedom that art making demands, and suggest a more democratic environment for personal and collective expression in the sense that there are fewer borders and more possibilities for the creative mind. Art departments are aware of such social and theoretical development, and they should respond to the needs of this new artistic and social perception. But, incomprehensibly, they have enclosed themselves within the archaic structure of disciplinary fragmentation, and have returned to the more traditional pedagogical scheme of art education and have limited themselves to techniques and disciplines. The experience we are having at Goddard attempts to challenge the present situation of the creative arts in higher education by offering a space for learning in which the central figure is the student and the creative process, not a set of parameters defined beforehand by predisposed theories and practices.

The Artist's Formation at Goddard

The arts at Goddard were always given equal status with other areas of the curriculum. They were seen as having personal and social importance, worthy of hard work, and discipline.

—Royce Pitkin

Our current cultural, political, and economic situation seeks to perpetuate the privilege of a few through the exploitation of many; art, from another side, seems to create a common space for reflection and possibility, if not comfort. Artistic practice and appreciation, defined in generous, broad terms—beyond the "art world" definitions—occupy a special place in people's lives. Goddard College was one of the first liberal arts colleges in United States to include arts as a major part of the curriculum, and, in fact, the original educational plan for Goddard states that education in the arts should be one of the goals of the college. As an educator working at Goddard I first discovered this tradition, the openness, and the generosity of vision of this community expressed in the desire to create a learning space that would address pertinent questions concerning the creative process in an open-minded manner. It was a special moment when many of my own concerns about the creative process and the education of artists found an adequate context for expression.

The difference I found at Goddard in relation to other traditional settings is that at Goddard nothing is taken for granted, and every question, every issue is put through a complex system of assimilation and digestion, initially by the faculty, and subsequently within the exchange between the advisor and the student. Because the basic format for an effective learning environment is dialogue, a lot of conversation takes place, either one on one or in groups. Students have an enormous contribution to make, especially because they influence the curricular formulation at Goddard in many more direct ways than at other institutions with which I have been involved. The students have the opportunity to design their own individual curriculum in close collaboration with faculty. Decision making in art is second nature. Having artists assume responsibility for their own artistic aspirations through personal choice is essential to their individual creative progress. Why not, then, give the opportunity to art students to trace their own artistic goals within the institutional framework?

The recent educational experiences developed at Goddard College in the field of the creative arts search to challenge the traditional ways that artists are educated. Students and faculty are constantly looking for learning strategies that respond to the fundamental creative interests of the students and to their need for new forms of practices, new forms of art criticism, and new ways to critique artworks. Students also need to talk about the artistic process and to be truthful in their art to the times in which we are living. Asking the harder questions in an open atmosphere and in a spirit of collaboration is crucial for the student's artistic development and critical maturity. Joe Fulop, who taught art at Goddard for many years, said that "teaching art is not merely giving a course in technique and skills at the same time that the artist is not exempt from a role as a citizen. There is no escaping the pressures and responsibilities of our time." In relation to the exclusive notion of artistic talent, and the importance of the presence of art in people's lives he continues, saying that "to remain human the common man has to become an artist" (Adams and Benson 1987, 142). Art, in this context, is viewed not simply as an instrument for individual expression, but, beyond the individual creative process, we are looking for ways to re-articulate, to reconnect art to the existing social environment in meaningful terms to the students and their communities. This is a constant problem that is experienced in traditional settings: art students are not adequately prepared to face artistic life after the academy; what we are trying to do is to advance that experience into academic life and make it a vital, consistent part of their learning process. Students are often encouraged to establish actual links with their communities by exploring ways to engage their work with a context beyond the college's, and this experience has allowed them to verify new relationships between art, reception and participation, as well as giving them opportunities to resolve problems — conceptual, technical, logistic, etc.—that otherwise would not be addressed in their creative process. This connection between art and community is an important feature of our program's philosophy, which greatly impacts our methodology and criteria.

A specific experience will be used here to describe this pedagogical experience in the creative arts: the new Master of Fine Arts Program in

Interdisciplinary Arts, and, within its curricular structure, the Study Plan as the core piece of the pedagogical strategy, and an experimental online seminar which intends to create a continuous communal space for low residency, off campus students, functioning, at the same time, as a critical stage for theoretical articulation. Before we get there, let me describe some of the pedagogical philosophies already in place, and how they can serve specifically art students, supporting their impulse for creative exploration.

The Student/Advisor Relationship

Even though Goddard is structured with both campus and low-residency, off campus programs, the new Master of Fine Arts Program in Interdisciplinary Arts is offered, for the moment, only to off campus students, due to the adult population it attracts. In the campus program the students spend the whole semester in residency at the college, and in the low-residency off campus program the students spend one week of intensive work at the college campus, at the beginning of every semester, and develop their semesters' work at home, in their local communities. During the residency specific workshops and activities are provided to fulfill the student's learning needs and to expand the cultural perspectives of the community in a friendly environment that supports a spirit of sharing and collaboration. The themes for the workshops vary from residency to residency, depending on the residency theme (stipulated collaboratively by students and faculty), but there are also foundation workshops that are offered in a regular basis.[5] The foundation workshop themes range from Critical Thinking, Research Methods, Creative and Research Writing, to Feminist Theory and Practice, Identity Politics, Social History, Technology, to Art Practices. In every residency there is a whole new range of workshop options facilitated by students and faculty; the students are encouraged to design their own residency according to their interests, using the workshops as a support system for their personal research. There are plenty of opportunities for discussion in a one-on-one basis between students and faculty members, and there are also organized encounters between a faculty member and respective students, which we refer to as the "advising group," that meets to discuss common interests.

This scenario of great proximity and communal living at the residency, followed by great distance during the actual semester when the students work from home, creates a unique relationship between advisor and student because it is a relationship characterized not by the collective and constant physical encounters that usually happen in traditional settings (the classroom), but instead is based on a one-on-one association. The individualized, one-on-one exchange happens through varied types of communication: letters, e-mail, telephone calls, etc., depending on the kind of communication the student needs at different times during the learning process. At the same time that this one-on-one communication deepens many of the discussions during the student's process, the student should develop skills for autonomous research, advancing in this case the future post-academic experience. Much pedagogical and social nurturing takes place to support this one-on-one exchange, and the subtleties and complexities are always different from student to student, from advisor to advisor, and in each student/advisor relationship. Beyond the pedagogical strategy created to respond to a specific student's needs remains a very basic human relationship between student and advisor, which is considered to be a consistent part of learning.

The position of the conventional instructor or, in our case, the "advisor," is naturally understood as being a position of authority. This authority figure sometimes reaffirms the traditional teacher's role, reinforcing, therefore, a position of power. Sometimes this dynamic is reinforced by the student's behavior: the misleading need of being guided or kept under control. Traditional educational settings constantly reinforce both behaviors: from curriculum planning and class structure all the way to the evaluation process. Shifting to a more balanced condition between "teacher" and "student," which means decreasing these power differences, represents a desire to build a healthier circumstance for a teaching/learning experience, characterized more by exchange than by the unilateral transmission of information. The designation of "advisor" at Goddard, instead of instructor, professor, or teacher, represents more than a simple, formal change of the terminology, but intends to indicate fundamental pedagogical concerns that support a more equidistant relationship between learner and educator. The student has a greater opportunity to exert control over the learning process, and the advisor's role is redefined as that of a supporter, rather than a leader.

Reciprocity, in this case, appears as an ideal condition of dynamic searching. Teaching happens as a learning experience to whoever seems to be in the teacher's position and vice versa: the student becomes a kind of a teacher. By taking responsibility over the learning process, it is up to the students "to teach" the advisor about the recurrent questions related to their personal learning process, and also to indicate the possible directions in their progress. That is when the exchange between student and advisor occurs. The construction of a personal critical discourse is encouraged to happen both ways, on both sides, between student and advisor. In this process both the student's and the advisor's individual experience constitutes the basis of the learning process. It is what I could call *preconception*: everybody knows something about something before being told about that same thing. More than transmitting a personal experience, the advisor would rather try to instigate and stimulate the hidden parts wherein lies the genuine knowledge of the student. Such a pedagogical format is possible only because of the individualized structure in place. In collaboration with the advisor, the student defines the learning goals, the ways to support these goals, and the procedures by which the student can achieve them.

In my experience as an educator, this pedagogical structure has been the most effective regarding the intellectual, spiritual, and creative progress of an art student. It corresponds to the autonomous, independent artistic spirit, preserves the creative freedom, and at the same time gives the necessary critical and technical support for the student's desire for achievement. As a confirmation of the effectiveness of this present structure, I realize that in the traditional university setting I have been more successful in conveying authentic learning only when, after struggling over the existing model—one teacher/many students/one classroom—and subverting the administrative/pedagogical organization of the institution, I finally create some isolated moments of individual engagement with students that can be, sometimes, truly transformative. The difference at Goddard is that the individualized structure is already in place, and responds positively and in more effective ways to the learning expectations of art students than the traditional university setting. The integral individual attention given to the student's learning process resides as the pedagogical foundation for the learning to occur. In the case of Goddard, the institution is less in the way of the student and represents instead a more supportive system for the student's learning and growth. This balance between artistic freedom and academic sponsorship is crucial for the success of art institutions.

The Study Plan

In the spirit of democratic decision making, the campus-wide pedagogical approach supports individualized education unconditionally. One of the most important pedagogical components that fosters the individualized structure at Goddard is the study plan. During the period of one week (that we call "residency") the whole community—faculty, the student body, service and administrative personnel—reunites at the college campus for an intense period of research and communal exchange. Drawing from the multiplicity of their own interests—that could range from painting to anthropology, from performance art to radical politics, from environmental issues to architecture, etc.—the art students are encouraged to design their individual study plans. They use the study plan as a drawing board to determine their own program of studies and select and adapt the fields of knowledge in which the personal investigation will take place. Because the vision imprinted in the curricular choices is informed by personal experience and motivation, there is a different sense of responsibility and engagement in place that nourishes the student's learning process from its genesis. In a certain way this is a model that is used instinctively by artists in their own creative processes. Self-motivation is a crucial component of art making, and the open choice of interests is always a given in any creative process.

The study plan functions as a learning guide for the student, and stipulates the student's learning goals for the work to be realized during the semester or for a whole degree, including research resources, readings, activities, field work, internships or practicum, workshops or conferences to be attended, and scheduling for the realization of the work. The student also indicates what products will result from the semester's research; for example, paintings, performances, journals, papers, research reports, creative writing, etc. The role of the educator is redefined not in relation to an existing, predetermined program of studies (program descriptions, course outlines and bibliographies), but is decided by the artistic intentions and learning goals of the students, coupled with their exchanges within the advising group (faculty and other fellow students). There is very little risk of intellectual or creative manipulation from the outset because the study plan is designed for each individual student in a collaborative effort between the student and the advisor. The role of the facilitator is emphasized and replaces the traditional role of the teacher that defines traditionally and discriminatorily "what to do" to a whole group of students (the traditional "course outline"). The opportunity to choose is the basis of a successful study plan; it is a more democratic learning method because students have a voice in the determination of their own curricular composition. Students use bibliographies to build theory about their projects; they expand an initial (and sometimes scattered) interest into a coherent research subject. During this "flowering" process (and at all the other moments of the learning process as well) there is constant dialogue between the student and the advisor, which is not exclusively limited by a one-on-one exchange. The students are encouraged to search for other sources by sharing their interests with other students, other faculty members, and even members of their local communities. Having defined the parameters of their creative investigations the students go back to their communities to realize their artistic and learning goals.

When at home, it is the responsibility of the student to inform the advisor about the work's progress. Usually, this part of the student's work consists of an elaborated piece of documentation that we call a "packet," which illustrates through different forms the artistic production (the medium as well as the kind of practice is the student's choice). In addition to the actual documentation of the artwork and its process, the students are invited to articulate the learning process through writing, bibliographical research, presentation of a portfolio, etc. Each of these products communicates each stage of the process and establishes the eventual theoretical connections with their own artistic practices. Such a formal base allows for a natural connection between theory and practice which resolves the struggle observed customarily in art education settings, where theory seems to develop in dissociation from the student's own creative process. The advisor is responsible for feedback about the student's process. The feedback is given in a letter of response to each related packet. The basic difference I find between writing a letter to a student and meeting the student at my office is that in the letter my own process of reflection and my own critical sense is articulated in a much more perceptible and critical manner. A letter is a more permanent document that requires careful, methodical consideration about the interpretation of someone's creative process, and it is more present, sometimes, than a quick verbal answer. A verbal response can assume a very ephemeral character during and after a conversation. Writing a letter requires more rigor and sensibility from the advisor, and at the same time can serve as a close reference to the student's process because the student can come back to it at any time during the learning experience. Through the letter exchange process the student has greater autonomy in the learning progress; he or she can decide which advising recommendations to bring to the work and choose the specific orientation to follow.

The study plan also becomes an instrument of negotiation between student and advisor, a form of contract upon which the evaluation of the work will be based. At the end of each semester the student and the advisor write evaluations that assess the progress of the student in the program, decide the student's future learning goals, and determine whether the student is entitled to credit during that respective semester. At this moment the study plan serves as an important evaluative tool as well. This evaluative process still gives some degree of authority to the advisor, who has a special decision making responsibility. This evaluative process has some complex factors, but it is still a direct, participatory evaluation process, because it is an appraisal of the work based on reciprocal dialogue.

The complete isolation of the artist and the art making process were fully defended by late modernist critics, who glorified the art object by separating it from its surroundings and the reality of its construction (materials, site, labor, technology, the sociocultural structures, etc.). They even isolated the art object itself from the artist's life circumstances, creating the extreme supremacy of aesthetics over life and meaning, the control of the mind over the body. The intention of a reciprocal process is to disrupt this barrier and create an ongoing active mode of experimentation, replacing the exclusive and alienated system of simplistic representation. When there is no experimentation, learning does not take place. As in science, artists should draw from the present concerns related to their practices, the practices of others, and the theoretical discourses that are available. At the same time art teachers shouldn't remain trapped in old forms of pedagogical methodology. A course that is taught twice in the very same way, for example, is an "old form." The repetition of models assumes that the subject (the student) is the same, when time, space, and individual experience will always bring a new perception into the learning experience. That's the reason for the student–centered approach: each student is a different student, with a distinct experience and aspiration. If the educator is constantly transforming from day to day, so is the student. Experimentation, which decides the particular qualities of the student's work, is the risk factor in a learning process. It is the necessary motivation to relate the content to be learned with the life reality of each student, making the learning process meaningful to the student. To understand that a student is not merely a student, but is a human being with many complexities is a fundamental asset to the definition of and application of pedagogical strategies. It is crucial for the educator to be open to being changed through the interactions with students. This process of mutual exchange is more easily achieved in an individual teaching context such as Goddard, where the study plan guarantees that the student and not the teacher is at the center of the learning process. The study plan is the pedagogical core and a democratic instrument that supports the exploratory, free spaces of individual discovery necessary to any creative growth. The study plan is democratic not because the student designs it; it also reflects our epistemological position that we do not define the content of a student's studies. There is no "core content" in the program, no mandatory, pre-defined learning that students are expected to acquire, indicating that democratic, individual choice comes also with initiative and responsibility.

Continuous Unfolding: The Zone of Interdisciplinary Arts

In the Goddard process the study plan is the foundation of the pedagogical structure, and interdisciplinarity could be considered the philosophy behind the structure. I reiterate by saying that interdisciplinarity keeps open the possibilities of creative exploration. Art practices, after all, evolve in the world independently from educational systems through the artist's own initiative, even when we consider that the majority of artists today go through formal academic education. Art has always existed despite art institutions. Artists who critically oppose the traditions prescribed by art institutions have consistently overcome the limitations of academic art education to affirm their own visions and attitudes. Why don't artists, then, challenge the institutions to evolve, to adapt to the changing times? Why do art institutions resist innovation and change so fiercely? And what is the role of the academy in challenging art practices and artistic definitions? Art institutionalization dominates the great bulk of art production (galleries, museums, magazines, schools, etc.), and students constantly follow this process of institutionalization by accepting the mandates of disciplinary philosophies that are inspired by market values and tradition, which still determine the base of most art departments and their insistence on sustaining single medium art practices, i.e., ceramics, sculpture, painting, photography, dance, music, theater, video, etc. Students need to be encouraged to define their own directions in the creative process despite academic impositions or the teacher's personal preferences. They might choose to respond to the original claims for artistic freedom suggested by Dada artists, for example. Hopefully their vision and creative ambition will overcome the limitations of the institutions that embrace them.

Often I walk into art studios just to verify that the disciplinary boundaries are gradually vanishing and are being replaced by creative strategies that blur the lines between concepts, techniques, forms of action, and display. A painter, for example, after considering the affinities between the canvas and the space of the studio, starts to create new spatial relationships by associating objects with the painting, or by simply changing the position of the canvas in the space, altering the lighting, or even the architecture. From this moment on, with the complexities encountered in the multiple relationships between the original artwork, the new conditions of display, and the new relationships the artist is able to create in order to present the work to the audience, the artist defies the initial assumption that the original work is "painting." This is just an example, but such an openness and creative boundary-crossing usually leads to new art forms and new definitions of one's own creative process. The artist could then consider the artwork as the total environment or experience created, and not simply the canvas alone, and so on. This form of linguistic interdependence usually creates a conflict between the student and the institution (when the student is expected "to paint" or "to sculpt," etc.), and the pursuit of the creative act tends to become a permanent subject of conflict. This type of learning is not typical of any natural and supportive learning process. I have met frequently with students who are looking for a context that will work in harmony with their creative processes. As individual artists they are looking forward to breaking the barriers of the traditional curricula through their creative imagination, from within the confines of traditional institutions.

Despite the potential to establish new standards and create new learning environments where assertive learning takes place, the difficulties in subverting the existing set of values of a discipline-based curriculum and the existing evaluation processes of this existing structure, takes most of the energy of both students and educators. It is typical to find students protesting that they spend more time and energy fighting to get their work done instead of having a support system that responds effectively to their creative needs. Art education, in this case, becomes an ordeal more than a chance to nurture one's creative process. It seems so natural that the orientation of the student's creative process should be relevant to the student's own choices, and not responsive to the personal demands of the teacher, the parameters of the academy, or, by extension, the premises of the art world. In art making the opportunity to have a choice is a fundamental part of the creative act, even if this choice is more and more taken collaboratively, or if it isn't in agreement with the teacher's agenda. In discipline-bound programs the array of choices are limited frequently to material or technique-based expectations, which often conflict with the vast conceptual openness and technical possibilities in art practices today.

It is not the intent of interdisciplinary art to annihilate the knowledge of separate disciplines or the knowledge of tradition. Instead, it proposes the valorization of the discipline's intrinsic qualities, drawing from the inherent attributes allocated to a specific medium to create a language in tune with the contemporary culture and the histories of our own times. A video maker draws knowledge from either television, photography, literature, philosophy, or film to articulate a language that can be found in between the boundaries of such disciplines. A sculptor, sensitive to the architectural character of the sculpture, addresses issues of scale, proportion, construction, and placement when relating the object to its surroundings; these include the spectator and the gallery as part of the same architectural entity. In this case, architecture and sculpture meet on a common ground in the creative process to compose new qualities imprinted on the object, and, as a consequence, on the spectators as well. Interdisciplinarity is not simply a consequence of understanding contemporary sensibilities (cultural, political, social, technological, etc.) from the artist's perspective; it also creates a new experience for the observer, solidifying the idea that the audience participates directly in the creation of the artwork.

A distinction should be made between what has been traditionally defined as "interdisciplinary art" and what has been commonly referred as "mixed media." Interdisciplinary art draws from the technical, conceptual or epistemological knowledge of different disciplines to result in a distinct, coherent work of art; mixed media is considered a formal, more simplistic procedure of adding two or more different mediums together (for example, a collage of drawings and photos), omitting the intrinsic meaning, the inner qualities of these elements, without considering "what's behind a drawing, what's behind a picture." That is what has been referred to as "formalism." Where a video could be intrinsically considered an artwork with interdisciplinary characteristics, a video simply placed beside a painting doesn't necessarily represent interdisciplinary art. Interdisciplinary art must include a strategy that is built in the process of articulating ideas or emotions, whereby the artist searches through an array of possibilities and does not regard the particular strategy he or she chooses to be the final product. An interdisciplinary artist who starts composing a musical piece could culminate with an opera or a film, and not necessarily conclude with a symphony or a sonata. A musician can draw from philosophy or pure science to achieve certain artistic intentions in composing a sonata, etc. In a disciplinary practice, however, the innate definition of the final product is decided prior to the creative decisions of the process. In such a case, a musician who composes a symphony will have a symphony at the end. The definition of interdisciplinary art is more closely tied to a process, and not necessarily or primarily to a single medium or a final product. Interdisciplinarity keeps permanently open the possibilities of creative exploration.

The MFA in Interdisciplinary Arts Program

It is common knowledge that existing educational institutions are not keeping pace with their students' perceptions and desires to develop their own creative potential. Responding to the challenges presented by a new generation of art students, and by the contemporary art environment, Goddard College has established a new program in the creative arts, the Master of Fine Arts in Interdisciplinary Arts (MFA-IA).[6] But, why the need for a new graduate art program? Although the MFA-IA draws in inspiration and philosophy from the traditions of artistic manifestations of the last thirty years or so, it doesn't intend to limit the explorations in the domain of the creative arts in any specific, singled-out direction. We can even say that the program is in constant transformation, especially because the students have a lot of room to define its character. Every new group of students has the opportunity to contribute to the growth of the program, to imprint their individualities on its constant development. The vision for an arts program that responds to the actual cultural reality is not something easy to come by, but the need arises from the lack of art programs that emphasize the uniqueness of the individual student and at the same time offer a context where the students are able to orient their own creative process with freedom, in a nurturing, supportive environment.

The MFA-IA program has devised a series of components that are part of the contemporary art practices, but are not necessarily present in arts education curricula. At the same time that the notion of interdisciplinary arts is the cornerstone for the program, its definition is left as broad as possible to accommodate the most varied needs of different students. The notion of interdisciplinary art is described as a process where the artist integrates several components in the artistic procedure, in the choice of materials, in the discourse of the artwork and its conceptualization, the context in which the work is conceived, realized, or performed, producing an experience that crosses boundaries of traditional art forms[7] (work that blends craft and political discourse, for example). The program's focus is on the artist and the practice. Other issues of importance in the artistic experience are then addressed in relation to the practice, the process, and the product. When we evaluate the student's work, we look at the quality of the practice as a whole. Whatever concern the student wants to integrate into the artistic process (personal, spiritual, political, scientific, anthropological, cultural, etc.) is valued. In that sense, we depart from traditional notions of art according to which only the aesthetic quality of the final product matters.[8] The premise of the MFA-IA program is to open the possibilities of creative exploration without limiting those possibilities in any way. A program of this nature seems to be a normal outcome of our contemporary cultural expansion. Even if it seems a contradiction, in order to protect such an open learning environment from institutional interference a new academic structure had to be created.

In addition to the general interdisciplinary orientation of the program, there is a constant interest in relating academic activities with the broader, outside world, by integrating the student's work with current art theories and practices. In the same way that the product is not valued differently than the process, we also do not give a different importance to the artistic tradition. In this sense, all kinds of art projects are welcome in the program, but there is a constant interest in embracing the notion of artistic practices that are relevant to our present time. One of these notions is the notion of transformation (personal and/or social), i.e., practices that are transformative in all possible ways, at the levels of intention, purpose, means, and result. Although the program's focus is not disciplinary, it does not exclude traditional, discipline-based work. However, we value any form of contemporary practice that searches for authentic change and transformation such as socially engaged art, autobiographical art, spiritual art, and any other form of nontraditional art.

Reiterating the notion of artistic autonomy and freedom in the learning process, another factor that contributes to the artistic growth of the students is the continuous association with their own local communities: the fact that they don't have to leave their communities in order to attend college. The idea that the local community is the one that profits the most from the artist's explorations contradicts the tradition of students relocating just to attend art school. This practice mandates geographic displacement to the larger metropolitan centers, to the detriment of the relationships students have developed and nurtured in their communities. The off campus structure, where the students come for a week-long residency twice a year, but which allows them to live in their local communities for the rest of the semester, permits a closer contact with issues of immediate relevance. The need for more direct contact with an immediate art community (the kind of peer relationship found in art schools) is met by an on-line seminar, which will be discussed later. As part of the degree requirement, and as a support to the MFA-IA pedagogical strategy, the students are required to fulfill certain components within their artistic experience, which include:

- a fully developed personal practice
- the ability to conduct rigorous exploration within the context of an art practice
- a practicum in a community-based art project
- an understanding of the nature of art and articulation of a personal theory of art
- the ability to develop critical discourse on one's own practice and the practices of others
- an understanding of the concept of interdisciplinary art
- an understanding of the cultural, social, and political context of one's artistic practice

Along with the notion of interdisciplinarity, an awareness of historic and contemporary art making and theory, in their own practices and in other cultures as well, is fundamental to the preparation of students for the challenges awaiting them in their professional lives. The contextualization of their practices within the current discourses in the arts, the development of critical skills, the ability to articulate issues of various natures (aesthetic, formal, social, economical, political, ethical, epistemological, linguistic, etc.), form a consistent basis for a valid, relevant, active, participatory artistic life during their studies and upon their graduation. This criterion is in place to encourage the students to develop a practice consistent with their artistic intentions; to engage in an active, relevant practice within their communities; and to expand their abilities to theorize about their work.

There is a practical component during the program of studies. The purpose of the practicum is for the students to explore ways to interact with their community, ways by which they will be able to sustain themselves as professionals and/or contribute meaningfully as artists, preparing them to face artistic life after the academy. The criteria described above should be demonstrated by a practical component during the program of studies. The student presents a portfolio that demonstrates his or her achievements during the academic experience. The portfolio consists of a body of work or the docu-mentation of a process, replacing a traditional thesis, degree exhibition, and so forth. The portfolio is consistent with our focus on the artist, where the practice and the person are at the center of this degree portfolio, instead of only their work, as in traditional institutions. The components of the portfolio could assume many different formats ranging from journal entries and essays to research notes that document the student's critical and theoretical work. In addition to the theoretical segment of the work, appropriate documentation describes the student's artistic practice: photography, video, slides, sound recordings, drawings, or any other alternative medium consistent with the student's artistic intention. As director Danielle Boutet states in the program's vision statement:

> We believe that the actualization of one's practice is not something that is achieved only during five semesters of graduate work: it starts long before the student enters the program, and continues long after graduation. The student's experience in the program is an important step in a lifelong journey, one during which the student's individual practice will take on new dimensions and significance. The goals of the program are to prepare the artist to achieve new levels of quality and create new means of interaction with society and community, to prepare the graduating student to fulfill a variety of responsibilities, such as in art production, teaching, community work, art criticism, curating, consulting, etc.[9]

This view echoes that of Joe Fulop, former Goddard art educator, who was quoted as follows in *To Know for Real*:

> Art is an outgrowth of the search for truth in everyday activities. It involves searching, finding, conceiving, giving shape and meaning to the eternal questions, who and where am I? Creative art represents a vision of listless imaginative possibilities in the bottomless pool of the unknown, where exists only the search, the play, and no pat answers or packaged sophistication. The challenge is the task of finding the initial glimpse, the original sensitivity which helps us integrate multiple values into an organic whole. It is a challenge to create, to make contact with one's inner life, to perceive one's dream. (Adams and Benson 1987, 142)

The apparent inconvenience of studying in a setting where the group does not physically meet often is addressed in the learning process through relationships established with the local art and social communities. By making those relationships a part of their plan of study, students can create new alternatives of social engagement with the arts, expanding beyond individual concerns for self-expression. Another benefit of a community-based practicum is to encourage the students to use practical experience to reflect upon their roles as artists within a community. We invite them to understand what they are able to contribute to the larger world, and to look deeply into their relationships to a community. We encourage them to go beyond the view of the community as an audience. The community-based component of the MFA-IA program attempts to subvert the art institution as the only intermediary between the artist and society.

The idea for a community-based practicum is an art project that is designed to create strategies that will link the artist's explorations and discoveries directly to their own communities. This is not a criticism of the public institution, but rather an attempt to redefine the institutional role of the art school vis-à-vis society. Institutions have a positive presence when they work to serve their communities. When the institutional commitment overrules the community's immediate needs it automatically loses its primary social function. The community-based practicum intends to initiate such a relationship during the student's academic years and to advance an issue that is usually addressed only after graduation.

This is not the only attempt to create community ties among the students. Our experience with the experimental on-line seminar searches to fulfill such a need as well, by bringing students together in a critical forum about issues of mutual interest. The experimental on-line seminar, a common ground for exchange, complements the student's learning process by constituting a forum where theoretical discussions take place.

Transformative Practices: an Experimental On-line Seminar

They [people] should be able to meet around a problem chosen and defined by their own initiative. Creative, exploratory learning requires peers [who are] currently puzzled about the same terms or problems. The most radical alternative to school would be a network or service which gave each man the same opportunity to share his current concern with others motivated by the same concern.

–Ivan Illich

There is no technology which is inherently democratic or no technology which is inherently oppressive for that matter, technology is usually a fairly neutral thing. The technology doesn't care really whether it's used for oppression or liberation, it's how people use it.

–Noam Chomsky

On-line exchange has proved to be an effective tool to bring people together. At Goddard, the use of electronic-based communication is almost second nature because students and faculty are spread geographically. The use of on-line communication matured from a persistent need to exchange questions and find answers quickly, a function that proved to be hypothetical when we used regular mail and too expensive when we used the telephone. The experimental on-line seminar was created with the initial intent to generate a long-distance community forum for the MFA-IA students. It started as a forum where students and faculty could meet and discuss issues related to interdisciplinary art practices through the articulation of concepts and theories common to all people engaged in the program. The seminar is proving to be an effective tool of intellectual, social, and spiritual exchange, qualities that evolve beyond a traditional seminar setting where students and teacher meet formally in a classroom. In traditional seminar settings there is a certain quality in the discourse that happens live, in the moment of the exchange, with the teacher physically present, psychologically shaping the space of reflection. In the on-line seminar we dissolve this power relationship, which provides a better sense of equality among participants. The sense of presence is different in this case. The ephemeral quality of the discourse is replaced by an articulation based on reflection and measured response, because participation occurs through writing (we use e-mail instead of a chat room). To write one's critical feedback requires a different level of reflection; with time and space (controlled by the student), allow for a more elaborated response than the usual verbal, immediate reply of traditional seminars. The words, in this case, acquire a more tangible quality. They are recorded, and become a real document in space and time, which makes the process of reflection somehow different from classroom participation. Technology, in this case, could be seen as an instrument for democratic practice, for bringing people together, for creating a real opportunity for public articulation. However, the technology per se cannot be translated into a democratic tool. Instead it is the use of the technology and the ways it has been used by someone that can be called democratic.

In my first encounter with electronic communication I remained suspicious of its effectiveness, but in a context such as the low residency, off campus structure at Goddard, technology fulfills the function of bringing students together in the most varied ways and interests. Even if the access to the technology remains a complex, unresolved issue, the experiment of the on-line seminar has indicated new and effective uses for a technology that is often considered to be distant and cold.

Our themes for the seminar are deliberately broad, designed to provide a forum for all students, across disciplines, to learn to frame and contextualize their practice, and to learn how to write about art and how to locate themselves within large issues. As the theme for this year's seminar is "What is art? For the Artist, For the Community...Who Decides?", the general theme for the first experimental on-line seminar in the program was "Transformative Practices." The theme challenged the notion of art as an exclusive self-fulfilling instrument, in a time when the closed values of aesthetics are perhaps gone. The crisis of contemporary art demands new meanings for artistic practices that are relevant to both the individual artist and society, moving beyond the institutional formalities of art to reach lives with a tangible difference. The readings for the seminar covered a broad range of themes that explored several definitions of "transformative." The readings brought into the scene a series of diversified interpretations intended to open the students to various forms of theoretical articulations, ranging from the historical view of Marcel Duchamp to the radicalism of Lygia Clark, from the marginality of Starhawck to the erudition of Edward Said. The general character of the readings brought together different theoretical speculations that challenge the modernist tradition and presented several alternative ways to approach the nature of art practices in the twilight of the century. The subthemes included the creative process, community-oriented art, public art, issues related to the body, and engaged art.

Program director Danielle Boutet states that

> transformative is a keyword for our focus on practice. We are looking for practices which are transformative, in all possible ways, at the levels of intention, purpose, means and result. One may argue that art practice is always transformative, and we agree with this. But we want to put the transformative aspect of art at the center, rather than viewing transformation as a mere side-effect of art.[10]

"Transformative" in relation to art practices suggests a critical distancing from the paradigms of modernism. Modernism neglects questions related to the subjective world of the artist, the audience, the social, spiritual, historic, cultural, economic, and political aspects of the artistic process. This reading of the artistic process created a partial and sometimes twisted view of the complex webs of relations we can find in art as a public event. The seminar created a chance to discuss how some contemporary artists, critics, and cultural activists are increasingly and meaningfully renewing the process of artistic practices, to respond to the paramount needs and understanding of today's society.

The experimental on-line seminar enlarges the context of investigation by creating a formal dialogue between all participants over a topic, enhancing everyone's critical and communication skills, and invoking a stronger sense of community among faculty and students. It has proved to be an efficient manner to trace a collective direction by articulating a group of common interests that represent the vision of the program. The theories and artworks that have been discussed are a reflection of the group's current interests; the structure proved to be organic enough to maintain an animate and flexible spirit of discussion. The seminar also triggered several alternative detours from the discussions in smaller groups that took place independently from the general seminar structure.

Goddard's Contribution

In his book *Teaching Art: Academies and Schools from Vasari to Albers*, Carl Goldstein concludes his thorough description on the teachings of art from Renaissance to today with two questions:

> About to enter not only a new century but a new millennium, can we say that we are clear about what art is and what role we expect it to play in our lives and in society? Are we clear enough about these crucial issues to say that art should be taught in one way and in that way only? (1996, 299)

Goldstein questions the influential events that have shaped the theory and practice during the past decades. The shift from modernism that transformed so much the patterns of art making of the last thirty or forty years suggested the end of an era of ethnocentric European dominance in the art world, a reclamation of the art of non-Western cultures, misrepresented groups, and women. Postmodernism claimed to be the responsible for the collapse of modernism by reinventing an avant-garde with social and political consciousness, aesthetically free from tradition. Postmodernism has survived more as a cultural phenomenon than as a philosophical notion set in stone that functions as a means to explain the radical changes in the artistic traditions of the second half of the twentieth century. Paradoxically, at the end of the process, postmodernism reinstated the notion of tradition, opening the creative process to many new possibilities of artistic scrutiny at the same time that it returned to values that were once rejected by modern artists. Modernity, in its most traditional understanding, goes back way before the tenets of twentieth-century modernism, and has indicated that it will influence the complexities of the cultural process for a long time to come, through the present tendency of revisionism in the arts, and the difficulty of creating art totally outside that same tradition. Maybe a lesson has been learned at the end of this process: that the institutionalization of art and its power of influence must be under constant critical inquiry, and that the institutional authority of the art establishment could, after all, become vulnerable to the power of creative freedom and the ideals of democracy that are associated with the artistic spirit.

But, where does the teaching/learning experience at Goddard stand in the face of these changing circumstances of art practice and education? Dada and Surrealism were not the only entities to claim the autonomy of the artist within the creative process. The Sixties represented a sociopolitical upheaval that moved toward equality and fair recognition that permanently influenced our culture. During the past thirty or forty years the art academy has resisted the opening the dogmas of art theory and history. Is this self-inflicted institutional blinding allowing the permanence of the institutional image of the art academy because society demands that it do so or is it because it lacks the adequate conceptual and pedagogical experience to support a free, exploratory, and genuinely experimental learning environment in the creative arts? Art institutions are an image of the society they represent. However, they represent the ambition of only a small part of this same society. Goddard does not intend to provide a definitive answer. But what Goddard College does provide is an alternative, positive learning space that clearly differs from other institutions in its philosophical and methodological basis. We put the student at the center of the learning process and, through an instrumentation that protects their creative visions (the study plan and self-evaluation), we give art students the opportunity to trace their own futures within their creative process. The teacher's role is constantly redefined through a consistent understanding that what matters in the learning process is, a priori, the student, suggesting, in this case, a "politics of reciprocity" in the exchange between student and educator that encourages and valorizes the learning process above all. Goddard's interdisciplinary pedagogical strategies are committed to the creation of a more democratic environment within the artist's formation. We hope that these ideals of democracy will move beyond the confines of the art academy, and that the students will infiltrate into the world through their presence and influence in their own communities.

Endnotes

1. A distinction should be made between popular mass culture and art, even if the lines that delimit these cultural manifestations seem to increasingly blur. One of the criteria to distinguish both are distribution and market value; another is the scale and quality of impact of these cultural products within specific communities. When popular mass culture aims, sometimes quite exclusively, for profits, art making doesn't necessarily achieve the same commercial success or popular acclaim of mass produced objects. Mass culture supports the perception of globalization by distributing cultural icons that will be eventually assimilated in any geographical area through the rapid advancement and exploitation of technology. The same does not necessarily happen with all kinds of artistic experiences.

2. In 1928, László Moholy-Nagy said in his letter of resignation from the Bauhaus: "Basically one can't object if human power wants to measure itself on the object, the trade. This belongs essentially to the Bauhaus program. But one must see the danger of losing equilibrium, and meet it. As soon as creating an object becomes a specialty, and work becomes trade, the process of education loses all vitality. There must be room for teaching the basic ideas which keep human content alert and vital. For this we fought and for this we exausted ourselves. I can no longer keep up with stronger and stronger tendency toward trade and specialization in the workshops. We are now in danger of becoming what we as revolutionaries opposed: a vocational training school which evaluates only the final achievement and overlooks the development of the whole man [sic]. For him there remains no time, no money, no space, no concession. I can't afford the continuation on this specialized, pure objective and efficient basis–either productively or humanly. I trained myself in five years for a specialty, the Metal Workshop, but I could do this only by also giving all my human reserves. I shall have to resign if this demand for specialization becomes more intense. The spirit of construction for which I and others gave all we had–and gave it gladly–has been replaced by a tendency toward application" (in *The Tradition of Constructivism*. Edited by Stephen Bann. New York: Da Capo Press, 1974). Moholy-Nagy's statement reiterates the need for a more integral relationship between technical, disciplinary skills and a more holistic approach to education.

3. The College Arts Association records over 180 MFA programs in North America, and only 20 of these programs are organized under an Interdisciplinary Arts structure. The CAA classification includes 36 different disciplines of specialization, ranging from Ad and Product design to Wood. (Lynda Emery, in The Directory of M.F.A. Programs in the Visual Arts. New York: College Arts Association, 1992, revised 1996.)

4. Clement Greenberg was one of the most influential American art critics of the postwar period. He championed Abstract Expressionism and the muscular mid-century heroic and individualistic American generation of

artists led by Jackson Pollock.

5. Recent residency themes have been Democracy; Restoring Community, Living Our Visions; and Art and Nature.

6. The accredited master of Fine Arts in Interdisciplinary Arts program at Goddard College was created in 1997, and it is now in its experimental stages, functioning initially as a pilot program.

7. Work, for example, that blends craft and political discourse such as Judy Chicago's Dinner Party, where craft, art, history, and feminism are integrated (Danielle Boutet, *Program Overview* handout, 1997).

8. Ibid.

9. Ibid.

10. Ibid.

References

Adams, F. and A. Benson. 1987. *To Know for Real: Royce Pitkin and Goddard College*. Adamant, Vermont: Adamant Press.

Chomsky, N. 1995. interview by RosieX and Chris Mountford for Geekgirl, Australia, http://206.251.6.116/geekgirl/002manga/chomsky.html.

Gablik, S. 1995. "Connective Aesthetics" in *Mapping the Terrain: New Genre Public Art*, edited by Suzanne Lacy. Seattle: Bay Press.

Goldstein, C. 1996. *Teaching Art: Academies and Schools from Vasari to Albers*. New York: Cambridge University Press.

Illich, I. 1970. *Deschooling Society*. New York: Harper and Row.

FOUR

Writing for Our Lives:
The Power of Memoir for Marginalized Students

Shelley Vermilya

in collaboration with students and faculty at Goddard College in the BA/MA Individualized Off-Campus Program

Introduction

"Silence Equals Death," we say today about lesbian and gay rights, and this concept of silence takes us quickly through history to the burning of witches, slavery, and the Holocaust. These are just a few of the genocidal moments in time. Silence is a death for students who don't know their history, their sociology, their culture, their assumptions, and how they internalize stereotypes about themselves. They enter into a silence that leads to prejudice and self-perpetuating low self-esteem. It can kill curiosity and the desire to learn, and it can lead to the death of a mind. "Knowledge Equals Power," I often say to my students. "Use yourself as an example and intertwine your life experiences as you write about the theory you are reading, the psychology, sociology, history, or philosophy." Such a request assumes that they have critical experiences and that their voices are important. It also assumes they can integrate academic work with their lives.

To reflect on one's life in writing is to relive and expose oneself to a public readership. The terms appear too radical at first. There is often doubt in a student's initial response to such a suggestion. I work with adults who have returned to college, some after a thirty-year hiatus, others only a few years out of high school. Their college experience is a low-residency schedule that includes fifteen weeks back at home working on a project they have designed. Alone. Alone with their families, jobs, and an already full-time schedule to juggle and cajole. Red Smith once wrote, "I sit at the typewriter and open a vein." I use Red to illustrate that writing one's life is not at all as easy as it sounds. However, the struggle is worth it, as Judith Barrington explains,

> For members of marginalized groups, speaking personally and truthfully about our lives plays a small part in erasing years of invisibility and interpretation by others. And for all of us, engaging seriously with the truth challenges our society's enormous untruthfulness—whether it comes from the family, which so often

denies its own violence behind closed doors, or from the national and international powers that deny their own violence and call it "peace-keeping" (Barrington 1997,14).

To tell the truth of our lives requires that we break silences and taboos that have been used to coerce and condemn, belittle and sabotage the full possibility of our lives and our place in the social structure. The cost of true expression may be family disruption, avoidance by neighbors and associates, and job loss. Despite candid talk shows, Internet access, and a variety of popular novels and movies, many students are still not acquainted with the stories of marginalized* people, even if they are one! (The closet doors must still be closed, because gay and lesbian students are often amazed to find their history and literary culture. Southerners are often delighted to be introduced to Southern writers...and the list goes on.) Although authors of color, incest survivors, women, gays, and lesbians have entered the canon, somehow their poignancy and reality have not been recognized by students and faculty. Students and faculty have yet to fully embrace all learners; to accept the complication that a multicultural perspective demands. To accept the danger of raw voices, to accept rage and passion, requires faculty to "open a vein" of their own and reexamine the terms of truthfulness and let these student voices speak. Faculty need to dare to listen to raw voices and engage in dialogue about issues that are deeply engaging to students that may be new and/or discomfiting for faculty.

Autobiography and memoir challenge the inequitable power relations between researcher and researchee. Autobiography offers one important way to explore differences and diversity, and it inspires an epistemology that is disobedient to the power relations inherent in the Western canon. It has much to offer as an epistemology of resistance (Wilton 1995, 170, 176). Such resistance instigates new curiosity and new definitions of truth and power. Such disobedience and resistance inspires explorations of power, privilege, gender, sexuality, the erotic, race, and class. Diversity.

Incest and sexual abuse survivors, lesbians, gay men, transsexuals, Native Americans, people of color, people with disabilities, low income people, fat people, the elderly, the young, Jews. All must write about experiences they have had growing up and/or living in "marginalized" circumstances. This is an epistemology/pedagogy of identity politics and identity writing. It is a pedagogy that includes spiritual and healing dimensions. It takes learning off the page and integrates it into the learner. The mind, spirit, body, and soul are recognized in this experience.

Identity pedagogy involves a patience, dedication, and perseverance usually not required of an advisor/teacher. New definitions of truth and power require a true paradigm shift for the traditional (and nontraditional) teacher. The teacher may have to accept that the student has a great deal more information about the

---

*   Marginalized" may be controversial; however another term is not readily as meaningful or available.

environment, the social and cultural definitions, and the racial, ethnic, and gender experiences about which the student is writing. The teacher has to find new approaches to "teaching" because the authority of knowledge has shifted. The teacher takes on new challenges of encouraging further detail, closer examination of experience, helping the student find the voice that most appropriately fits them. S/he must create an environment of trust and acceptance in order for students to reach heights and depths they may never have considered possible for themselves. One of the inherent problems is evaluation, because who can disclaim a life? The discourse among our faculty about self-referential studies, the use of autobiography and memoir, continues every semester.

Autobiography/memoir dismantles the concept of authority/expert and the power of knowledge *over* the learner. The student describes her/his experience and consequently claims that experience in an integral way. The effort and ability to write inspires a deeper way of knowing. Students reflect the learning they have acquired as it relates to their personal experience. The facts fit their life, and their life is enlightened by the facts they find. "500,000 children experience sexual abuse each year" (Bluj 1998,6).

> The limbic system is over-stimulated and interacts with the prefrontal cortex in the brain to process the stimulation. Two consequences occur; there is a heightened intensity to the response and a lessening of counter-responses that might help to resolve the alarm state. The result is the disorganization of responses. This disorganization affects the neocortical pathways in the brain which are basic to cognitive mapping. Consequently, when the limbic system is compromised, the evolving meaning system in the neocortical pathways is also compromised. This is one explanation of why children allow the abuse to keep happening. (12).

Knowledge becomes empowerment. Writing her story, the abuse survivor realizes the abuse of power. Realizes it was not her fault. Realizes the physiological and psychological implications. Realizes that the skills she learned to survive demonstrate her true strength.

Judith Barrington provides my favorite definitions of some frequently confused terms.

> An autobiography is the story of a life: the name implies that the writer will somehow attempt to capture all the essential elements of that life. A writer's autobiography, for example, is not expected to deal merely with the author's growth and career as a writer but also with the facts and emotions connected to family life, education, relationships, sexuality, travels, and inner struggles of all kinds. An autobiography is sometimes limited by dates (as in *Under My Skin: Volume One of My Autobiography to 1949* by Doris Lessing), but not obviously by theme.
>
> Memoir, on the other hand, makes no pretense of replicating a whole life. Indeed, one of the important skills of memoir writing is the

selection of the theme or themes that will bind the work together (Barrington 1997, 22/23).

Barrington quotes Gore Vidal in *Palimpsest,* "A memoir is how one remembers one's own life, while an autobiography is history, requiring research, dates, facts double-checked" (24).

Memory is a funny, slippery, malleable thing. "Truth" pivots or shifts dramatically in the memoir writing and whole new perspectives are realized by the student due to their remembering. The student must have a deep motivating factor in order to begin this work. It may be the slaying of demons, the desire to break cycles, or the sheer energy that comes from starting a project that has deep, personal meaning. The descriptive devices help the writer to acknowledge the "truth" of the situation and their continued research will enhance the diversity and complexity of their understanding of their experience.

Lisa Townsend, in her undergraduate final product, wrote of her experiences as a single mother on welfare, the welfare system in Vermont, and the intrinsic class issues and stereotypes of the welfare mom. Suggestions for change in Vermont's public policy evolved through her writing. She included many pages of creative writing and journaling she had done over the course of her college experience. "The purpose is to free up the clutter in one's brain, to act as a creative processing plant for life's struggles and triumphs." She also included them in order to provide the reader with

a deeper understanding of the day to day struggles inherent with parenting solo and in poverty. I am certain that the self-doubt I so often express within these pages is directly related to the negative attitudes in our culture about single mothers in poverty. Creativity is an important combatant to those negative messages.

Lisa Townsend found that her daily experience did not equate with what she was hearing about welfare mothers in the media, nor did the image of herself as she wrote in her journals resonate with what she was hearing about herself from colleagues, fellow students, and teachers. Through her academic quest and her personal writing she was dismantling the stereotype of welfare mothers, dismantling the negative images of herself, and thus finding empowerment and self-fulfillment.

There is a dilemma in being entrusted as faculty with the responsibility to uphold standards while just such standards and expectations may impede the empowerment of students as self-directed learners. One of the areas in which the conflict takes place is that empowerment and self-fulfillment are not necessarily a degree criteria, though Goddard does rely on the Dewey trilogy of "knowing, being, doing," and what better fulfillment than empowerment as lifelong learners? Consequently, as an advocate of memoir/ autobiography, I frequently find myself defending a position that challenges my colleagues to reconsider the appropriateness of standard English for a marginalized student. Reading such work requires faculty have clear standards and expectations for college-level work, English as a second language expectations, reasonable learning-difference accommodations, and that they encourage reasonable creative license. All of these are pedagogical, political, and social considerations that take time to sort out and agree upon. I wholeheartedly agree that there are standards and expectations that must be maintained. My staunchest opposition to this work comes from grammatical sticklers who would rather have a comma in the proper place than allow poetic justice. I will conclude with some of the thinking our faculty have done in this regard.

The pedagogical goal of using autobiography in an educational framework is then multifaceted:

- It places the learner in a larger context of meaning. Examples are research in women's development, civil rights legislation, history, psychology, literature of the marginalized group.
- It integrates the learning for the learner. Parallel research in the field, as suggested above, gives the learner an immediate connection that is personal and community based and makes the learning more real, owned by the student.
- It encourages the learner to write and learn beyond the surface. The integration of the knowledge of the greater context grants the writer permission to reveal more and opens up expressive avenues. The facts and the emotions are intertwined for a richer dialogue on paper.
- It establishes learning as an integral part of being. This integration of knowledge is new for students. They often express how much more they retain than in prior learning environments where tests were the only gauge they had for knowing. Realizing they have the tools to find knowledge and that new knowledge is interesting and inspiring sets up a desire in students to continue risking, learning, knowing more.
- This new understanding clearly situates a student in profound self-esteem. When students realize all the factors that actually compose the life experience, they chose to write about what gives them a greater understanding of their responses, the actions of others, the systems of social injustice that perpetuate cycles.

One particular drawback of the work as an advisor is that there is no template response, no blue-plate special for this kind of work. Each individual has a unique story to tell and will find her/his voice through nurturing, relentless encouragement, and tough love. The rapport between advisor and student must include a blend of compassion and an insistence on quality so that degree criteria are met. The advisor must be agile and thoughtful, and must break the dominant discourse and response in order to respond to a unique story. It is a very risky undertaking for both parties in the learning partnership. Chanda Martin wrote in a note on May 28, 1998:

> I really hated doing the autobiography, it wore me down and out. I hurt so many people when I wrote that, but it was my first step to healing. It, though mediocre, was the most powerful thing I've ever done. Yes, I hated doing that piece, I even entertained hating you and Danielle (the

second reader and advisor), but I am soooo glad I did it and now all I
can say is thank you to you both.

I hope to reflect the vigorous nature of this work; the academic,
psychological, and political demands of memoir/autobiography for those who
undertake it. I will quote colleagues and students in order to mirror the dialogue
and the willingness that is required to dive into complexity and the
unwillingness to be singularly defined that is, in essence, the occupational
hazard that comes, for both teacher and student, when engaging in this
pedagogy.

Liberation and Education

I would say that my sub-heading is oxymoronic. I see students who have
experienced education as standardized, sanitized, homogenized, one size fits all.
Until I started working with my students on incorporating autobiography into
their college studies, I would say liberation was the furthest possible outcome of
education because students worked to please professors, to pass tests, or to do
what they thought was expected, not to think and integrate knowledge.
    bell hooks writes in *Teaching to Transgress: Education as the Practice of
Freedom,* that her thinking about education has been influenced by Paulo Freire
and Thich Nhat Hanh who talk about engaged pedagogy and engaged
Buddhism. This combination of liberation theorists yields the concept that
"education can only be liberatory when everyone claims knowledge as a field in
which we all labor" (hooks 1994,14). Knowledge as a holistic endeavor for the
mind, body, and spirit engages the entire student. The teacher must also be
actively committed to well-being and must be on a constant quest to understand
her/his essential self. This is a very demanding pedagogy!
    Most of my students are in midlife transition. They have had careers in
education, retail, as counselors in the recovery field, or they have been in a
marriage and find themselves at a crossroads that suddenly requires a degree. I
have worked with straight white men, straight white women, Native American
women, African American women, bisexuals and lesbians (white and of color),
women in recovery (in all of the above categories) from drugs and/or alcohol
and/or sexual abuse and/or incest, women with disabilities, combinations of all
of the above and more. I have included the story of a pre through postoperative
male to female transsexual.
    I work *with* learners, and we work hard to find the language that tells the
truth about our lives. These are all people who often have disappeared and or
have been denied or degraded in the shadow of standard texts, Standard English,
and legislation. These are also people just starting to question their privilege as
white, upper-class, male, female, straight, or homosexual people.
    My role as a facilitator of learners who are using autobiography/memoir as
the premise of their study has been to inspire writing beyond general reference,
memory recitation, or ego-based "I love Me in this!" Writing beyond the
comfort level, writing to the bone (to misquote a Natalie Goldberg title), writing

a truth that hasn't yet been heard, either from the writer or in public discourse. The student has to be prepared: this is very hard work conceptually and creatively. Although this work has therapeutic value, students in need of in-depth therapy need to work with professional therapists. Furthermore, because this work pushes people beyond themselves in a greater context, one needs to understand one's story in a historic, social, developmental, and/or political perspective. I encourage students to look at psychology, philosophy, history, or a combination of fields, that will illuminate their strengths and help them interpret their stories.

This process also requires advisors to constantly reassess the function of education and what balance of self-reflection best serves the students. My colleague, Ralph Lutts, has asked,

> What is our vision of the kind of "educated person" that Goddard wants its graduates to be? My sense is that a liberal arts student should have a broad knowledge, critical thinking skills, learn how to learn, gain depth in some area and be able to place this within a wider intellectual and cultural context. Too great an emphasis on self-reflection and/or studies within a narrow, self-reinforcing field does not empower students; it disempowers them.

A handout he gives his students clearly states his expectations:

> Given Goddard's emphasis on combining knowledge with experience, it is understandable that some students might want to base a portion of their studies on self-reflection. This can be an important element in some students' work. However, if you want self-reflection to become a significant part of your studies, it is very important to place it within the larger academic context. This larger perspective is central to liberal arts studies and is required by Goddard's criteria for graduation.
>
> One might, for example, want to explore one's own autobiography. If you want to focus on autobiography as writing, then it is appropriate to also read a number of published autobiographies and become familiar with the theory and critical literature of autobiography. If you are interested in autobiography as psychological self-examination, then it is appropriate to read published autobiographies of this sort and become familiar with the literature and theories of the formation of self, personality, the life cycle, and psychobiography.
>
> Similarly, if you want to explore your own spiritual and religious beliefs and experiences, it is appropriate to also place this within an academic context. This might include examining the psychology, philosophy, and anthropology of religion and myth, as well as the history and theology of your own religion and of other religions. The goal of this broad exploration is not to undermine one's own religious beliefs, but to strengthen one's knowledge and understanding by placing them within a larger context. (Jan. 22, 1997)

This message from Ralph inspired others among the faculty to then consider the issue of critical writing as the lens for interpreting the greater world.

Another colleague, Caryn Mirriam-Goldberg, continued the dialogue with these comments,

> When I think about students who resist critical writing, I think about what fear might lie beneath the resistance. I don't think it's a fear of research as much as it's a fear of organization. They find all this great stuff, but then how do they put it together? Especially if they're trying to blend the self-referential into the research-from-beyond-the-self. And since many people have been beaten and berated earlier in their formal education, the fear of being able to write something that speaks true for them and meets the requirements can overwhelm.

Some students are indeed overwhelmed by the task of organization and writing, while others lose their bearings as facts and new comprehension or contexts meet old ways of thinking of themselves. Discarding old ways of seeing themselves is often difficult and adopting new perceptions (of oneself and the circumstances and the world) takes time.

This is the "context" of autobiography/self-referential studies: the question or concern that the student brings to the research. The writing asks/explores/dives into the answers *for the individual.* This is critical writing from the very deepest motivation for the individual and for an audience. To be heard, seen, and read contextualized the writing further.

"When it was pointed out to one of my students at Goddard that he was no longer a 'victim' of his social class because in the act of writing he had 'solved' that dilemma, he cried," writes faculty member and writer Cherry Muhanji. Cherry suggests that the issue that leads to finding one's voice is self-esteem. "Critical writing and the resistance to same represents, I think, all those critical voices that have told us for so long that we are not worthy (not my language), that we are a piece of s--t" (January 29, 1997).

Through autobiography and memoir a student can re-vision their experiences and claim their authority. They can re-write endings to strengthen their sense of health and well-being, their self-esteem. This is a revolutionary act because it completely dispels the lies, myths, and silences that have made collaborators in oppression of all of these students.

The following examples from recent Goddard College off-campus graduates and faculty show the value of autobiography/memoir as one means of acquiring an engaged pedagogy that inspires risk taking. What some find, however, is that autobiography/memoir is not a magical cure but the beginning of lifelong learning.

Terry Stoeker found that writing her life, fictionalizing some events in short story form and creating a body of multimedia pieces was the beginning of dispelling family myths. She writes a year after submitting her senior study "Breaking the Fourth Wall of the Self,"

It started out as a burning desire to "get my story out!" I felt driven to tell, to speak, to heal. The task at times seemed too painful, too large, too overwhelming to accomplish. But, still the desire led the way. The residual result of the end product (I cannot say finished product, since there is much more to do) was empowering beyond any expectations. I, naively, thought that one of the healing benefits of writing down the story of my early childhood would be to feel cleansed or free from the negative aspects of surviving sexual abuse. The bad habits left over from days of lying, hiding, physical pain and emotional undoing would be lifted, magically. A profound healing did take place and continues to work in my life, but it was not a magic lifting, it was a gradual unfolding of love.

The healing arose out of a restored and clear path back to the natural love of self that was so long ago defiled. This path, at times, is still strewn with the debris of abuse and the residue of self-loathing that blocks me from fully functioning to my highest expectations. Through the writing, I have learned to love the woman I am, where I am, along with the blocks in her path and who has accomplished so much despite the terrible things that happened in her past. I have come to embrace and laugh at my need for perfection and control. I recognize my path toward always finding what is true for me and to live that truth everyday. And I have learned to accept and love the part of me that gets very tired from all that I have to fight against. I have moved through the verb "to survive", though the elements of survival will always be a part of me, to a healing verb "to thrive". I have also, through continued writing and inquiry, made a decision to talk with one of my primary perpetrators. I would not be at this place in time, if I had not done the autobiographical writing, which at the time, I never considered to be autobiographical. It was just my need to tell my story, to help other women, to discover and realize my self-worth and to work toward my womanhood. The writing process, itself, taught me that my work is a process to embrace and encourage.

Terry Stoecker worked with three-dimensional multimedia, performance, and writing to create an interdisciplinary final project. It was an artistic and psychological undertaking that resulted in over 250 pages of poetry, short stories, and essays. Autobiography was a driving force, not necessarily a conscious decision.

Cherry Muhanji takes autobiographical writing into her fiction and uses her craft to dispel racism and racial myths and to reclaim her power. She says,

In my creative work I often create scenes that echo the "real" events. For example, much of what happens to us in places and spaces where we are disempowered we do not realize to what extent or that anything happened till much, much later. How did I know at seventeen that what I represented to my community was the hi-yellah who would that what I represented to my community was the hi-yellah who would get all of the benefits from white culture because I was "light bright and almost white"? How could I know that? How could I know that I was perceived as a trophy, not someone with a mind? It would take years, girlfriend, years. How do I empower myself now when so much has happened that told me I was shit (dominant culture), and that I was a piece of "yellah throwed away" by my own? (I didn't, in the final analysis, have Euro hair and features).

I write. I can control the terrain. I can introduce all that pain through my characters and work it out by having whomever I choose be victorious. And yes, there is an emotional honesty in that the characters work out in the world of the book things that I could not and cannot in the "real" world.

Sometimes in the development of a certain character or situation the mind suddenly remembers a feeling—an emotion—a real something "going down" that has been forgotten, but now I can do something about it. Therapy? Well—yes. Not only has a working-class Black female lesbian grandmother come to voice but she has found a way to have power. Writing. The empowerment is not only in coming to voice but the struggle to work out what has happened and to "actively" do something about it.

"Actively *do something about it*," says Cherry. How do we get students to such a point? bell hooks honors both Paulo Freire and Thich Nhat Hanh for leading her to the concept of an "engaged pedagogy" (hooks 1994, 14/15). The emphasis for these two teachers, notes bell, is on " 'praxis'-action and reflection upon the world in order to change it" (14). The praxis in memoir/autobiography writing sometimes requires pages and pages of raw, cathartic material that are revised and revised until the reflection can occur.

bell hooks admits that engaged pedagogy "is more demanding than conventional critical or feminist pedagogy" (15). And it is through such demand (by both student and teacher) that freedom comes to the writing and authenticity comes into consciousness for the writer. Identity pedagogy is engaged, feminist, resistant, and very demanding because it requests authenticity from the writer as well as an examination of the essential self and all the qualities of that personal essence.

Authenticity. Internalized fear and oppression. Duality.

This is "The tragic dilemma of the oppressed which their education must take into account," writes Paulo Freire in *Pedagogy of the Oppressed:*

The oppressed suffer from the duality which has established itself in their innermost being. They discover that without freedom they cannot exist authentically. Yet, although they desire authentic existence, they fear it. They are at one and the same time themselves and the oppressor whose consciousness they have internalized. The conflict lies in the choice between being wholly themselves or being divided; between ejecting the oppressor within or not ejecting them; between human solidarity or alienation; between following prescriptions or having choices; between being spectators or actors; between acting or having the illusion of acting through the action of the oppressors; between speaking out or being silent, castrated in their power to create and re-create, in their power to transform the world. This is the tragic dilemma of the oppressed which their education must take into account. (Freire 1970, 30)

Freire points out other attributes of the oppressed that are frequently qualities found in the student before s/he undertakes an autobiographical/memoir writing project:

- Fatalistic attitude
- Magical belief in the invulnerability and power of the oppressor
- Emotional dependence
- Drinking and drug abuse

People of color, alcoholics in recovery, survivors of incest or sexual abuse unwittingly prove Freire's theories. Again and again we hear marginalized students tell of being in relationships with whites, family systems, men that are either emotionally and/or physically abusive and how long it took them to a) understand that it was abuse, b) understand that they did not "deserve" to be treated thus, and c) figure out how to "get out."

The repetition of patterns, of self-deprecation and self-inflicted abuse among marginalized peoples becomes palpable. Students discover the patterns through repetition as they write their memoir/autobiography and this leads them (and us as readers) to their own experience of authenticity. Lisa Townsend writes,

My own journey of unearthing my voice has been painful, exciting, tedious at times, but almost always worth the effort. What I have unearthed in my dig has simply been astounding to me at times; leaves me breathless, frightened and in awe of what lays below the surface of my fear. I have found that hidden underneath my seemingly damaged shell, is a gem, a glorious gem that has been laying there dormant all this time, protected deep inside my psyche since I was born. ("No More Offerings to the Porcelain Goddess," 2).

Freire says that we believe in ourselves when we find the oppressor out and become involved in organized struggle. And reflection leads to action and authentic liberation, which is the process of humanization.

That reflection leads to action is imperative. Action for the learner, first, is writing their story in a way that is authentic to them. The story often highlights the student's disenfranchisement. The full circle from reflection to action often inspires participation in community. Community may begin as a recovery group and then expand to job-related community, then to social and political participation in local/national community. Claudia Conlan is a good example.

She did drugs, got into recovery, wrote about her incest experiences for her undergraduate work and slipped back into taking drugs. It was not until she wrote about women's history in her graduate work and found the greater context for her experiences that she took her recovery into another level. I've worked with other students (especially incest survivors) who demonstrate time and again that identity politics are crucial for authentic liberation.

Many of my students, as you will see in the following excerpts of senior studies, demonstrate the educational/experiential continuum that liberation of the self leads to participation in the greater world. The initial period of separatism required for Claudia to research the history of women, lesbians, and women with drug addictions in fact provided her with a self-affirming basis from which to go on and participate more fully in the world. She is now considering a Ph.D. in theology and work in hospice.

Separatism, for a period of time, can be a good thing! Our curriculum ought to establish one's identity. Then the student, with self-confidence and esteem, has a great desire to explore all fields and disciplines, has the skills to critically examine social and political issues, and the commitment to actively engage in changing the world around them. The following students declare the importance of autobiography/memoir as engaged/identity pedagogy.

David is in his late forties, a white, gay man who has come through the AIDS pandemic. Although he is HIV negative, he has lived with the conflict of survival while watching hundreds of friends and acquaintances die.
David Boyce writes in the preface to his 1996 senior study, "A Crowd of Incidents,"

In employing an autobiographical narrative form, I have found a broader canvas on which to paint, and a larger vocabulary of tools with which to work. Personal anecdotes could be expanded into passages of emotional richness that seemed to allow the reader a fuller and more human experience of my story, and recreate scenes, sensorial descriptions, and bits of dialogue that may in fact not be fully accurate, but are the essence of the truth as I remember it, and evoke in me the appropriate emotions as I recall them. That emotional honesty felt more important than any factual detail, and has, I believe, made my story more accessible and authentic to a reader.

The form allowed me greater creativity, a more assured sense of authority, and perhaps more importantly, a sense of choice and control in and over my life. Innately, I know I did not choose my sexuality, but as a gay writer using this form, I could reinvent the world from my own perspective, making it into one in which my marginalized status as a gay man is, to varying degrees, less proscribed by the dominant culture. No matter how different my life is deemed to be by anyone else, for the most part, it is normal to me. In attempting to make approachable, believable, and palatable what may be extraordinary for some readers, it is my hope they will relate to it with less intimidation, bias, and fear, and with more compassion and understanding. I also hope and presume many gay readers will recognize and identify with a fellow traveler.

As a result, I have come to better understand where I fit as the main character in my life. All these stories have me as a common element, but previously I hadn't been able to grasp the accumulated subtleties and shadings of their combined effects. I think we tend to look at our lives as a series of individual events, often grouping incidents of similar theme, without necessarily assessing how their linearity impacts on us as an accrued whole. The chronologic autobiographical narrative form readily permits such a reading, and is more accurately reflective of how life transpires, though perhaps not as it is perceived.

I have found this form both enjoyable and more valuable, as a personal writing experience. In their retelling, I have relived these stories, and made connections, had revelations, and seen possibilities that were previously inaccessible or unavailable. In many cases, I have been able to reach a peace with myself through self-forgiveness, taken long overdue responsibilities for past actions in which, because of callowness or ignorance, I was unable to ascertain my own complicity or culpability. If my writing has matured in the process, and I think it has, it is because I have matured as I have written, and accepted my experiences as those of a human being who errs, and eventually learns.

Marisa is Southern, white, married with children. She was radically adamant about not wanting to "get over" her eating issues, rather she wanted to claim them, keep them, use them to empower her life.
Marisa Durden, writes in her 1997 senior study, "A Bite to Die For,"

I think that the development of my anorectic personality, as a subconscious attempt to resolve my silent conflicts and personal frustrations, has been one of my most mystifying, enigmatic, terrifying, confidence building and enlightening educational encounters of this life. *To study, understand and/or define my experience has been soul-rending and heart-aching because so many different levels of thinking and emotion, from the initial spark of life, and forward, are pureed and whisked until they become one's new personality.* I say "new" personality because the first personality I demonstrated wasn't really my own. It was the product of all those experiences I had as I lived each day. It was during the course of trial and error, success and failure, and exhaustive self-examination that I began to realize that there might possibly be a personality that was just mine!

Chanda is a white, Southern woman who, while talking with another Goddard student about her life, came to recognize the battering and abuse of her marriage relationship. She then changed the course of her study to examine the truth of her situation.

Chanda Martin wrote in the introduction to her 1997 senior study, "A Journey Away from Southern Traditions,"

> The writing of this autobiography has been an all-consuming project. In many ways, it has unraveled the very fiber that held my family together. And no matter how tainted that fiber has been, it has bound the family, always. Now that has changed. In revealing the warp of the family fabric, I've uncovered some of its flaws. The sharing of that knowledge with some other members of the family has upset what has been a carefully maintained balance of secrecy. Now I feel I'm dangling like a loose thread in the wind, trying desperately to hang on to the broadcloth.
>
> I haven't yet been able to change the attitudes of my family, nor do they yet understand the changes that have taken place in me. My connectedness to them has become clouded. I thought because I had been so hurt by members in my family, they did not matter to me, but I find they do. I am growing tired of trying to explain my reasons for being where I am, and I am growing even more nervous about losing my family because I cannot explain myself in a way they understand. I am also concerned for Carley's sake. She misses her grandparents, and my sister. I do not want her to be without the love that she felt from them, even if it is a love that harbors prejudice. While I see the women in my family choosing to remain the victims of their circumstances, I chose to leave that role behind. Sometimes this choice feels lonely, but sometimes I find it very powerful.

April is a white artist with Dissociative Identity Disorder. We came upon the idea of having each personality write letters as a method of communication for April as well as for audience understanding. Autobiographical information is revealed through descriptions within the letters.

April Faye's 1996 senior study "The Crowd" describes the experience of the theoretical and personal implications of Dissociative Identity Disorder, the new term for Multiple Personality Disorder. We meet the cast of male and female characters who will lead us to comprehend the complex and creative world of "The Crowd." Seven characters play crucial roles in enhancing the life and the survival of April. Horrible circumstances lead to the creation of each character but April, as narrator of this story, explains the ways in which horrors are surmounted, truths are told, and healing is achieved.

Through letters and dialogue April introduces each character and slowly the reader comprehends the circumstances each shared and had to overcome. This is a very imaginative approach to explaining a baffling set of circumstances to readers of all interests.

April includes a theoretical approach and explains DID in psychiatric terms and continues to offer herself and her alters as examples. She weaves each character back into the theoretical explanations so we deepen our understanding;

our commitment to the characters is cemented in the initial autobiographical storytelling.

This is a truly hopeful account of recovery from addictions, abuse, and the story of living with DID. April concludes by saying that writing this has been an amazing experience and *"the whole experience has been quite moving and we are ready to move on."* She leaves the reader sitting in admiration and hopeful that The Crowd will continue to do more writing and lots of art work.

Single parent of a son, African American, lesbian, artist, poet, and very shy, Yolanda found an audience that really listened to her when she read her poems or presented workshops. She is now a candidate for the Masters in Art Education and Teacher Certification K–12 at Miami University, Oxford, Ohio.

In her 1995 senior study "Temples: Mind, Body, & Soul," Yolanda presents a collage of artistic formats that speak out about body image, self-image, women of color, single women raising children and working, grandparents, neighborhoods, depression, joy, and humor. Universally this collection speaks to readers about issues women face privately that come from social constructions that oppress women (i.e., the medical system, sexism, body image, money, racism).

There are so many images in this manuscript that stay in my mind's eye several years after reading it: walking Grandmother to the bus stop, a screen door slamming, the alley where she hurt her knee, too tight jeans, soupy oatmeal, book bags, being "the only." Then there is the list of thirty daily challenges she faces as a woman of color that put theories about feminism and oppression in the total reality of daily life. Here are just three examples from the thirty:

> 1. I am not allowed to be anti-social and/or a racist. I can not be found in the company of people of the same race and/or lifestyle exclusively, without being judged.
>
> 7. My skin color gives the oppressor and capitalist the right to copy my culture and commodify it, and then sell it back to me.
>
> 13. I have to teach my son to be prepared to defend his intellect, culture, and body.

She also includes drawings that are of the power, strength, and courage of women of color.

Yolanda writes that "women authors of color also celebrate racial victory as well as acknowledge defeat to insure that we all learn. . . . Acknowledging the source of one's pain and reconciling oneself to be responsible for it" is part of the profound insight of this manuscript. Further she says, "the idea of human dignity is the reward of personal responsibility."

Writing of her own experiences as a Native American, single woman, Kathleen found the voice with which to guide women in sweat lodges. Alcoholism, sexual abuse, and the impact of internalized racism on Native American woman were most poignantly revealed through this study. Learning disabilities framed some of her style but the need for a woman's tongue was very clear for this particular study.

Kathleen Hope wrote in her 1995 senior study about the construction of a sweat lodge at a women's correctional facility and about conducting sweats with the inmates. "My goal was to complete an in-depth study of how Native Americans healing ceremonies are effective in treating indigenous peoples contemporary illnesses, trauma, and disease (alcoholism and drug addiction). The work also covered the cultural, historical, and political aspects of the native peoples' spiritual practices."

Kathleen's descriptions of alcoholism and sexual abuse illustrate the profound impact of societal oppression and internalized oppression on a Native American woman. Kathleen shares glimpses of her own story to encourage the women in the sweats to do the same. The healing techniques and skills of her heritage contrasted with the sheer devastation of a culture are profoundly described in this work.

Kathleen Hope graduated from Goddard and completed a MA in education in December 1996. She is finishing a second master's degree in counseling and will start a doctoral program in leadership.

Tom entered the BA program at Goddard and graduated as Lauren. A male-to-female transsexual from the steel mills of Pittsburgh, Pennsylvania, she was an active participant in early gender discussions. Disowned by her biological family but tenacious, she entered the Goddard MA in Psychology program. Lauren D. Wilson died, it appears by her own design, less than one year after sexual reassignment.

Lauren D. Wilson writes in the 1993 preface of "The Valley Spirit: Sexual Reassignment in Process,"

> This writing is my testament to my life as I have lived it. I feel that an issue like transsexualism, which lies outside the boundaries of common experience in our culture, need be heard in subtleties and nuances, in whispering winds, in the slow moving water of oxbow loops; be divined in the varieties of shape, color and texture in art museums, in the variegated hues of stained glass windows—all of which are integrated in the quintessential magical art of women being women.

> As the Tao Te Ching states:

> SIX
> The valley spirit never dies;
> It is the woman, primal mother.
> Her gateway is the root of heaven and
> earth.
> It is like a veil barely seen.
> Use it, it will never fail.
> (Feng and English, 1972, n.p.).

I am currently negotiating one of the more fascinating transitions available to humankind. I am certainly doing something outside the pale of what our culture would conceive of as a choice for a man. I find that as I have embarked upon the actual path of transformation, that is, actually taking hormones and presenting myself in public "as a women," that this transition is resonant and supportive and therefore speaks out of the rich sense of rightness which enables me to continue my process of change.

And later:

This conclusion is necessarily pre-emptive, since I have not yet fully crossed over the divide. I am well on my way though. Therefore, I can draw no absolute conclusions as to the appropriateness and efficacy of sexual reassignment in my case. It is conceivable (remotely) that I am making a mistake.* I am willing to take that risk. I might die on the operating table. I don't say this ghoulishly, but to state a conceivable, albeit extremely unlikely possibility. Frankly, I'm not sure I could live much longer as a man, anyway.

Being a man, raised as a man, was a purgatory, oftentimes a hell, for me. In this essay, I have tried to describe the experience of being "trapped in the body of the opposite sex." This description, while perhaps inaccurate in describing gendered subjectivity, and rendered facile by virtue of being overused and appropriated by pop culture, nevertheless clearly portrays the sense of distance and confusion that I, then Tom, now Lauren have felt.

I see my journey as a journey back to myself. I felt outside the boundaries of this culture. I choose to rejoin it as a spokeswoman for the potential for a culture where all sex and gender possibilities are open to choice and mutual respect.

I have been through a great deal of pain and suffering as a result of being transsexual, I neither wear this as a badge nor diminish it. Today, I have a resiliency not based on status or position, but most importantly one that does not exclude others, for then it would not be strong, only fragile vainglory. I bring the "valley spirit" into the world, to remind others that it surrounds and holds them too.

* I doubt it though. Just look at my eyes shining in the photographs. No one can fake this energy.

Friends of Lauren in the transsexual community disclaim her choice of suicide by saying, "Oh, she had other pathologies. It wasn't because she was a transsexual."

One can be empowered by writing autobiography and memoir, but having done such writing one finds that life is still in process and indeed, disempowerment can occur. I think once we are empowered we are quicker about reclaiming our power if we do find ourselves in disempowering situations.

Autobiography/memoir may have the power to empower an individual, but Lauren demonstrates that such work may not necessarily save a life.

Implications/Applications for the Learning Process

The shattering of stereotypes—not just the creation of new vocabulary for labeling them—is the only way we will stop the perpetual violent cycles.

Education that feeds the mind, body, and soul is radical and thus transformative. Frequently my students *look* different after a semester of this work. The implications are that students are no longer doormats, no longer scapegoats, no longer held hostage to internalized or horizontal hostility. Suzanne Pharr suggests this formula in *In the Time of the Right:*

Stereotypes=scapegoating=internalized oppression=horizontal hostility

Pharr writes

When we think of ourselves and our people as lacking in value - as being inferior and incapable, as being at fault for our lack of equality - then we begin to hold contempt for one another. We exhibit rage and frustration and despair in our daily lives rather than toward the more distant/abstract institutions and forces that harm us (Pharr 1996, 35).

The Brazilian educator Paulo Freire writes of horizontal violence (synonymous with internalized oppression), and suggests that striking out at comrades for the pettiest reasons is common behavior. He also states that self-deprecation derives from internalization of the opinion the oppressors hold.

In order for stereotypes to remain, we require a social system that relies on scapegoating to justify power inequities. Those who are scapegoated must be convinced of their diminished worth. This propaganda, the constant demeaning messages received by marginalized people who are driven by perpetual power inequities, is so invasive that it produces a self-loathing and consequently an equal loathing of all "others" as well (internalized and horizontal). Examples: Gay people frequently hate themselves and other gay people, particularly drag queens and bull dykes, or those who take the images of gay to extremes. African American males shooting African American males. Alcoholism among Native Americans. The occupational hazard of adolescent girls has become anorexia/bulimia and is now rising among boys. This clearly demonstrates the power of propaganda to appropriate body image.

In effect our educational system is still under the reign of white supremacists who insist on a canon that is designed to perpetuate stereotyping and scapegoating. I've worked with students from the South who had never read southern writers. Every semester I introduce women to women writers and thinkers, and I introduce all students to gay/lesbian writers, artists, and activists and artists of color.

The issue of supremacy is relevant when we discuss an identity pedagogy: there is a need for students to defy stereotypes, define themselves, and, despite all odds, break the cycles. Progressive, self-defined, and inspired education can work with victims and perpetrators. Education is not the landscape of the elite. Marginalized people must participate in the discourse and prevent the mainstream from becoming stagnant and non-nurturing.

The application of autobiography/memoir can be visual, emotional, and spiritual. The results define the cycle of oppressions that can then shatter stereotypes. From this point of view, adding to the discourse encourages tangible learning that contributes to building communication and community and to negotiating creative change and development within and between disparate groups.

Jay Parini, professor of English at Middlebury College, concludes his article "The Memoir Versus the Novel in a Time of Transition" thus:

> I believe my students understand, intuitively, that when they read memoirs they are learning things that cannot as easily be acquired by reading fiction. They are learning quite explicitly how to construct a self, how to navigate the world, and—perhaps most usefully—how to gain some purchase on the world through the medium of language. The more they know about this process, its history and dynamics, the more tangible their education will have become.

In her essay "The Master's Tools Will Never Dismantle the Master's House," Lorde urges us to disrupt the competitive academic ethos and really contemplate how we are enmeshed in perpetrating oppressive ways. She writes,

> In a world of possibility for us all, our personal visions help lay the groundwork for political action. The failure of academic feminists to recognize difference as a crucial strength is a failure to reach beyond the first patriarchal lesson. In our world, divide and conquer must become define and empower (Lorde 1984,112).

Lorde calls upon us to take responsibility for the ways in which we perpetuate oppression through even the language and means we say we're using to dismantle it. It behooves us to bring our attention to all the places where we inadvertently continue to use the master's tools.

> Women of today are still being called upon to stretch across the gap of male ignorance and to educate men as to our existence and our needs. This is an old and primary tool of all oppressors to keep the oppressed occupied with the master's concerns. Now we hear that it is the task of women of Color to educate white women—in the face of tremendous resistance—as to our existence, our differences, our relative roles in our joint survival. This is a diversion of energies and a tragic repetition of racist patriarchal thought. (Lorde 113)

This is a call from a great poet and thinker to stretch ourselves as teachers and students to learn beyond all our comfort zones, stretch ourselves to encourage the voices and stories be written and then really listen to all the voices of our diversity. Hear our multicolorful chorus. She is also asking us, as teachers and students, to be tornados that touch the ground. Do some damage to patriarchal thought and racism.

Caryn Mirriam-Goldberg, faculty member, poet, mother and prairie reclaimer writes in a letter (May 8, 1997) to student, Amie Ziner:

> Tornadoes Don't Have Impact Unless They Hit the Ground.
> Think of a tornado (okay, a Kansas image for sure although I haven't yet seen one). Unless it touches down and grounds itself, it does no damage. Poems are like that, too. They need to be grounded in real and original details, in a context that tells the reader where she is and what it looks/smells/sounds/feels/tastes like in that place. Give your poems a context. (Give all writing a tornado.)
>
> Let the Truth Show Its Face. Especially if you don't know what the truth is anymore (all the better for the poem). Let the truth surface and show itself. Be afraid and do it anyway.
>
> Words Invents Word, Way Leads Onto Way (quoting from Robert Frost and William Stafford). The word you write invents the word that comes next. Trust. Or pretend you trust until you actually do.

Conclusion

Be afraid and do it anyway. Trust.

Chris Remick, multimedia artist, newspaper columnist, entrepreneur, wife, mother, caretaker of elderly, writes in her 1996 senior study, "How I Learned to Stop Cleaning and Start Creating: A Look at Women, Art and Domesticity,"

> Women have to live despite and beyond the patriarchy. They cannot be subject to control and must triumph over the predictability of the female paradigm. The management difficulties inherent in the artistic life surrounded by domesticity result in resiliency, determination, and perseverance. These strong qualities add texture and invention to a woman's life (111).

All marginalized people "must triumph over the predictability" of the oppressor/oppressed paradigm. As Chris says, the "resiliency, determination, and perseverance" do indeed add "texture and invention" and such qualities inspire hope and creativity for each generation.

To weave the essence of an identity pedagogy with the rather radical notion that the true purpose of education is liberation/authenticity teaches people to think and makes graduates truly dangerous to the status quo. I tell my students to go ahead, be dangerous. Women started telling the truth of their lives and laws against sexual abuse and battered women's shelters came into being; teachers of literacy were beaten or murdered during slavery in the United States and more recently in Brazil and people learned to read. There is danger in the words of heartfelt people and their truths. To remain truly dangerous, we must continue to speak our lives, to write for our lives.

Closing Thought

There's an idea that there's this great mainstream, which may be wide but is shallow and slow-moving. It's the tributaries that have the energy.
—Grace Paley

References

Barrington, Judith. 1997. *Writing the Memoir: From Truth to Art.* Portland, Oregon: The Eighth Mountain Press.

Bluj, Allison M. 1998. "The Effects of Sexual Abuse on a Child's School Experience." MA in Education final project for Goddard College.

Freire, Paulo. 1996. *Pedagogy of the Oppressed.* New York: Continuum.

hooks, bell. 1994. *Teaching to Transgress: Education as the Practice of Freedom.* New York: Routledge.

Lorde, Audre. 1984. "The Master's Tools Will Never Dismantle The Master's House." In *Sister Outsider: Essays and Speeches by Audre Lorde.* New York: The Crossing Press.

Parini, Jay. "The Memoir Versus the Novel in a Time of Transition," *The Chronicle of Higher Education* (July 10, 1998), A40.

Pharr, Suzanne. 1996. *In the Time of the Right: Reflections on Liberation.* Berkeley: Chardon Press.

Wilton, Tamsin. 1995. *Lesbian Studies: Setting an Agenda.* London: Routledge.

FIVE

Toward a Pedagogy of the "Oppressor": A Freirian Approach to Anti-Sexist Education for Men

Steven A. Schapiro

. . . The situation of oppression is a dehumanized and dehumanizing totality affecting both the oppressors and those whom they oppress. . . . To surmount the situation of oppression, men [sic] must first critically recognize its causes, so that through transforming action they can create a new situation, one which makes possible the pursuit of a fuller humanity.

—Paolo Freire

Introduction: Posing the Problem

Wanted: a faculty member in education and psychology, with expertise in human development and in men's development toward a non-sexist world.

So read part of the job advertisement that brought me to Goddard College in the fall of 1985. Having recently completed my doctorate in education with a focus on human development and social justice education and with a dissertation on men's identity development and anti-sexist education, I was intrigued by the possibility of working at this small progressive college that was explicitly interested in what I had to offer. As I began my work there, I found that Goddard, with a strong feminist studies program and a high degree of commitment among many faculty and students to addressing issues of sexism and other forms of oppression, both at Goddard and in the world at large, was a very hospitable environment for those, such as me, who were already committed to such goals. But it is a very challenging place to be for others, particularly men, who do not share this perspective. A campus with many women who are becoming aware of and angry about their oppression as women creates a context in which it sometimes feels wrong or bad to be a man. How can we help men deal positively with such a context? This is the question that no doubt prompted the job advertisement quoted above and to which I have tried to respond.

How can we engage men in the study of gender issues and of men and masculinity in ways that can help them to critically examine traditional gender roles and structures and to consider alternatives, without having them feel attacked and threatened in ways that lead to defensiveness and resistance? How in general can we help people to grow and change in regard to such issues without subjecting them to coercion, indoctrination, or other forms of political correctness? How can we do these things in a student-centered way that at once raises issues of social justice and also involves learners in genuine inquiry and collaborative construction of knowledge in regard to issues of real and meaningful concern? These are the questions or problems to which this chapter responds.

In what follows, I describe the pedagogical model and course design that I have evolved over a number of years in order to address such concerns. That design builds on work that I first developed in the early 1980s in the context of the then nascent social justice education program at the University of Massachusetts at Amherst. The approach developed there has recently been described at length in *Teaching for Diversity and Social Justice: A Sourcebook for Teachers and Trainers* (Adams, Bell, and Griffin 1997), which includes a chapter on anti-sexist education that I co-authored with Diane Goodman. The model that I present here also draws on other relevant theories and practices, including, most explicitly, the T-group approach to human relations training and Paolo Freire's education for critical consciousness. The work is therefore situated within the wide array of progressive approaches to education that have been developed over the last half of this century to responding to the most pressing challenges to democracy in our times, to issues of diversity, to domination, to oppression and to liberation. These approaches, such as feminist pedagogy, experiential education, multicultural education, black studies, gay and lesbian studies, and critical pedagogy both build on and move beyond the contributions of Dewey and his contemporaries.

In describing this model, I suggest a set of general principles that could serve as the basis for a "pedagogy of the oppressor"—a necessary corollary to Freire's pedagogy of the oppressed—a pedagogy that is designed to help those in more privileged positions in society to recognize their stake in working toward a more just and humane world, and to join with "the oppressed" to create a world in which we all can be more free and more fulfilled as human beings; a world, in Freire's words, "in which it is easier to love." The course and the model are also a manifestation of an integrated approach to education for democracy, as it has been discussed earlier; education that promotes individual human development while also recognizing that such development occurs within a social context—a community. A commitment to education for human development therefore requires us to also work to improve and change that context—to make it more conducive to such development. Education for democracy must help people to understand and overcome both the internal and the external blocks to human development, our internalized oppression/domination/subordination and the externalized structures of society.

In what follows, I will first of all give a brief overview of the course goals and methodology as it has evolved, describe at some length the pedagogical theories on which the design is based, outline an integrated model for a pedagogy for men's consciousness raising, illustrate the impact of this course on some of the men who have experienced it, and finally, discuss some of what I have learned over the years in doing this work.

The goals of this pedagogy are to help men to re-examine and if appropriate reconstruct their sense of what it means or should mean "to be a man" and in so doing to begin to develop new ways of being male that are less oppressive to women and more fulfilling to men themselves. Such a pedagogy is needed because: (a) masculinity is in transition—in response to the feminist movement, the gay liberation movement, and to social changes that are making traditional forms of masculinity more and more obsolete, our society's definitions of what it means or should mean to be a man are changing, and (b) existing approaches for educating and counseling men in transition and for helping men to unlearn old roles and behaviors and learn new ones are either inadequate in terms of the changes they attempt to facilitate or inappropriate for working with men because they are not based on a full understanding of men's identity and consciousness in regard to this issue. An approach is needed that can help men to recognize the relationship between, on the one hand, the limitations of the traditional male role on both their self-actualization as full human beings and their opportunity to have authentic and fulfilling relationships with women and with other men, and, on the other hand, the social structures and behaviors that support sexism and heterosexism and lead to the oppression of women and gay men.

In an earlier study (Schapiro 1985), I developed a preliminary model for the goals of such a pedagogy that integrated three alternative models of masculinity: the "liberated man," the "androgynous man," and the "anti-sexist man." Although these models were articulated some years ago, I believe that they still represent the clearest statements of the various points of view on this issue, and I think they incorporate more recent visions, such as that of the "wildman" or the mytho-poetic man as articulated by Bly and others. They do not incorporate the model of the "promisekeepers" but I think they do address the need for meaning, for male community, and for expression of feelings that are in some ways embodied in the promisekeepers movement, but do not include its return to patriarchal gender roles. These goals are summarized with the terms autonomy, androgyny, awareness, and activism, which can be defined as follows for the purposes of this discussion:

- *autonomy*: freedom from culturally imposed models of masculinity and femininity, the ability to make self-directed choices about how to express oneself
- *androgyny:* an integration of traditionally "masculine" and "feminine" aspects of the self that potentially combines the best qualities of each
- *awareness:* social/political consciousness about how masculinity and sexism are institutionalized, about the relationship of masculinity to our socioeconomic system, and about the changes that may be necessary to create a more just and equitable society
- *activism:* a demonstrated commitment to struggle against sexism and other

related forms of oppression on both the personal and societal levels.

At this point, it will be useful to look at a brief overview of the course as it has been presented to students. This will enable us to refer back to that description in the discussion that follows:

ON BEING MALE: Men and Masculinity in Contemporary Society

Facilitator: Steve Schapiro

Objectives: To increase the extent to which participants:

- *Understand the impact of male socialization on psychological development, interpersonal behavior, and social attitudes.*
- *Recognize some of the costs and benefits of that socialization.*
- *Understand the basic dynamics of sexism at individual, cultural, and institutional levels.*
- *Explore and experiment with alternative ways of being male through which we can be more complete and whole and less hurtful to ourselves and others.*
- *Make more conscious and informed choices in our lives about what it means or should mean to be a man, and to be able to help others to do the same, intrapersonally, interpersonally, and institutionally.*

COURSE STRUCTURE AND METHODOLOGY

This course will be run as a structured consciousness-raising group in which, in a nonthreatening and supportive atmosphere, we will learn about masculinity by exploring together our experience of being men, or of being women in relation to men. Class time will involve a combination of discussion, structured experiential activities, and possible films and guest speakers. The processes through which we communicate and develop as a group will also be treated as an important source of learning. Journal writing and a series of learning papers will serve to stimulate and supplement the personal reflection and sharing through which we expect most of our learning to come. Weekly readings will be used to stimulate discussion and provide a theoretical framework from which to analyze our experience.

TENTATIVE GENERAL OUTLINE (The specific content and order of topics may vary, depending on the interests of the group.)

Session 1: Introduction

--Who we are, goals and expectations, hopes and fears

Sessions 2, 3: Growing Up Male

--Stereotypes. role models, fathers and sons, personal histories, learning to deal with emotions

Session 4: The Dynamics of oppression

--Sex roles, sexism, dominant-subordinate roles

Sessions 5, 6, 7: Men and Women

--Patterns and games, power, intimacy, dependency, sexualiity, violence against women

Session 8: Male sexuality

--Physical and emotional intimacy, heterosexuality, homosexuality,

pornography
Sessions 9, 10, 11: Men and Men
--Fathers and sons, male friendships, male bonding, effects of competition and homophobia
Session 12: Men, Class, and Race
--Men and work, classism, racism
Session 13: New Directions
--Personal and social change
Session 14: Closure
-- Where do we go from here?

PROPOSED EXPECTATIONS

- *Attendance: Because of the experiential nature of the course, attendance is critical. It is expected that everyone will attend all class sessions.*
- *Journal: A personal journal, in which participants will write during class and for homework.*
- *Readings and written responses: participants will be asked to write one- or two-page written reactions and responses to the weekly readings.*
- *Learning papers: Four three- to four-page papers, in which participants will be asked to write thoughts, feelings, and responses to what we're doing in class.*
- *Book review/presentation: Written and verbal report on a book or books about a topic of special interest.*
- *Action plans/reports: A plan for a way of working toward some kind of personal or social change in regard to this issue, and a report on the plan's results.*
- *Final paper: A reflection, summation, and integration of one's learning in the course.*

The main topics explored in the course, their sequence, and the specific questions and problems explored within each have varied with the needs and interests of each group with which it's been conducted. However, a basic logic of the course has been consistent, based on Borton's "What? So what? Now what?" principle of sequencing (1970), that provides one useful overlay for looking at the logical flow of the course as a whole. "What, so what, and now what?" are colloquial expressions for what Borton identified as three basic information processing functions: the sensing or perceiving function through which information is gathered (what?), the transforming or conceptualizing function through which generalizations are made and patterns of meaning are found in the information that has been gathered (so what?), the acting function through which decisions are made about how to act on the new information and patterns that have been discovered (now what?). In this group study, the basic "information" that is being processed is the concept of masculinity of the participants, with all of its implications for their male role behavior and attitudes about sexism. Through the logic of the "what/so what/now what" sequence, group members are given the opportunity to identify what that concept is, to analyze how the actualization of that concept affects them and others, and to begin to develop and to put into practice a new concept of masculinity.

The course can be divided into three main sections, each basically addressing one of the three questions: What? (sessions 1–3), So what? (sessions 4–12), and Now what? (sessions 13–14). More specifically, the "what?" in this case is: What is traditional masculinity? How have the norms of traditional masculinity affected course participants as individuals? Thus the first three sessions of the course are devoted to identifying and exploring the norms of masculinity, the ways those norms were learned by members of the group, and some aspects of their behavior and personality that were shaped by those norms. Within the basic "what?" of this first section is therefore a first "so what?": How did those norms affect the people in the group? The basic "so what?" addressed in sessions 4–12 is really: How do those "masculine" qualities affect and relate to our relationships with women and with other men? How do those qualities support and how are they supported by institutionalized sexism? How do those qualities relate to and support racism, classism, and other forms of oppression? Some "now what?" questions are considered in the course of considering each of these topics individually, but in the final two sessions the "now what?" question becomes paramount: What do you/we want to do about what you/we have learned? What kinds of personal and social changes do you/ we want to work for? How?

In working to develop this pedagogy and course design, I have drawn on and integrated principles and practices from three educational approaches noted above, laboratory and human relations training groups (T-groups), Freire's education for critical consciousness, and anti-oppression education (recently called social justice education). The principles underlying those approaches (including their origins, participant objectives, and learning theories) will be described in some depth in the pages that follow, which will lead to the articulation of an integrated model that draws on each of the three in a synthesis of education for personal growth and social change. The synthesis creates a model of a pedagogy for liberation that can potentially be adapted and applied to help motivate the more privileged members of society from various social groups to join with the less privileged or oppressed in working toward the creation of a new social order that is more just and more fulfilling for all. After reviewing these principles and explaining the development of the model, I will revisit this course design to explain how it puts that model into practice.

Laboratory, Inter-group, and Human Relations Training

The T-group, or basic human relations training group, can be broadly defined as a small learning group that brings people together for the purpose of learning about themselves, about their impact on others, and about group dynamics and development through the process of analyzing their own behavior as it occurs in the group (Benne, Bradford, and Gibb, in Cooper 1971). Within that broad definition, such groups vary in the extent to which they concentrate on learnings about the self, interpersonal relationships, group and organizational processes, or intergroup conflict resolution.

The fundamental goals or outcome objectives of the basic T-group experience are to enable participants to achieve increased personal autonomy— greater freedom to choose how they want to respond in their interactions with others— in order to enhance their interpersonal effectiveness and their ability to function more effectively in face-to-face situations. The particular learnings and skills involved in increasing that person-to-person effectiveness will of course vary with the individual learner.

The T-group as a form of human relations training developed out of the work of social psychologist Kurt Lewin and three of his associates, Kenneth Benne, Leland Bradford, and Ronald Lippit (Benne et al., 1975, 110), and has since been adapted to a wide range of teaching and training applications. T-group emphasis on learning through analyzing and processing group interactions has been integrated into many forms of human relations training, including a variety of approaches to diversity training and multicultural education. Because I have integrated and adapted some of the basic methodology of T-group education into this pedagogy, it will be useful to explore in some depth the pedagogical principles and model of change on which it is based.

This "laboratory method of changing and learning," which is how this type of education has come to be identified, includes a wide range of approaches for helping people to "diagnose and experiment with their own behavior and social relationships" (Benne, Bradford, and Gibb 1979, vii). Underlying this method are a broad set of values, goals, and assumptions about how people learn and change. This "innovation in education" grew out of the conviction among its founders that in our world of rapid social and technological change, it was necessary to develop ways to help individuals to "correct dysfunctional effects of early socialization" (Benne 1975a, 36) and learn how to be more effective in reconstructing the social environment. In Benne's words: "In a rapidly changing society, people must assume greater responsibility for consciously and selectively directing the process of their own socialization" (1975a, 37). In so doing, it was hoped that individuals could not only enhance their own personal effectiveness in one-to-one and group situations, but also learn how to create and work in groups that are conducive to the personal growth and development of all of their members. The T-group is one approach that has been developed to help people work toward these goals, goals that are fundamental to the development and functioning of a democratic society.

Many theorists have described the kind of change and learning that goes on in a T-group as a form of re-education and re-socialization (Lewin 1948; Bennis 1962; Dennis 1975; Sargent and Kravetz 1977; Shepherd 1970). In a paper entitled "Conduct, Knowledge and the Acceptance of New Values" (1945), Lewin presented perhaps the first formulation of the general principles of the re-education process, a formulation that is still very useful today. Those ten principles are based upon the assumption that effective re-education affects a person in three ways. It changes one's cognitive structure"—ideas, facts, beliefs, one's "valences and values," and one's "motoric action"—behavior. The whole person must be involved in the process.

Three of Lewin's ten principles are particularly relevant to our concern about how people change in such groups. These are:

1. "The re-education process has to fulfill a task that is essentially equivalent to a change in culture."
2. "A change in action-ideology, a real acceptance of a changed set of facts and values, a change in the perceived social world—all three are but different expressions of the same process."
3. "The individual accepts the new system of values and beliefs by accepting belongingness in a group." (37)

The key assumption or belief behind these principles is that we become people— learn our characteristic pattern of values, attitudes, and behaviors— through growing into membership in various associations and relationships, from family to school to peer groups. It is through internalizing the norms and beliefs of these groups as cultures that we become enculturated and socialized. Therefore, it is in becoming part of a new group that is based on alternative norms and values, that re-enculturation and re-socialization can occur and we can develop a new set of attitudes and behaviors. The implications of that idea for the use of the small group as a context for a limited and focused re-socialization process should be clear.

Seeing people not as isolated individuals but as existing, in Lewin's terms, in a social field, or in other terms, as part of a system or systems, it follows that if the field or system changes, the person must change as well. According to this perspective, because social fields and systems have a natural tendency to seek equilibrium, changing the field in a particular way will have a repercussion somewhere else in the field. In other words, if we change a person's field or put them in a new one, they need to reach a new orientation to that field in order to reach a new equilibrium.

Lewin described three phases within this change process: unfreezing (disequilibrium), changing (finding a new equilibrium), and refreezing (restabilizing). I will use this model, which has been amplified by many theorists, to try to understand and explain the theory of how people in T-groups change and become re-socialized, because such a process is fundamental to the change process involved in the pedagogy that I am describing in this chapter.

Unfreezing can be conceived of as an experience of "being shook up" or shaken out of one's present complacency and equilibrium, an experience that must precede any new learning. When a person's present equilibrium of personal constructs and behaviors is upset or altered, he or she will experience a felt need for change. The unfreezing process must involve a *combination of heightened anxiety* (the motivation to change) and *reduction of threat* (which allows for an openness to change rather than a defensive rigidity).

In T-groups, people seem to get "shook up" and unfrozen because the group is a new, ambiguous situation in which there is a confusion about norms and about the expectations about what is appropriate. This leads to heightened anxiety. The givens of behavior now become choices. Because their old patterns and models may not work effectively in this setting, people are forced to think about their behavior and become aware of the ways in which they are choosing to act. What makes it possible for this unfreezing process to lead to change instead of defensive refreezing is the creation of an atmosphere of safety and freedom in which participants feels free to experiment with new behaviors. Facilitators (trainers) can help to create such an atmosphere by modeling caring and unconditional acceptance of others and by encouraging the feeling that people are mutually engaged in a group learning project in which they can learn by experimenting with their behavior and analyzing together the impact of their behavior on each other and the group. Also, through modeling appropriate use of self-disclosure and feedback, trainers can help the group to learn how to learn from its own behavior.

Changing involves the development of new behaviors, attitudes, and ideas that will enable the members of the group to re-establish an equilibrium. As they join the attempt to resolve the dilemmas with which the group confronts them, people search for behaviors that will be effective in making the group into the kind of community in which their needs can be met. Group members discover a discrepancy between their back-home behaviors and those behaviors that seem most effective in the group and search for more effective behaviors to emulate, behaviors which may be exhibited by other group members or by the trainers. People will then try out these new behaviors to the extent that they feel safe to do so. Such experimentation is often much safer in the group than outside the group because of the accepting atmosphere and reduction in the fear of disapproval and rejection. It is often much easier to try out new behaviors in a group of relative strangers than in an ongoing relationship that may be disrupted or even destroyed by the change.

Refreezing—stabilizing and integrating the new behaviors and perspectives into one's personality and life systems—must occur if the changes that people experiment within the group are to be long-lasting. In Lewin's terms, the field must become relatively secure against change. In these terms, it appears that there are really two fields that must reach a new equilibrium; our internal field (composed of our personality, attitudes, and beliefs) and our external field (our social context). Schein and Bennis (1965) provide a framework that breaks down the refreezing process into two such components, the personal and the relational. For personal refreezing to occur, the changes must somehow fit or be consistent with the rest of one's personality and attitude systems. If there is not a good fit, either refreezing will not occur or another attitude or behavior will have to change in order to accommodate the first change. It is in this internal refreezing process that the introduction of new cognitive frameworks or ways of thinking may help people to make sense of their experience and to refreeze their new behaviors and attitudes into a new consistent framework. Similarly, relational refreezing, which involves integrating the new patterns into one's significant relationships, will occur only when these significant others in some way confirm or validate the changes. If that confirmation does not occur in at least one supportive environment it will be very difficult to sustain the new repertoire of interpersonal competencies and attitudes.

From this discussion of how people learn and change in such groups, we can discern the basic principles of this model for training and education, presented here in terms of two primary aspects: the *structure* and *leader behaviors*, which together comprise the *teaching principles* of this approach; and the sequence of behavioral and affective *objectives for the participants*. For the sake of clarity and to make the sequential nature of the approach apparent, the teaching principles and learning objectives will be presented in outline form for each phase of the learning process—unfreezing, changing, and refreezing (see chart 1).

It is important to note that the T-group was created essentially by and for men to help them increase their sensitivity, self-awareness, and interpersonal competence. As such, it has, in Rossabeth M. Kanter's words, "long been viewed as a particularly effective method to help men develop new behavioral repertoires and self-insights counterbalancing the stereotypical tendencies of the male role" (Kanter 1979, 72). Indeed, most of the basic T-group principles, such as discussing the processes of group interaction and engaging in self-disclosure and feedback, run counter to traditional male norms. Where the male role emphasizes instrumental leadership (a task and power orientation), T-group norms and the female role emphasize expression of feelings, support for others, and a process orientation. The behaviors that are disconfirmed, unrewarded, and unfrozen in the T-group are often some typical male ones, such as coolness, competitiveness, toughness, and self-reliance, behaviors which may be rewarded in the traditionally male, patriarchal, competitive culture of our dominant institutions, but are not rewarded in the alternative culture of the T-group. As men search for alternatives to these disconfirmed behaviors, they often learn that the behaviors they lack that are effective in this setting are some stereotypically feminine ones.

This is not to suggest, however, that men tend to reject all of their "masculine" behaviors and take on all "feminine" ones, but that they have an opportunity in the group to develop and experiment with a more balanced repertoire of interpersonal skills. Indeed, in looking to the group for models of alternative behavior, they may notice that it is people who are most androgynous who are the most effective group members (Bem 1976; Sargent 1979, 1980).

In Sargent's words:

> The effective group member is typically someone who possesses
> leadership skills and supportive helping behaviors, who has both
> masculine independence and feminine nurturing, helping skills,
> spontaneity and playfulness. (Sargent 1979, 115)

Within the safety of the group, men can begin to try out and practice using the behaviors that they lack, making it possible for them to become more

CHART 1: MODEL OF T-GROUP EDUCATION

TEACHING PRINCIPLES (including structure and leader behaviors)	PARTICIPANT OBJECTIVES (behavioral and affective)
UNFREEZING *Deroutinization*—to be achieved through a lack of clear structure or leader direction, leading to ambiguity about tasks and roles. *Here and Now Focus*--an emphasis on learning from what people are experiencing in the group. *A supportive climate/atmosphere of safety and freedom*—to be established through modeling by the trainers of empathetic listening and other caring responses. *Norms Encouraging Self-Disclosure and Feedback*—in regard to feelings about self and others, to be established through modeling by the trainers, and attempts to elicit that behavior from others.	Generate behaviors for analysis and learning Experience feelings of heightened anxiety. Experience feelings of dissonance and disconfirmation in regard to some typical behaviors and attitudes. Engage in self-disclosure of feelings about the group, self, and others. Experience feedback in regard to one's impact on others and on the group process.
CHANGING *Norm of Experimentation with New Behavior*—to be modeled and encouraged by the trainer. *Opportunity to Plan and Make Application of Learnings to Back Home Situation* *Provide Cognitive Maps*—theories, explanations, concepts with which to interpret new experience.	Experiment with new behavior. Continued self-disclosure and feedback. Continued practice and application of new behaviors. Integration of new behaviors and attitudes into personality and attitude structure.
REFREEZING (may not be planned for in typical T-group, and may need to occur outside the group after it is over) support in ongoing relationships and from organizational/institutional context	Integration of new patterns of behavior into ongoing relationships and organizational/ institutional context.

intentional in their behavior, more able to choose how to behave under what circumstances; to become, in the terms used in this discussion, more autonomous and more androgynous.

But to what extent and under what circumstances will the development of a more androgynous set of behaviors, as described above, also lead to parallel changes in attitude (e.g., the attitude that it is good for men to express feelings, co-operate, support each other; increased awareness of the causes and effects of sexism). In the traditional T-group, with its emphasis on interpersonal effectiveness in the "here and now" experience of the group itself, nothing is necessarily done to encourage the development of such awareness. However, the chance that these behaviors and attitudes will be maintained and will lead to further attitude change can be enhanced if people are offered a coherent new cognitive framework, such as a feminist analysis, with which they can replace their now dissonant and dysfunctional system of beliefs about appropriate interpersonal behavior. Indeed, when one adds to the traditional T-group experience a presentation to participants of a framework that will help them interpret their new behavior in terms of overcoming the limits of gender role stereotyping, it seems possible both to enhance the possibility that the changes occurring in the group will refreeze and to use the group experience to stimulate the addition of a point of view that transcends gender roles. Sargent (1975, 1977, 1979) and others (D. Kravetz and A. Sargent 1977; Kanter 1979) have described just such an approach, utilizing the small group as a laboratory in which gender role expectations can be brought into awareness, new behaviors experimented with, and new cognitive maps offered that redefine the meaning of "gender-appropriate" behavior. In the discussion that follows in regard to other pedagogical approaches I will also explain how other perspectives can be introduced that can help men to develop a critical understanding of the institutional and cultural context of sexism in which those behaviors occur.

To conclude, the T-group approach in and of itself can potentially help men to become more autonomous and more androgynous. In pursuit of those objectives, the basic T-group teaching principles that facilitate the process of unfreezing and changing are applicable and necessary. That is: deroutinization; focus on the here and now; an atmosphere of safety and freedom; norms of self-disclosure and feedback; norms of experimentation with new behavior. Beyond the basic T-group experience, it also appears that in the refreezing process there is the potential to stimulate an increased awareness of sexism and of anti-sexist activism. The teaching principles involved in that contextual refreezing process, principles not normally utilized in the basic group, can be added: provide new cognitive maps (that offer an analysis of sexism); provide opportunities to plan and make outside applications; find support in ongoing relationships and from the organizational/institutional context. The level and extent of awareness and activism that result from such a process would seem to depend on the nature of the disequilibrium or cognitive dissonance brought on by the experience and the kinds of cognitive maps offered with which to make sense of the experience.

The pedagogical model I present below integrates these principles from the T-group approach and the additional cognitive reframing principles noted above with a Freirian and student-centered approach to the process of learning how to critically examine and transform the social reality in which we are immersed.

Freire's Education for Critical Consciousness

Paolo Freire was a revolutionary Brazilian educator who developed a method for teaching illiterate peasants how to read, and in the process how to transform themselves and their world. In describing the methodology he used in this work Freire (1970, 1971, 1973) described the principles of a general "pedagogy of the oppressed", a pedagogy whose goal is not to teach people how to read and to become literate in the traditional sense of the word, but also to help people to develop what has been called "social literacy" (Alschuler 1981); the ability to join with others in collectively naming, analyzing, and changing the social reality in which they are submerged. In Freire's words, that social literacy develops through what he called "conscientization—the process through which men [*sic*], not as recipients, but as knowing subjects, achieve a deepening awareness of both the sociocultural reality that shapes their lives and of their capacity to transform that reality" (Freire 1979, 27)

The principles of Freire's pedagogy can therefore be applied not only to teaching reading, as Freire did in Brazil before he was exiled in 1964, and as he later did in Chile, but to the educational process in general. Freire himself, for instance, later applied his approach to the organization of the educational system of a newly liberated African country (Freire 1978), and after his return from exile to the school system in Sao Paolo. Several American educators (Giroux 1981; Harmon 1975; Alschuler 1980; Shor 1980, 1992; hooks 1994) have attempted to apply it in a variety of other contexts, including, for example, the organization of community action groups, teaching English in a community college, and helping students, teachers, and administrators in urban schools to collectively solve their "discipline" problems.

Freire's pedagogy is based on his belief in the value of human development and in the right of people to personal and collective self-determination. "Man's vocation," he says [using male-dominant language], "is to become more fully human" (1970, 4). His pedagogy is fundamentally aimed at helping people to pursue that end. For him, the essential quality of our humanness relates to our ability to become conscious of our own consciousness and to develop our power and ability, in collaboration with others, to rename and recreate the social world in which we live and act. As Alschuler explained Freire's position, "the more we consider the world, criticize it, and transform it the more human we are . . . since that is the essential quality of humanness" (1980, 93).

Because for Freire the essence of being human is thus related to choice, intentionality, and self-determination, that which denies or limits choice and self-determination he considers to be oppressive and/or dehumanizing. Those limits can be on both our powers of reflection and thought—(through myths, mystification, and false consciousness that we internalize in our minds, which then limit us); and on our power to act—(through coercion, regulation, violence, and the structure of society).

Although in these terms, the truly oppressed in any society are limited in both of these ways (internally and externally) even the oppressors—those who objectively benefit from the socioeconomic structure and existing power relations—are themselves limited and dehumanized by having to live in a society in which it is difficult to love, to engage in dialogue, and to relate to people as equals; a society in which they too internalize rigid and false images of themselves and the oppressed. As Freire puts it, "no one can be authentically human while preventing others from doing so." (1970, 42). Full humanization for anyone is therefore possible, according to Freire, only in a context, a society, in which the oppressor/oppressed contradiction has been overcome.

A pedagogy whose goal is to promote and facilitate people's "vocation of becoming more fully human" must therefore help them to overcome the limitations on their powers of thought and their powers of action, to help them create a world in which such humanization is possible - "a world in which it is easier to love." It is with such goals in mind that Freire developed a pedagogy aimed at helping people to develop their consciousness and ability to create such a world, an "education for critical consciousness."

With a "critical transforming consciousness," in which people are able to understand the systemic causes of their problems and the underlying structure of society, as the goal of his pedagogy, Freire described two other phases of consciousness that he observed in the people with whom he was working. In the magical-conforming phase people see their situation as either unoppressive and nonproblematic or as an unchangeable fact of existence. Therefore, they conform to the situation. In the naive-reforming phase people believe that problems are caused by bad individuals, not by faults in the system. They therefore blame other individuals or themselves for the problems they experience. Freire's pedagogy attempts to help people to move from a magical to a naive to a critical phase of consciousness.

Although Freire addressed himself primarily to the question of how to help facilitate such changes in people's consciousness and not with specific action plans and blueprints for social transformation, his methodology for facilitating those changes in consciousness is based on the notion that consciousness and society do not exist apart from each other. He saw instead a dialectical relationship between the two and explained how our consciousness affects the kind of society we create and recreate, and how the social structure and our experience within it affect our consciousness.

Given this view, Freire believed that people can become unsubmerged from the reality they are in and begin to overcome their oppression through a combination of reflection and action that he called praxis. Through acting, reflecting, and acting once again, a new consciousness develops as a new social reality is created. Through such a process people realize, in Freire's words, that "we have to make our freedom together with others" (1976, 225); that we can not, in other words, be self-determining by ourselves—that it is only through collective struggle, not individual adjustment or reform, that real solutions can be found.

Freire's methodology for engaging people in such a struggle and such a process is based on a dialogical relationship between teachers and students who collectively attempt to solve problems. The dialogical nature of that process is based on Freire's belief that the educational process is itself inherently political and that it contributes either to domination and oppression or to liberation and freedom. The approach that he suggested stands in contrast to what he described as the "banking form of education" in which the knowledge, ideas, and beliefs that are to be transmitted to students are predetermined and the role of the teacher is to deposit that knowledge into students' minds. The process of this banking education, with its strictly hierarchical, authoritarian relationship between teachers and students, its concept of what knowledge is, and its delegitimization of the culture, ideas, and feelings of students contributes to the domination of consciousness and oppression of the students involved regardless of the content involved in the "banking" transaction.

Dialogic education, in contrast, is based on democratic social relations between teacher and students, and on respect for and faith in what students can potentially be. Through this dialogical process students can realize that knowledge is not something to be handed down from on high, but is something that people can find and create by themselves in their struggle to understand and change their world. Such dialogue can help people to free up their powers of reflection, powers which they can then apply to naming, analyzing, and trying to change their world as they struggle to overcome the limitations on their powers of action. It is through that struggle to understand and solve the problems that confront them that people's liberated consciousness can develop into a critical transforming consciousness. Within such a dialogical relationship, it is the role of the teacher or leader to engage students in such a problem-solving process through what Freire calls problem-posing or problematization of education. The role of the leader in that dialogue is not only to listen and facilitate discussion, but also to actively present his or her view of reality and to help students to examine and to act on their own reality. From the point of view of the leader/facilitator, that methodology can be broken down into five phases: 1 investigation, 2 codifying, 3 problem-posing, 4 dialogue/decoding, and 5 action. These steps, which will be explained below, are carried out in the context of a learning group that is composed of people who have in common some aspect of their social existence.

During the *investigation* or listening phase, educators study and analyze the life situation of the group in order to identify key limit situations—aspects of the social reality which limit their growth and development. Listening to people tell their own stories and describe their own experience can also serve to affirm their power to name themselves and their reality. The key limit situations, or themes, are then *codified* by the facilitators in such a way that they can be posed *as problems to be solved*, not as unchangeable aspects of reality. In other words, the leaders take what they are told by the people and give it back to them in a way that defines their world as a situation to be transformed, a way that gives people a sense that things could be different and better.

The codifications may, as in basic literacy training of peasants, be in the form of pictures—(pictures, for example, of a landlord beating a peasant), or in the form of written articles, stories, or films. These codifications attempt to call attention to the *why* of a situation and to challenge people to act to change it (e.g.,Why do landlords beat peasants? What gives them the right to do it? What would it take to create a situation in which they did not have that right?). These codifications, or problems, must involve contradictions that represent the key factors in the oppression reflected in the situations (e.g. the fact that the landlord owns the land and the peasants must work for him).

The codifications also must be posed in such a way that they help people envision an alternative to the limit-situation (e.g., the landlord not having the right to beat the peasants if the peasants owned their own land, either individually or collectively). In other words, according to Freire, in order to help people emerge from the oppression and domination they experience, we must not only help them to see what is wrong—or limiting and dehumanizing to them—about their reality, but we must help them to visualize an alternative as well, as we help them to discover and articulate the utopian negation to their present reality. In then analyzing the constraints between the *is* and the *ought to be,* people raise their consciousness about what they need to do to get from here to there.

In Freire's words, we must both denounce and announce in order to create hope, "denouncing oppressive structure and announcing humanizing one" (1976, 220). In Freire's pedagogy, in a combination of process and content, that announcing can come in part through the affirming, dialogic educational experience itself. As people experience that process and see that people can relate differently and can respect one another and collaborate to solve problems, and as they feel themselves affirmed and fulfilled in so doing, they experience a microcosm of the sort of society that they can go on to struggle to create—a society with conditions that would make such dialogic communication and democratic problem-solving the norm.

In the process, people can "experience change as a collective endeavor, not just a theoretical possibility" (Whitty 1976, 110). When they engage in such critically conscious thought and action in a dialogical, loving community, people are not only working toward a less oppressive and more humanizing society, but they are also experiencing what it might feel like to live in a world in which such dialogue and action were the norms. In that sense, Freire's education for critical consciousness is both the path to liberation and liberation itself. For Freire, it is not simply the new nonoppressive reality that will lead to self-actualization and human fulfillment, but rather the continual process of creating and recreating it. For him, it is when we engage in such critically conscious thought and action that we are being most fully human.

Thus, as the codifications are presented, the problems are posed, and the alternatives are envisioned, the group engages in a process of *dialogue* through which people de-code the codifications in a manner that leads them to a deeper understanding of the causes or roots of the situation and a realization of their collective power to rename the reality and to act to change it. It is through the collaborative dialogical process of identifying problems, analyzing them, *and taking action to solve them, reflecting on that action, and acting again,* that people engage in the sort of praxis that is at the heart of Freire's pedagogy, and through which he believed they can develop critical consciousness. As a group engages in such praxis and as its members develop the ability to engage themselves in critically conscious thought and action, the teacher or *leader can wither away,* allowing the group to lead itself.

Chart 2 summarizes the basic principles of Freire's approach as described above, including the suggested structure, leader behaviors, and sequence of participant objectives.

CHART 2: MODEL OF FREIRE'S EDUCATION FOR CRITICAL CONSCIOUSNESS

Teaching Principles	*Sequence of Participant Objectives* (behavioral and affective)
Dialogue	
Demonstrate and create norms of non-judgmental listening and unconditional acceptance.	Feel affirmed and accepted.
	Become aware of human power and rights.
Share authority and power.	
Problematize	Become aware of self as a person in the process of becoming.
Investigate life of the people; identify themes and limit situations.	Become aware of what is dehumanizing in a situation.
Abstract situations by codifying them.	
	See the inner structure of reality, the contradictions,
Problematize the limit-situations by presenting codifications and posing questions, based on a reality to be produced, directing people's attention to the problem side of a situation, helping them to decode the codification.	Envision a different situation.
	Envision alternative routes to that vision.
Action-Praxis	Take action to achieve that vision.
Dialogue with the group about possible courses of action.	Reflect on/analyze results and experience of acting.
If appropriate, join group in acting to solve the problems.	Experience change.
	Feel hope in the possibility of internal and external change.
Wither away, turning over leadership to the group itself.	

When we consider the applicability of Freire's pedagogy to the goals of this project for anti-sexist education with men, there are really two aspects of that pedagogy to consider: the *process*—which is based on dialogue, democratic social relations, and praxis; and the *content*—what people dialogue and problem-solve about, which is based on the limits they experience to their human growth and development. The effects of that educational process would appear to be just as applicable to men as to women. The effects of the content are more problematic.

The process of Freire's pedagogy, which gives people an experience of dialogically, democratically, and collaboratively naming, analyzing, and acting on their social reality, can make two contributions to the development of critical consciousness. 1) It can help people to realize that knowledge and social reality (including social rules and social institutions such as gender roles and male-dominated institutions) are not absolute and given, but are historical creations, which people have the collective power to rename and recreate. 2) It can serve the "announcing" function of giving people an experience in a more fulfilling and affirming social reality and a sense of the kind of human relationships and kind of society that they could struggle to create. Because everyone in the society, oppressors as well as oppressed, is socialized to believe that the present social reality is essentially unchangeable—that is, that it is the only and the best one possible—these emancipatory effects of Freire's process can and should be experienced by members of both social groups.

Since the content of Freire's approach is based on the particular limit-situation, or aspects of social reality, that block an individual's or group's ability to be self-determining and to fulfill their human potential, the power of Freire's pedagogy to help men to develop critical consciousness (awareness and activism) about the nature of sexism must be based on the extent to which the solutions to that which limits or dehumanizes men in their roles as men are related to the oppression of women. In other words, to what extent must men's liberation from those limitations be based on women's liberation?

This is a complex question, but it seems safe to conclude that some limits that men experience are related to sexism and women's oppression and some are not, or some limits are more directly related than others. Some limits that men may feel and talk about may in fact be caused in the short term by women's liberation and empowerment as men lose some of their privileges, freedom, and opportunity to pursue their self-interest that those privileges made possible. On the other hand, those limits that men experience through the constraints of the traditional male gender role can be traced directly to sexism and women's oppression, and as Freire himself has pointed out (1970, 25), there is the dehumanization which all oppressors experience when they are in dominant/subordinate relationships and treat others in dehumanizing ways.

Because some of the limit-situations that confront men as men are much more directly related to women's oppression than others, it would seem to make sense for the Freirian educator to:
- focus, if possible, on the more directly related limit-situations
- be careful about helping men to see the less direct connections in regard to other limit situations by codifying and presenting those limits in appropriate ways, including limits that involve class and race
- avoid focusing on limit situations whose solutions would appear on the surface to require more rather than less oppression of women

A discussion of some specific examples will make these points clearer. One area in which many men feel limited and dehumanized as a direct result of women's oppression involves the difficulty of having equal, authentic, and satisfying relationships between men and women. Because problem-posing and problem-solving around these issues would lead men most directly to see the need to overcome the contradiction between oppressors and oppressed limits and themes in regard to this issue are probably the most appropriate and most promising to be worked with, and it would make sense to help men to get in touch with and identify the limitations they feel in this area. Many other limits that men experience are based on gender roles, which, as described above, involve various prescriptions about the personality traits and social roles men should have, or on problems in relationships between men and men. On a superficial level, it can often appear that many of these limits can be resolved by a simple "change of heart" or personality without necessarily impacting on women's oppression. When we work with men who are most concerned about these kinds of limits, it is therefore important to help them to identify the connections between those limits and roles, on the one hand, and sexist and heterosexist ideologies and the social structures that support them, on the other. Although men are not oppressed as men, many are oppressed as members of other subordinate groups, for example as working class men, gay men, and men of color. It can make sense, if men in a group are concerned about their oppression in these areas, to begin with these generative themes, but then to continue to present codifications or analyses of these limits that can help men to see their connection to sexism and patriarchy, just as it is also important to see, in the other direction, the connection of sexism to racism, classism, and heterosexism.

To conclude, all of the key principles of Freire's approach are clearly very applicable and useful in helping men to develop more awareness and activism about sexism if the limit-situations focused on are those related to the oppression of women, or if a special effort is made to help men see the connections of other limits to sexism. The most relevant principles (with key provisions or qualifications in parentheses) are:

- set norms for dialogue (nonjudgmental listening, unconditional acceptance)
- identify themes and limit-situations (related to sexism and oppression of women)
- codify limit-situations (showing connection to sexism and oppression of women)
- problematize--present limits as problems to be solved
- praxis--plan actions, act, reflect, act.

These principles, with their emphasis on the development of awareness and activism, can be used effectively in tandem with those of the T-group, which can help men become more autonomous and androgynous. The third approach that I have drawn on in developing this pedagogy, anti-oppression education, provides a framework into which these other two approaches can be integrated.

Anti-Oppression Education

Anti-oppression education (AOE) involves the integration and application to issues of oppression of teaching principles that are derived from various streams of progressive educational thought and practice, including humanistic education and human relations training, psychological education and cognitive developmental theory, and feminist, multicultural, and Freirian approaches to consciousness raising and critical pedagogy. In blending these streams together, AOE is able to "attend to specific psychological issues of the learner as they encounter the educational process" and to "utilize a developmental frame of reference for determining outcomes and instructional procedures" (Bell and Weinstein 1982, 13). In the recently published book, *Teaching for Diversity and Social Justice: A Sourcebook for Teachers and Trainers* (Adams, Bell, and Griffin, 1997), Adams describes the basic principles of this approach, which she and her co-editors call "social justice education," as follows:

- *Balance the emotional and cognitive components of the learning process*: Teaching that pays attention to personal safety, classroom norms, and guidelines for group behavior.
- *Acknowledge and support the personal (the individual student's experience) while illuminating the systemic (the interactions among social groups)*: Teaching that calls attention to the here-and-now of the classroom setting and grounds the systemic or abstract in an accumulation of concrete, real-life examples.
- *Attend to social relations within the classroom*: Teaching that helps students name behaviors that emerge in group dynamics, understand group process, and improve interpersonal communications, without blaming or judging each other.
- *Utilize reflection and experience as tools for student-centered learning*: Teaching that begins from the student's worldview and experience as the starting point for dialogue or problem-posing.
- *Value awareness, personal growth, and change as outcomes of learning*: Teaching that balances different learning styles and is explicitly organized around goals of social awareness, knowledge, and social action, although proportions of these three goals change in relation to student interest and readiness. (42-43)

In applying these principles to teaching about oppression, AOE attempts:

to have people confront the misconceptions, myths, or prejudices in their own thinking and behavior. . .that lead to and reinforce unequal treatment of certain groups in our society. . .to clarify and communicate the prevalent contradictions in how we say people should be treated in a democratic society and how they are treated: how we as individuals, groups, and systems collude in maintaining such contradictions; in effect, how we maintain oppression. . .to interrupt such maintenance by attempting to change attitudes and behavior so that they are more congruent with our democratic ideals. (Weinstein and Bell 1983, 1)

As it works toward these goals, AOE utilizes a combination of structured experiences whose goal is to stimulate disequilibrium and cognitive dissonance by introducng new cognitive organizers or frames of reference that can resolve the contradictions. As such, the approach is similar to the work of other educators who see the need for individual and social change and have applied various principles of humanistic education and human relations training to oppression issues. See, for example, the work of Katz (1978), Schneidiwind (1975, Schneidiwind and Davidson (1983, 1998), Sargent (1977), Carney and Mcmahon (1977) and Derman-Sparks and Phillips (1997). In so doing, this approach also provides a useful framework for integrating principles from the laboratory training and Freirian approaches discussed above.

The anti-oppression pedagogy is designed for use with members of all social groups, dominant as well as subordinant, and in that sense should be applicable to work with men about the issue of sexism. The learning theory upon which AOE is based reflects the belief that the change process involved in reaching the goal of "learning attitudes and behaviors more congruent with our democratic ideals" (Weinstein and Bell, 1983, 1) is analogous to the change process involved in moving to a higher stage of cognitive development, as described in various forms by Piaget (1926), Loevinger (1976), Selman (1980), Kegan (1983) and Weinstein and Alschuler (1984), all of whom describe stages of development in making sense of experience. That is not to say, however, that the changes promoted by the AOE approach are equivalent to or are dependent on cognitive development, only that they involve a similar change process. Therefore, what Weinstein and Bell describe as the cognitive developmental conditions for learning apply to their approach to consciousness raising as well. Those conditions are:

> Growth takes place as a consequence of a dialectical interaction between the organism and the environment. . . .Development proceeds as a consequence of contradictions, which challenge present modes of perception. . . .Growth involves exposure to more adequate means of making sense of reality (8-9).

In providing a context for that interaction, in raising those contradictions, and in offering that exposure, AOE attempts to create those conditions.

In order to provide a framework for describing the various elements of this approach, Weinstein and Bell adopt Kegan's three-phase formulation of how developmental change is experienced and can be facilitated. According to Kegan, that process involves a movement through phases of *defending*, during which people feel embedded in a present equilibrium and try to fend off or deny stimuli that cause disequilibrium; *surrendering*, during which one allows the contradictions to enter one's consciousness, which brings on feelings of anxiety, loss, and disequilibrium; and *reintegration*, in which a new balance is reached that is based on a new way of making meaning of one's experience.

According to Kegan, each of these phases requires a certain kind of facilitating environment: *confirmation*, which involves "holding on" to someone, giving them the feelings of safety and validation that they can lean on as they allow themselves to experience disequilibrium; *contradiction*, which presents the individual with disconfirming information and experiences; and *continuity*, which facilitates staying put or reintegration as it provides an ongoing, stable, consistent system of beliefs and interpersonal relationships.

Weinstein and Bell (1983) describe various strategies and principles that can be used in the context of this approach to create each of the facilitating environments, and in so doing facilitate the desired learning and change:

Confirmation: The learning process must begin with the creation of a "holding" or confirming environment, an environment in which participants experience feelings of safety, trust, and affirmation that will allow them to begin to engage in self-analysis and self-disclosure as they articulate and consciously examine their understanding of the issue. The goal here is to create an environment in which individuals can explore where they currently are on the issue. Only when we accept people where they are, and help them to articulate and become conscious of their current position can we help people to engage in a process of critically examining that position. In order to "establish a climate of trust and openness, as well as group norms of dialogue, interaction, and self-disclosure" (23), leaders must "insure that each person is acknowledged, that people feel invited to participate, validated as individuals, and listened to with respect" (28). By modeling such behaviors, leaders can help to set these norms for the group as a whole. Specific activities and suggestions for structuring the environment include posting a clear agenda and objectives, beginning with introductions and expectations, acknowledging feelings that arise in the course of this kind of learning, providing activities early on that require people to interact and share both thoughts and feelings, validating and rewarding personal risk-taking, allowing dialogue to develop and continue, and allowing contradictions and tensions to exist. Although it is especially important to establish a confirming environment at the outset, such an environment and such an atmosphere must be maintained throughout the learning experience if people are going to allow themselves to experience, confront, and work through the contradictions, loss of self, and self-doubt that the approach in some ways is designed to provoke.

Contradiction: The purpose of the contradicting environment is to facilitate the interaction of participants with each other and with new information and perspectives through which they can broaden their knowledge and awareness about the issue, gain experience in taking the perspective of other people and other groups, and as a result, experience feelings of contradiction, dissonance, and disequilibrium. As "the environment gradually shifts from a focus on confirmation to a focus on contradictions," activities are introduced which are "designed to unbalance and challenge people and to explore contradictions in their previous way of thinking about oppression" (28). The suggested general sequence of steps involved in each activity or encounter include: *the introduction of new information or cognitive organizers*—concepts or ideas which give people an organized way to examine the issue; *an encounter or structured activity*, which might be a role play, guided fantasy, lecture, film, discussion, etc.; *processing* the activity through personal reflection and analysis; *discussion and dialogue* around questions, thoughts, and feelings generated by the activity. Depending on the nature of the encounters, which are designed to engage learners on the affective as well as cognitive levels, participants may recognize contradictions in their previous ways of thinking and/or acting in regard to the issue and also may be exposed to different ways of thinking and acting that they find more satisfying. In this contradicting environment then, the crucial change and learning take place.

Continuity: Finally, an environment must be created that can facilitate continuity and reintegration by providing participants with opportunities to synthesize and summarize their learnings and to plan ways of integrating their new awareness and behavior into their daily lives. With such goals in mind, suggested activities include writing summaries of relevant learning, the creation of support groups, and the development of plans for taking future action outside of the learning group. Through such a process, people are encouraged to make connections between awareness and action, and to become "engaged in an ongoing process of transforming themselves and their social environment" (18). In addition to the basic strategies described above for structuring the learning environment, AOE is also based on a series of principles in regard to the appropriate sequencing of instructional activities: personal-institutional, concrete-abstract, low risk-high risk, and "what? so what? now what?". The personal to institutional sequence refers to each activity as well as to the workshop or learning experience as a whole. Each begins with the personal content, gradually introduces an institutional focus, and then cycles back to the personal from the perspective of institutionalized forms of oppression and their impact on individual perceptions and behavior. The concrete to abstract sequence "reinforces the personal to institutional sequence and also grounds each new learning so that abstractions are firmly connected and rooted in concrete examples" (34). The low-risk to high-risk sequence provides the obvious function of helping to build trust and safety, and introduces people to high risk activities only when they are ready to engage in them. The "what/so what/now what" principle provides a rationale for the logical sequencing of content and course activities. Such sequencing helps participants to ground their learnings in the concrete personal experience of their lives and to build generalizations and conclusions on that base of personal knowledge. In this emphasis on moving from concrete personal experience to generalizations and to institutional/political analysis, these principles are analogous to those of Freirian and feminist consciousness raising.

The basic teaching principles (structure and leader behaviors) and sequence of participant objectives of AOE are summarized in the chart below:

CHART 3: MODEL OF ANTI-OPPRESSION EDUCATION

Teaching Principles	*Sequence of Participant Objectives*
Confirmation Sharing of agenda/objectives Introductions Comfortable setting Sharing of fears/expectations Warm-up/interaction	Feel comfortable and safe Articulate and consciously examine one's current understanding of the issue
Contradiction Leaders present advance organizers, new information, definitions Activity (role play, guided fantasy, film, discussion, etc.) Personal processing of activity, with focus on personal reactions and learnings. Discussion/dialogue—sharing responses, perspectives, etc. Synthesis—leaders provide avenues for resolution of contradictions at more "reality-based" levels of thought and action	Stretch and broaden one's scope of knowledge about the issue Experience taking on the perspective of another person and social group culture Experience contradiction about the present way of making meaning about the issue, including feelings of disequilibrium and cognitive dissonance
Continuity Synthesis Wrap-up/summarizing—by participants and leaders. Feedback (i.e., responses to the design of the learning experience and to each other) Support groups (for use in the workshop setting and after) Reading (to provide for continued synthesis)	Resolve the contradictions with the adoption of a new way of making meaning about the issue Become engaged in transforming oneself and one's environment in pro-active ways.

Unlike Freire's education for critical consciousness (which was explicitly designed for use with members of oppressed groups) and unlike T-groups (which were not designed with issues of oppression in mind at all) the AOE model described above is designed to be used with members of any social group to raise their consciousness about oppression issues. In that sense, it is indeed applicable for helping men to learn about sexism. T-group education and Freirian pedagogy, both of which include (using different terms) phases of confirmation, contradiction, and continuity, can also be fit into the AOE framework, with various strategies drawn from each approach for creating confirming, contradicting, and reintegrating environments applied in the appropriate phase. What this AOE model offers that supplements the other approaches is both the clarity and generic nature of the design and specific principles for successfully integrating cognitive, affective, personal, and political education.

A Pedagogy for Men's Consciousness Raising: An Integrated Approach

The approaches reviewed above provide the building blocks that I have used to outline an integrated pedagogy that is theoretically capable of helping men to become both "liberated" and anti-sexist," to develop more autonomy from the dictates of gender role prescriptions, more balance of the stereotypically "masculine" and "feminine" in their repertoire of personal behaviors, more awareness of the dynamics of sexism—personal, cultural, and institutional—and more activism in opposing it. Through an integration of some approaches that promote personal growth and others that promote political awareness and activism, it has been possible to develop a pedagogy that is both personal and political, that promotes both personal growth and social/political activism.

From the T-group approach come principles for helping men to become aware of the limitations of some of their traditional "male" personality traits and to develop a more androgynous repertoire of interpersonal skills. When they increase their understanding of the roots of these attitudes and behaviors, men can develop more ability to freely and autonomously choose whether or not they wish to follow the script that has been written for them. Freire's education for critical consciousness offers principles that can be used to help men to identify the factors in the social/economic/political environment that limit their growth and development, to see the connection of those limits to the oppression of women, and hence to motivate them to act against personal and institutional sexism. Anti-oppression education offers strategies for helping men to recognize the contradictions between their current attitudes and behaviors and the democratic principles of equality and social justice. When men's awareness of the effects of sexism on women and on men themselves is increased, it can help motivate them to take anti-sexist actions.

This integrated pedagogical model makes use of frameworks found within the learning theories of two of the approaches. Anti-oppression education offers a broad framework for conceptualizing the consciousness raising process based on the phases of confirmation, contradiction, and continuation and on teaching strategies to provide the appropriate learning environment for each phase. The learning/change theory that underlies the T-group approach (Lewin's model of unfreezing, changing, and refreezing) can be used to integrate the participant objectives of all of the approaches.

Below is a simple schematic representation of the relationship between these facilitating environments and participant objectives:

Facilitating Environment (from AOE model)	*Participant Objectives* (from T-group model)
confirmation	unfreezing (feeling safe, feeling anxiety)

changing   contradiction
continuity   refreezing

I have found that further differentiating this model in regard to the relationship between the environment and the objectives can make it even more clear and precise. Unfreezing must involve a combination of a feeling of safety and a feeling of heightened anxiety and disequilibrium. Because different kinds of environmental factors or teaching principles elicit those different categories of feelings, it will be useful to subdivide the unfreezing category into two. That change will make the objectives more parallel with the environmental factors. A confirming environment will lead to feelings of safety and confirmation, and a contradicting environment will lead to feelings of dissonance and anxiety.

Confirmation → Feelings of Safety

Contradiction → Feelings of Dissonance and Anxiety

On the other side of the equation, what is described as the contradicting environment really seems to be performing two discrete functions: creating disequilibrium and dissonance in regard to current behaviors and ways of making meaning, and offering means of resolving those contradictions and reaching a new equilibrium. That latter function can be facilitated through the creation of what I would call a *creating environment*, in which people are exposed to or themselves discover alternative behaviors and ways of thinking about the issue. The cognitive developmental learning theory from which this framework is adopted points out that development or movement to a new stage is facilitated by exposure to higher levels of reasoning or meaning making. Once people see the inadequacy of their present system of beliefs and behaviors, they must see or develop alternatives if they are going to change instead of retreat into a defensive rigidity and shut out or deny the disconfirming information or experiences. It therefore seems useful to include the provision or development of such alternatives as a fourth category of facilitating environment. A more differentiated framework would look like this:

Facilitating environment: *Participant Objectives*:

confirmation   (unfreezing)   ⟶   feeling safe and affirmed
contradiction   (unfreezing)   ⟶   anxiety, disequilibrium
creation   (changing)   ⟶   changed behavior, attitudes,
                                            and consciousness
continuity   (refreezing)   ⟶   reintegration, equilibrium

Although this model appears to be sequential and closed-ended, the change process is probably more cyclical and open-ended; all four kinds of facilitating environments exist to some extent at the same time, and change occurs all of the time. If we picture the change process as occurring within an environment which is always in some ways confirming, a schema of a more cyclical change process might look like this:

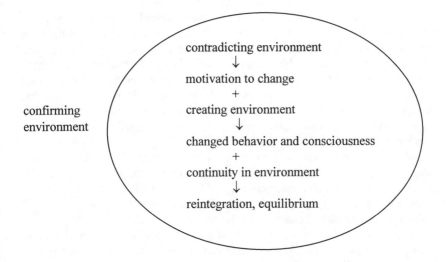

To put this schema into words, within a confirming environment, which can lead to an openness to change, a contradicting environment will create the motivation to change, which, if one is aware of alternatives and options, will lead to change itself. In an environment that offers continuity, some of those changes might lead to reintegration and equilibrium, while other changes will themselves lead to new experiences and new information that might lead to new contradictions and the motivation to change, which could, as the cycle continues, lead to more change. Such a cycle of action for change leading to the discovery of new contradictions, leading to more action for change, is another way of conceptualizing Freire's concept of "praxis": action—reflection—action.

Within this broad framework or schema, it is the application of particular teaching principles in the creation of each sort of facilitating environment that can create conditions that are conducive to the particular objectives of this pedagogy. The various teaching principles applied in creating the contradicting and creating environments in particular will determine the particular changes that will result from the process. It is important to remember that if this pedagogy is to lead to the personality changes involved in increased androgyny, as well as the changes in attitude, consciousness, and behavior that are involved in increased awareness and activism, then contradicting and creating must occur in regard to interpersonal behavior and to ways of making meaning about sexism. The model below therefore includes teaching principles drawn from the three approaches reviewed, designed to facilitate changes in those aspects of men's identity and to help men to see the connections between them.

What follows is an outline of the teaching principles to be used in the development of each kind of environment, the objectives to be achieved, and some examples and illustrations of their application in practice.

1. Development of an Environment that Offers Confirmation

All of the approaches reviewed above are premised on the creation of an environment that helps participants to feel safe, supported and confirmed; an environment in which they can open up and share their personal feelings and experiences in and out of the group, and articulate and examine their current understanding of the issues. The creation of such an environment involves setting norms regarding the process of communication in the group and the content of the communication—which must center on the personal experiencing of the learners. The various means that can be used for setting such a climate can be combined into the following principles:

a) Set norms for nonjudgmental dialogical communication. These norms can be set by the leader through personal modeling, clearly announced guidelines, and monitoring and enforcement. Guidelines, which a group can help to create for itself, may include such practices as active listening, use of "I" messages, confidentiality, and no put-downs.

b) Set norms that make the personal experience of learners the basic content of communication. These norms can be set by announcing that people will learn primarily from themselves and each other, not from the leader, and demonstrating and engaging others in the sharing of personal experiences from inside and outside the group. Beginning the exploration of each topic with journal writing and discussion about individual experiences with, for instance, growing up male, relationships with women, relationships with men, followed by reading various analyses of such issues, can support the development of such norms.

c) Structured experiences that build trust and dialogue. Activities that move from personal reflection to paired sharing to small group and then large group discussion can help to build trust and dialogue as people build relationships and gradually become comfortable sharing information and feelings with larger groups of people.

2. Development of an Environment that Offers Contradiction

The contradicting environment must function to help participants to experience feelings of anxiety, dissonance, and disequilibrium in regard to their interpersonal behavior and their way of making meaning about sexism. The necessary means for facilitating such dissonance are expressed in the following principles:

a) Process interpersonal behavior in the group, in regard to its effects on others and the group process, and its relationship to male role socialization. This processing can be facilitated by focusing attention on such behavior, asking processing questions, setting aside group time for it, and demonstrating and setting norms of self-disclosure and feedback. For instance, such processing and feedback may help some men to notice how much they may monopolize discussion, interrupt others, or intellectualize issues instead of expressing feelings.

b) Present new information, definitions, and cognitive organizers about gender roles and sexism. Examples might include information about the relative status of men and women, statistics on rape and violence against women, videos on images of men and women in advertising and on date rape and theories about the dynamics of oppressions.

c) Structure activities through which participants encounter contradictions in their present behavior and consciousness. Examples of such activities may include (depending on the consciousness and identity development of those in a group) brainstorming about stereotypes of women and men, role plays involving images of men and women, feedback on interpersonal patterns of behavior, confrontation in regard to lack of action in support of professed beliefs.

d) Problematize—pose limits to men's growth and development as problems to be analyzed and solved. For instance, limits such as lack of ful-filling relationships with women or difficulties with expression of feelings can be linked to gender roles and to inequalities of power between men and women.

3. Development of an Environment that Offers Creation—New Models and Visions

Once people's attitudes, beliefs, and interpersonal behaviors have become "unfrozen," the next step is to create an environment that offers them the means for change, means which will help them to resolve the contradictions and reach, if even only temporarily, a new equilibrium. In order to facilitate that change, the learning environment must offer some idea or vision of what that change might be. Those alternatives, or models for new ways of thinking and behaving, and new forms of social organization can be developed by participants themselves, or be presented in some form by the leaders. The principles involved in creating this sort of environment involve ways of either helping participants to develop and articulate their own alternatives or ways of modeling and presenting alternatives.

a) Modeling alternative interpersonal behaviors. As individuals search for alternatives to what they may discover to be their ineffective repertoire of male-stereotyped interpersonal skills, they need to see examples and models of new more effective behaviors, such as, for example, empathic listening, making sure that others in the group have a chance to speak, talking with other men about their relationships with one another.

b) Dialogue/discussion involving the analysis of the causes of the limits men experience, the connection of those limits to sex roles and the oppression of women, and the envisioning of solutions to those limits. Through a problem-posing and problem-solving process, it may be possible to some extent to help men to discover for themselves new ways of thinking about these issues, and to themselves envision alternatives and solutions. For instance, a focus on the limits a man may experience in his relationship with his father may lead to an analysis of male socialization toward the value of work and away from the family, which may in turn lead to a vision of more equitable gender roles in regard to the balance of family and work responsibilities.

c) Present alternative cognitive maps/forms of consciousness. In order to facilitate the discovery process mentioned above and to help people to sort out and make sense of the other contradictions they are experiencing it is often helpful to present through lecture or discussion new frames of reference. For instance, a framework that explains the relationship between heterosexism, sexism, and rigid gender roles can help men see their stake in opposing both of these related and interlocking forms of oppression. If these new "maps" do help people to resolve the contradictions they see, they will then appropriate and internalize these maps as their own, The presentation and internalization of different ways of thinking about sexism and gender roles can also help people internalize into their self-concept the new, more expressive behaviors they may be experimenting with.

d) Provide structure for planning actions for personal and social change. Once problems have been identified and analyzed and long range solutions have been uncovered, the next step is to plan how to get from here to there. That planning may involve simply thinking about when to try out a new interpersonal behavior or it may involve carefully analyzing a series of action steps to work toward one's vision of a new society, At any level of change, the learning environment must encourage people to think through those actions and envision concrete steps that they can begin to take. That encouragement can range from asking participants to set personal goals, objectives, and plans for change to engaging the entire group in creating plans for how to change or facilitate their own interaction, or how to take some political action together. Actions can take place, and be planned for, at a variety of levels.

e) Praxis—Engaging participants in action to transform themselves and their society. Once alternatives have been envisioned and actions planned, the next step is encourage and support people in taking action. Those actions may involve personal change in, for instance, one's level of self-disclosure in the group or way of relating to women friends, or social action such as forming an anti-pornography task force or joining a march against rape. Such actions can be encouraged through such means as setting a group norm of experimenting with new behavior, or asking people to take some action and report back to the group about it. As individuals reflect on that action and its results, their understanding and awareness will continue to increase, and they can go on to plan for and take more action.

4. Development of an Environment that Offers Continuity

If the changes in behavior and consciousness that individuals experience are to be integrated into their life outside of and after the learning groups, an environment must be created which offers them some means and structure for facilitating that sort of integration on both the cognitive and affective levels.

a) Summarizing and synthesizing. At various points in the learning process and especially at the end, it is important for participants to summarize and synthesize their learning. Such written and verbal synthesizing can reinforce learnings and help people to gain clarity and perspective. In the course design presented here, these opportunities are presented in three interim learning papers on some of the main focus areas, such as growing up male, relationships with women, and relationships with other men, and in a final paper in which students are asked to reflect on and synthesize in writing their learnings from the course as a whole.

b) Support groups. Support groups in and after the group can provide people with the interpersonal support they need to maintain and nurture their changing selves. On at least two occasions, for instance, this group study led to the creation of ongoing men's group outside of the class itself, and to participation in regional and national conferences of NOMAS, the National Organization for Men Against Sexism.

c) Continued praxis. Action planning, action, reflection. A full integration of the changes that are desired necessarily means that people will become engaged in an ongoing process of critical reflection and action to change themselves and their world. Once underway, it is a process without an end.

d) Gradual disengagement by the leader. As individuals and the group develop more and more of a capacity for critical thinking and action, it is important to gradually "wither away" and turn over more and more leadership functions to the group so that it and the individuals involved can function for and by themselves. In this way, the study can be an empowering experience for the participants rather than one that leads to dependence on or idolization of the group leader.

A model that outlines the basic principles and objectives of this pedagogy is presented in Chart 4.

Like the more schematic model of change outlined earlier in this discussion, this model for men's consciousness raising may appear to be necessarily sequential and closed-ended, but the change process is probably never that tidy. In fact, all four kinds of facilitating environments may need to be present throughout the learning experience as participants cycle and recycle through the change process in different ways. A course or learning experience may have sequential phases during which confirmation, contradiction, creation, or continuity are most emphasized, but within that overall process, each class session or meeting may in and of itself need to involve the same cycle. In regard to sequencing, it is also important to note that this pedagogy adopts from the anti-oppression approach principles regarding the appropriate sequencing of instructional activities, moving from personal to institutional, concrete to abstract, low risk to high risk, and what, so what, and now what. These guidelines for sequencing must often be applied within each class session or unit, as well as in regard to a course as a whole.

CHART 4: MODEL OF A PEDAGOGY FOR MEN'S CONSCIOUSNESS RAISING

Learning Environment/Teaching Principles	*Participant Objectives*
1.*Confirmation* a) Set norms for creating a nonjudgmental dialogical communication process. b) Set norms that make the personal experiencing of learners the basic content of discussion. c) Structure activities that build trust and dialogue and facilitate personal sharing.	1. *Unfreezing, Part 1:* Feeling safe and affirmed a) Feel comfortable, safe, affirmed, and accepted. b) Open up and share personal feelings and experiences regarding: (1) the here and now experience in the group; and (2) there and then experiences in the past and outside of the group relating to masculinity, gender roles,

2. *Contradiction*
a) Process interpersonal behavior in the group.
b) Present new information, definitions, and cognitive organizers about gender roles and sexism.
c) Structure activities through which participants encounter contradictions in their present behavior and consciousness.
d) Problematize—pose limits to men's growth and development as problems to be analyzed and solved.
e) Praxis—engage participants in action to transform themselves and their society, and in reflection on that action.

3. *Creation*
a) Model alternative interpersonal behaviors.
b) Dialogue/discussion involving an analysis of the causes of limits and problems, and envisioning of alternatives and solutions.
c) Present alternative cognitive maps
d) Provide structure for planning actions for personal and social changes

4. *Continuity*
a) Summarize and synthesize.
b) Support groups.
c) Encourage continued praxis.
d) Gradual disengagement by the leader.

and sexism.
2. *Unfreezing, Part 2*: Feeling anxiety and disequilibrium.
a) Experience feedback about one's effect on others and the group process.
b) Feel heightened anxiety, dissonance, and disequilibrium about some stereotypically male interpersonal behaviors.
c) Recognize connections between some of those dissonant behaviors and male socialization.
d) Stretch and broaden one's scope of knowledge about gender roles and sexism.
e) Recognize some of the dehumanizing effects on self and others of gender roles and sexism.
f) Experience feelings of dissonance and disequilibrium regarding one's current way of making meaning about gender roles and sexism.
3. *Changing*
a) Recognize interpersonal effectiveness of a more androgynous range of behavior.
b) Recognize some of the socio-economic-political causes of some of the limits that one experiences as a man, and the connection of those limits to gender roles and sexism.
c) Recognize or envision alternative personal behaviors and alternative forms of social organization.
d) Experience more satisfying and fulfilling ways of being with other men.
e) Recognize and adopt a new cognitive map about these issues that resolves the disequilibrium one was experiencing.
f) Engage in praxis—action-reflection-action—in trying to change oneself and one's environment, in and out of the group.
4. *Refreezing*
a) Integration of new behaviors and consciousness into relational system.

Chart 5 on the following page presents an overview of the course design in which this model was applied, outlining a) the what, so what, now what sequencing of questions and problems, both within the overall design and within each session; b) the basic questions and problems posed within each session, which, in Freire's terms can lead to the sort of dialogue, decoding, and analysis that can lead to the development of critical consciousness; and c) the primary

CHART 5: COURSE OVERVIEW

SESSION/TOPICS	QUESTIONS/PROBLEMS	ENVIRONMENT
Phase I: What?	What is this course about?	Confirming
1. Introduction	Who is in the group?	
		Confirming
2. Growing up male, I	What messages did I/we learn about how to be a man?	Contradicting
		Confirming
3. Growing up male, II	How did those messages affect us?	Contradicting
4. Men, emotions, and self-disclosure	What messages did we learn about feelings? How do those affect you/us?	Confirming Contradicting
Phase II: So What?	What are the dynamics of oppression?	Confirming
5. The dynamics of oppression		Contradicting
	What have been the problems/limits in your own relationships with women?	Confirming
6. Man-woman relationships and the dynamics of oppression	How do gender roles affect m/w relationships, your relationships? How do issues of power/ dominance/ subordinance affect m/w relationships, your relationships?	Contradicting Creating
	Why are men violent against women?	Confirming
7. Violence against women	What can we do about it?	Contradicting Creating
	How do issues of dominance/ subordinance affect your sexuality? Male sexuality? What is the relationship for you and other men between sexuality and intimacy? What would you like to change about how you express your sexuality?	
8. Male sexuality		Confirming Contradicting Creating
	What are the barriers to close male-male relationships? How are those affecting us in the group?	Confirming
9. Men relating to men, I		Contradicting Creating
	How can we overcome those barriers, in general and in the group?	Confirming
10. Men relating to men, II		Contradicting Creating
	How do classism and racism affect you,us other men? How do they relate to/ support sexism?	Confirming
11. Men, class, and race		Contradicting Creating
	What changes would you like to make, are you making in your way of being a man, relating to men and women, dealing with sexism, etc.?	Confirming
Phase III: Now What?		Contradicting
12. Personal change		Creating Continuing
	What social changes would make those personal changes more possible and overcome the various problems/limits identified above.	Confirming
13. Social change		Contradicting Creating Continuing
14. Closure	What did you/we learn?	Continuing

learning environments (based on the confirmation, contradiction, creation, and continuity model described above). This overview is presented as a generic model that can and should change in response to the particular interests, problems, and questions of concerns of those in the group. It is at that point when the men in the group, in response to the sorts of broad questions posed above, engage with specific concerns and questions regarding significant issues and limits in their own lives, that the real process of change and learning can occur. Therefore, the detailed session-by-session course experience will vary significantly in response. For a detailed description of an early version of this course design see Schapiro (1985); for a detailed course design on sexism for mixed gender groups see Goodman and Schapiro (1997).

Men in Transition: Experiences of Change

The pedagogical model and course design as presented above may be theoretically sound, but the real test has come as that theory and model have been put into practice, and again and again, revised in response. The strongest evidence of success has come in the words of the participants themselves, as they have reflected, both during and at the end of the experience, on what they have gained from it. In their words, which I have excerpted below from some of their self-evaluations and reflection papers, I think we can hear a transformation process at work, a process that connects the personal and the political.

M: There is an issue that is of crucial importance to the way I view myself, and deal with others that I am just barely now starting to recognize and deal with. That issue is homophobia. Six months ago I would have said that I was not homophobic. . . . That was only part right, some of it was a lie. I was lying to myself, because I was afraid to face the possibility that I might have a homosexual side. As I said, I was just starting to deal with that now, and I don't have very many answers, mostly, I just have a lot of questions. . . . In order to free myself of these feelings, I need to first face the possibility that I may be attracted to some men.

C: Probably the most important thing that happened as a result of this study, however, was my examination of my family as a dysfunctional system. This arose directly from the suggestion to examine my relationship with my father and ask myself what did I not get that I needed as a child. Once again, I see all of the issues in my life connecting and my emotional work being facilitated by my learning experiences. . . .

If we begin now to resist domination, competition, and traditional capitalist-defined success in our lives, if we refuse to oppress women on a personal level, if we remember our father's suffering while we raise our sons and remember our mother's oppression as we raise our daughters, if we learn to connect with and feel our own pain and share that pain with other men who feel the same pain, if we talk to other men at work, at the bus stop, at the bar and at the game about these issues, if we refuse to work for companies that oppress minorities and refuse to buy products that exploit third world labor, and if we are public about our efforts and encourage our peers to follow our model, then, in the generations that follow, our social environment will change for the better.

K: One of the most important portions of this group study was to learn the fundamental concepts of power, dominance, subordination, hierarchy and patriarchy, socialization and internalization. I believe that understanding the fundamentals of all relationships is the basis for analyzing the roots of problems and promoting change both within ourselves and in society and roots of problems and promoting change. . . . Another very important result I have seen is the way I have improved my discourse and conversations with women. I was able to almost completely absorb the concepts of emotional empathy, sympathy and compassion and have watched my conversations with women grow to new heights. . . . I think that one of the most important ways that I could change how I express my masculinity is to be a better communicator in a clear and precise way. . . . As a person I feel that I have become more compassionate and empathetic toward myself and others. This empathy and compassion has helped me in many ways to struggle with my own sadness and feelings of guilt and powerlessness caused by letting go or changing my traditional masculine role. . . . hope that I can be an agent for change socially by educating not only other men about masculinity but my own children and students that I educate as well.

D: The most important career learning manifested itself in a pedagogy of communication skills. . . . Realizing the difficulties in making the transition from inner city street life to a Goddard classroom, I next became aware of my modes of speaking and listening. . . . I hypothesize that if I have become too blunt and abrasive, then my counseling style . . . could do an injustice to my clientele. Interacting in the group precipitated these thoughts. . . .

T: At the beginning of the semester I was asking myself why men could not emote or be expressive of affection physically. Now the question has changed to, with the information that I now possess, what can I do about this?. . . Being in this class has given me a new understanding of the male condition in society today, and this understanding has given me an idea as to how we can break out of the cycle of oppression. Men oppress women, but we also oppress ourselves. We compete, and in competition we find ourselves as males. If we can manage to diffuse the feelings of competition and the need for emotional deadness we will be better able to relate to each other, and thus be able to better relate to women and other oppressed groups. But to do this we will have to change our entire idea of how children should be raised. . . .

C: Upon reflection, three major concepts or ideas stand out as most important to me. First, the impact which male socialization has had on me

*personally and other men in general. Second, the idea that gender is an
artificial product of society and not wholly determined by sex. Third, the limits
of masculinity that exist within the context of a hierarchical and capitalist
society. . . . I have never thought of myself as very "masculine," but I
understand now that indeed I am masculine and that many of my interpersonal
difficulties have their roots in this masculinity. Second, I have a deeper
understanding of the need to radically reconstruct the environment in which
boys grow up in order to achieve a society that is free of sexism and
homophobia. . . . I have learned that a vast amount of what society considers
masculine and feminine is not a result of sex but rather culturally imposed
models. . . . The fluidity that I have allowed to permeate my concepts of
masculinity and femininity has helped me to relate differently to both men and
women. By learning to reject those aspects of "masculinity" that have been
harmful to me and others and to embrace those aspects of "femininity" that will
further my emotional and spiritual growth, I am developing relationships in
entirely new directions. I have become more expressive with emotions and am
learning to listen to people without judgement or feeling the need to "fix"
situations. . . . I have discovered that there are definite limits to gender and
masculinity within the context of our present society. . . . Religion, education,
and the family act as agents of reproduction with regard to gender roles. As
much as personal growth is needed, without radically altering society's
institutions or economic system gender can be transformed only so far.
Therefore, in order to achieve a non-sexist and non-homophobic society, we
must affect a systematic change that reaches to the roots of oppression:
capitalism and hierarchy. . . . After all has been said, the single most important
thing that I have gained through this study is a new lens through which I can
view society, myself, and my relationships. This lens is that of masculinity. . . .*

We can hear in these men's words their movement away from confronting
and acknowledging their personal limitations and constraints, to seeing the
connections of those limits to systems, structures, and forms of consciousnsess,
and their engagement in working at once toward personal and social change.
The connections are there; it is our role as critical progressive educators to help
people to discover and unravel those connections for themselves, and to do so in
ways in which they can find a personal stake and a personal motivation to
change. I believe that people have an inner drive to be whole, to relate to others
in authentic and meaningful ways, to live in relationships based on mutuality,
honesty, trust, and collaboration rather than on exploitation, deceit, competition,
dominance, and subordinance. As we help others and ourselves to uncover the
connections between our personal dilemmas and frustrations and the systems of
oppression in which we live, we lay the groundwork for the sorts of personal and
social transformation that can help us all live more satisfying and meaningful
lives. As Freire has taught us, no one is free while others are oppressed.

I hope that the pedagogical principles and course design outlined in this
chapter can contribute something to a vision of how in the classrooms of our

colleges and universities we can engage in transformative educational practices, practices that promote social justice and democracy, practices that can help us to change relationships and social structures based on dominance and subordinance into those based on mutuality and equality. In working toward these ends, there is a rich array of progressive educational theory and practice that we can draw on, developed over the last quarter century of engagement with education for diversity and social justice. The pedagogy that is described here represents the application, integration, and adaptation of this new array of progressive educational practice to work with men about issues of sexism.

As I reflect on my personal learning through this experience, I realize that this work has helped me come to some important realizations along the way. One of the things that my students have helped me to learn is the need to move away from normative concepts of "masculinity" based on the white middle-class heterosexual experience. In earlier iterations of this course, most of the readings and discussion were based around that normative concept of masculinity, and even though our purpose was to critique that concept, I came to realize how that very notion was marginalizing to gay men, men of color, and others outside of that dominant paradigm, including those who consider themselves to be "transgender." Broadening my own concept of the norms of masculinity and the masculine experience; recognizing that there is not one masculinity to critique and transform, but many masculinities, has helped me to broaden and deepen my own sense of what I am and can be as a man and a person. Working to help other men to reflect on and transform their understanding of gender, to become more whole, and more able and willing to confront social injustice, has kept me doing all of that for myself. I have allowed myself, in Freire's words, to enter into dialogue which, "as a democratic relationship…is the opportunity I have to open myself up to others' thinking…" (1994, 119) and to the possibility of being transformed in the process. For that, I am grateful.

References

Adams, M., L. Bell, and P. Griffin, eds. 1997. *Teaching for Diversity and Social Justice: A Sourcebook.* New York: Routledge.

Alschuler, A. 1980. *School Discipline*, New York: McGraw-Hill.

Bell, D. 1982. *Being a Man: The Paradox of Masculinity.* Lexington, Massachusetts: Lewis Publishing Co.

Bell, L. and N. Schneidiwind. 1989. "Reflective Minds, Intentional Hearts: Joining Humanistic Education and Critical Theory." *Journal of Education,* 167 (3): 9–26.

Bem S. 1974. "The Measurement of Psychological Androgyny." *Journal of Clinical and Consulting Psychology* (42):155–162.

———.1975. "Sex Role Adaptability: One-Consequence of Psychological Androgyny." *Journal of Personality and Social Psychology* (31):634-643.

———.1976. "Probing the Promise of Androgyny," in *Beyond Sex Role Stereotypes: Toward a Psychology of Androgyny,* edited by A. Kaplan and J. Bean. Boston: Little, Brown.

———.1977a "Beyond Androgyny: Some Presumptuous Prescriptions for a Liberated Sexual Identity," in *Exploring Contemporary Male and Female Roles: A Facilitator's Guide.* edited by C. Carney and S. McMahon. La Jolla, California: University Associates.

———.1977b. "Psychological Androgyny," in *Beyond Sex Roles*, edited by A. Sargent. St. Paul, Minnesota: West Publishing Co.

Benne, K., L. Bradford, and R. Lippit, eds. 1964. *T-Group Theory and Laboratory Method: Innovation in Re-Education.* New York: Wiley.

Benne, K., L. Bradford, J. Gibb, and R. Lippit, eds. 1975a. *The Laboratory Method of Changing and Learning.* Palo Alto: Science and Behavior Books..

———.1975b. "Conceptual and Moral Foundations of Laboratory Education," in *The Laboratory Method of Changing and Learning, edited by* Benne et al. Palo Alto: Science and Behavior Books.

Bennis, W., K. Benne, R. Chin, and K. Corey, eds. 1976. *The Planning of Change.* 3rd ed. New York: Holt, Rinehart, and Winston,

Bly, R. 1990. *Iron John: A Book About Men.* Reading, Massachusetts: Addison-Wesley.

Borton, T. 1970. *Reach, Touch and Teach.* New York: McGraw Hill.

Brod, H. 1987. *The Making of Masculinities: The New Men's Studies.* Boston: Unwin Hyman.

Carney, C., and S. McMahon, eds. 1977. *Exploring Contemporary Male and Female Roles: A Facilitator's Guide.* La Jolla, California: University Associates.

Creane, J. 1981. "Consciousness Raising Groups for Men," in *Men in Difficult Times*, edited by R. Lewis. Englewood Cliffs, New Jersey: Prentice Hall.

Derman-Sparks, L. and C. B. Phillips. 1997. *Teaching/Learning Anti-Racism: A Developmental Approach.* New York: Teachers College Press.

Farrell, W. 1974. *The Liberated Man.* New York: Random House.

Fasteau, M.F. 1975. *The Male Machine.* New York: McGraw Hill.

Freire, P. 1970 *Pedagogy of the Oppressed.* New York: Herder and Herder.

———.1973. *Education for Critical Consciousness.* New York: Seabury Press.

———.1976. "A Few Notes on Conscientization" in *Schooling and Capitalism,* edited by R. Dale. London: Routledge.

———.1978. *Pedagogy in Process.* New York: Seabury Press,

———.1994. *Pedagogy of Hope:* New York: Continuum.

Gilmore, D. 1990. *Manhood in the Making: Cultural Concepts of Masculinity.* New Haven: Yale University Press.

Giroux, H. 1981. *Ideology, Culture, and the Process of Schooling.* Philadelphia: Temple University Press.

Goldberg, H. 1979. *The New Male: From Macho to Sensitive But Still All Male.* New York: New American Library.

Heilbrun, C. 1973. *Toward a Recognition of Androgyny.* New York: Knopf.

hooks, b. 1994. *Teaching to Transgress: Education as the Practice of Freedom.* New York: Routledge.

Hornacek,, P. 1977. "Anti-Sexist Consciousness-Raising Groups for Men," in *For Men Against Sexism,* edited by J. Snodgrass. Albion, California: Times Change Press.

Kanter, R.M. 1977. *Men and Women of the Organization.* New York: Basic Books.

———.1979. "Women in T-Groups: Norms and Sex Role Issues," in *NTL Reader.* Menlo Park, California: University Associates.

Kaplan, A. 1979. "Clarifying the Concept of Androgyny, " *Psychology of Women Quarterly* 3 (3): 223–230.

Kaplan, A., and J. Bean, eds. 1976. *Beyond Sex Roles: Toward a Psychology of Androgyny.* Boston: Little, Brown.

Katz, J. 1978. *White Awareness.* Norman, Oklahoma: University of Oklahoma Press.

Karsk, P., and B. Thomas, B. 1979. *Working with Men's Groups.* Columbia, Maryland: New Community Press.

Kegan, Robert, 1982. *The Evolving Self.* Cambridge, Massachusetts: Harvard University Press.

Keith, J. 1974. "My Own Men's Liberation," in *Men and Masculinity,* edited by J. Pleck and J, Sawyer. Englewood Cliffs, New Jersey: Prentice Hall.

Kimmel, M.S. 1979. *Changing Men: New Directions in Research on Men and Masculinity.* Newbury Park, California: Sage Publications.

Kirshner, D. 1977. *Masculinity in a Historical Perspective: Readings and Discussions.* Washington, DC: University Press of America.

Kivel, P. 1992. *Men's Work: How to Stop the Violence that Tears Our Lives Apart.* Center City, Minnesota: Hazelden Books.

———.1996. *Uprooting Racism: How White People Can Work for Social Justice.* Philadelphia: New Society Publishers.

Kohlberg, L. 1966. "Cognitive Developmental Analysis of Children's Sex Role

Concepts and Attitudes," in *The Development of Sex Differences*, edited by E. Maccoby. Stanford, California: Stanford University Press.

Levant, R.F. 1996. *Masculinity Reconstructed*. New York: Penguin Books.

Levant, R.F. and W.S. Pollack. 1995. *A New Psychology of Men*. New York: Basic Books.

Lewin, K. 1948. *Resolving Social Conflicts*. New York: Harper and Row.

————.1951 *Field Theory in Social Science*. New York: Harper and Row.

Lewis, R., ed. 1981. *Men in Difficult Times*. Englewood Cliffs, New Jersey: Prentice Hall.

Moreland, John. 1976a. "A Humanistic Approach to Facilitating College Students Learning About Sex Roles," *Counseling Psychologist* 6 (3): 6–64.

————.1976b "Facilitator Training for Consciousness Raising Groups in an Academic Setting." *Counseling Psychologist*, 6 (3): 66–68.

Mosher, R.L., and N.A Sprinthall. 1970. "Psychological Education in Secondary Schools: A Program to Promote Individual and Human Development." *American Psychologist* 25 (4): 911–924.

Nichols, J. 1974. *Men's Liberation: A New Definition of Masculinity*. New York: Penguin.

O'Neil,, J. 1981. "Patterns of Gender Role Conflict and Strain: Sexism and Fear of Feminity in Men's Lives," *Personnel and Guidance Journal*, 203-210.

Sargent, A. 1975. "Consciousness Raising Groups: A Strategy for Sex Role Liberation." Ed.D. diss. University of Massachusetts at Amherst.

————.1977. *Beyond Sex Roles*. St. Paul, Minnesota: West Publishing Company.

————.1979. "Training for Androgyny," in *NTL Reader*. Menlo Park, California: University Associates.

Schapiro, S. 1985. "Changing Men: The Rationale, Theory and Design of a Men's Consciousness Raising Program." Ed.D. dissertation. University of Massachusetts at Amherst.

Schapiro, S. and D. Goodman. 1997. "Sexism Curriculum Design," in *Teaching for Diversity and Social Justice*, edited by M. Adams, L. Bell, and P. Griffin. New York: Routledge.

Schein, E., and E. Bennis, eds. 1977. *Personal and Organizational Change Through Group Methods: The Laboratory Approach*. New York: Wiley.

Scher, M. 1981. "Men in Hiding: A Challenge for the Counselor," *Personnel and Guidance Journal*.

Schniedewind, N. 1975. *A Model Integrating Personal and Social Change in Teacher Education: Its Implications in a Racism and Sexism Training Program*. Ed.D. dissertation. University of Massachusetts at Amherst.

Schniedewind, N, and Davidson, E. 1998. *Open Minds to Equality: A Sourcebook of Learning Activities to Promote Diversity and Equity*. New York: Allyn and Bacon.

————.1983. *Open Minds to Equality*. New York: Allyn and Bacon.

Shepherd, H. 1970. "Personal Growth Labs: Toward an Alternative Culture," *Journal of Applied Behavioral Science* 6 (3): 37-50.

Shor, I. 1980. *Critical Teaching and Everyday Life.* Boston: South End Press.
———.1992. *Empowering Education: Critical Thinking for Social Change.* Chicago: University of Chicago Press.
Solomon, K., and Levy, B. 1983. *Men in Transition: Theory and Therapy,* New York: Plenum Press.
Snodgrass, J. 1976. "Four Replies to Radical Feminism: Marxism, Revolutionary Effeminism, Gay Marxism, and Men's Liberation." Paper presented at the Pacific Sociological Association Meetings, San Diego, California.
———.1979. "Critique of the Men's Movement," in *The Men Say/The Women Say,* edited by E. Shapiro and B. Shapiro. New York: Dell.
Snodgrass, J., ed. 1977. *For Men Against Sexism.* Albion, California: Times Change Press.
Sprinthall, N.A.1976. "Learning Psychology by Doing Psychology, A High School Curriculum in the Psychology of Counseling," in *Developmental Education.* edited by G.D. Miller. St. Paul, Minnesota: Minnesota Dept. of Education.
Staples, R. 1978. "Masculinity and Race: The Dual Dilemma of Black Men." *Journal of Social Issues* 34 (1): 169-181.
Stein, T. 1983. "Men's Groups," in *Men in Transition: Theory and Therapy,* edited by K. Solomon and B. Levy. New York: Plenum Press.
Stoltenberg, J. 1977a. "Refusing to be a Man," in *For Men Against Sexism.* edited by J. Snodgrass. Albion, California: Times Change Press.
———. 1977b. "'Toward Gender Justice," in *For Men Against Sexism,* edited by J. Snodgrass. Albion, California: Times Change Press.
Weinstein, G. and L. Bell. 1983. "Anti-Oppression Education." Unpublished manuscript. University of Massachusetts at Amherst.

SIX

But I Don't Read Poetry: Relearning to Read Literature

Nora Mitchell

"You Know How Such Things Get Around"

For over twenty years, I have handed drafts of my poems to friends for critical feedback. At first, they balk and say, "But I don't read poetry." When I insist, they read my rough drafts and respond—at first tentatively, and then with increasing confidence and sophistication. I do not do this to convince them that they can read poetry but because I need responsive readers, people with whom I can talk about poems, people for whom the choice of this word or that word matters. From confirmed nonreaders of poetry, some of my friends have turned into readers. They seek poetry on their own now, buy a collection occasionally, and read for pleasure.

These same friends revel in fiction and nonfiction and join reading groups where they discuss the finer points of character and point of view. Why is poetry not part of their reading?

As far as most people in the United States are concerned, poetry is highbrow, weird, unnecessarily difficult. Of all the arts, poetry may be the most suspect—as it has always been in this most pragmatic of countries. Herman Melville's wife wrote to her mother, "Herman has taken to writing poetry. You need not tell anyone, for you know how such things get around" (Rukeyser 1996, 10). Novels are bad enough, but poetry? The fact is that poetry scares people, and their judgments are largely defensive. People think a poem is like a trick question with only one right answer, or like a dirty joke told at a party. If you don't get the joke, you bluff. If you don't get the poem, you reject it.

Poetry may only be the extreme case, however, since most people shy away from "literary" books in favor of romances, thrillers, mysteries, and science fiction adventures, books that entertain but rarely challenge. Most of these books are formulaic entertainment products in book form.[1] There is nothing wrong with these books—they are fun and diverting—as long as their broad market appeal does not lead publishers to neglect the more complex, questioning books that both entertain *and* challenge. (Publishers, however, are neglecting the more complex, questioning books as they keep their corporate eyes on the bottom line.) As a teacher, I ask myself some hard questions as well. Does our teaching somehow move literature out of the reach of students and discourage them from becoming lifelong readers? How can we teach students to engage with literary art in ways that really matter to them, so that they can, in educator Louise Rosenblatt's words, "come intimately and lastingly into their literary heritage" (Rosenblatt 1976, 65)?[2] I approach this topic as a poet who teaches at the college and graduate levels. This is not to say that I am a teacher whose "real work" lies elsewhere. I doubt that I would write as I do were I not deeply engaged with teaching. My teaching, likewise, is deeply engaged with writing. My experiences as a writer have shaped my pedagogy as much as my graduate training has, and I continue to puzzle over the troubling implications of that nearly automatic response, "But I don't read poetry." What does it mean to write poems in a culture that barely reads poetry? Am I some kind of anachronism? What does this say about my culture?

Democratic Practice and Friendship

As I have approached this chapter, I have had some anxieties about the application of the phrase "*democratic practice*" to the teaching of poetry. What is "democratic" about teaching someone to read a poem when the reader may experience that poem as elitist?

These anxieties stem largely from the way I was taught in college. Though I was introduced to Freudian, Marxist, and feminist literary criticisms in college, most of my teachers approached poems from a New Critical perspective with a fierce insistence that what mattered was *the poem itself*, not the poet, the poet's historical context, or the reader. New Criticism, a post–World War II pheno-menon, helped English professors stake out a professional territory for them-selves when science and scientific methods were ascendant. New critics treated the text as something autonomous, complex, and wondrous—an object worthy of expert study. I was taught to read closely, to mine the text for everything.

As a young writer, I benefited from this training, but there was something puzzling and mystifying about the process, too. Recently, I ran across a critique of the New Criticism that resonated with my experience as a student. Russell Hunt was trained in historicist theories and methods, but welcomed New Criticism because it worked better in the classroom; its methods seemed to make literature more readily accessible to a new generation of students than did the older historicist methods. But he notes that he failed to realize that his historical training continued to inform his own reading, that his reading of "the text itself" in fact included a great deal more: "when we assured (students) that if they just read closely enough they'd get it, what we really did was to make it seem like magic to most of them" (Hunt 1991, 110). It seemed like magic to me, especially in poetry courses. Poetry, which had always seemed vitally connected to the life of my times, was presented as something highly technical, elite, mystical. To read poetry properly you had to be an expert.

I have also continued to mull over what went right in the learning experiences of my friends and how to connect their experiences to the larger concern of this book—democratic practice in higher education. Why were they able to learn so quickly? What is democratic? Is there a connection between their learning and the egalitarian nature of friendship? In order to make a first pass at answering these questions, I will try to analyze the positive learning experiences of my friends through the metaphor of relationships. As my friends read and appraised my poems, they were engaged in several relationships: with the discipline of poetry, with the text in front of them, with me as a poet and "authority" on poetry, and with me as a friend who had asked for help. They grew freer to learn about poetry as the power imbalances in these different relationships evened out.

Friendship was key. On the basis of our friendship and my explicit trust in them, they undertook something that was unfamiliar and intimidating. Not only did I ask my friends to read a poem, but I also asked for their critical judgments. I placed them in an awkward position, because they perceived me as the poetry expert and felt exposed. How could they tell me what was right or wrong about a poem? Because I was asking for help, however, my role as the "poetry authority" shifted and they started to feel authorized, too.

The fact that the poem was still in process also made a big difference. Reluctant readers feel more comfortable when they know that the work is still fluid. This changes their relationship to the text; because the poem may contain mistakes, it is no longer the authority. Furthermore, my friends know more about poetry than they know they know. As soon as they feel authorized, as soon as the authority shifts from the poem to the reader, they can exercise their intelligence. Then they are not in relationship with the monolith Poetry but are in relationship with a single poem.

To view a piece of art or to read a book is to create a relationship. It requires that the viewer or the reader imagine a way into another's perspective while continuing to acknowledge and to appreciate his or her own perspective; it involves dialogue, a kind of intimacy.

Last year, the United States Postal Service issued a Georgia O'Keeffe commemorative stamp, and with the stamp it printed a wonderful quotation from the artist: "Nobody sees a flower, really—it is so small—we haven't time, and to see takes time, like to have a friend takes time." Is reading, then, like having a friend? It takes time and involves give and take. Good teaching should make this relationship possible.

Defining Some Problems

Most of the students whom I encounter in classrooms have been badly educated when it comes to reading literature in general and poetry in particular. Some tend to leap to abstract answers to a question that I never ask: "*what does this poem mean?*" Others tend to be harshly critical. Still others remain immersed in inarticulate feeling and observe only, "*I like it.*"[3] These responses are characterized by impatience, inattention to what is actually on the page, and inability or unwillingness to use the full range of their resources. In the classroom setting, these readers close down and rush for answers or opinions; their ability to pay attention to literature seems limited. In fact, it may be more difficult to teach people about poetry inside the classroom than outside it.

The primary problem is that they have learned about literature in a hierarchical framework based on personal achievement. School is a long competition, organized around a series of performances: quizzes, written tests, coming up with the right answer in class discussion, term papers, labs, achievement tests, PSATs, SATs, essays, research papers, midterm exams, final exams, lab reports, GREs, LSATs, MCATs, MATs, comprehensives, boards, dissertations, dissertation defenses. All these performances are scored, and records are kept: the higher the score, the higher the accomplishment, the better the student. Performance itself becomes the point.

Poststructuralism focuses on the power of our discourses—the *ways* we talk about the world—to determine not only what we say but how we think. Within English classrooms, by and large, four kinds of literary discourse operate: the right-answer discourse, the reading-comprehension discourse, the realist discourse, and the field-of-knowledge discourse. Other kinds of literary discourse also operate in individual classrooms, depending usually on the teacher's interests, tastes, and training. Ruth Vinz identified seven kinds of literary language in use in an eleventh-grade class, all of which could be associated with the teachers the students had had in the past (1994). Each shapes the ways students learn to think about reading and literature.[4] Here, however, I will focus on larger discourses, three educational and one literary.

I will begin with the right-answer discourse. When a right answer ostensibly exists, the teacher and the text become its sources. Students feel a constant pressure to be right, and this pressure is felt even in freewheeling class discussions. More important, this pressure intrudes on the intimate reading relationship between a reader and a text. "Instead of plunging into the work," Rosenblatt remarks, "and permitting its full impact, he is aware that he must prepare for certain questions, that his remarks on the work must satisfy the teacher's already crystallized ideas about it" (1976, 62–63). The poem becomes something from which meaning must be wrested, and the student peers *through* the language in search of it.

Good students are adept performers. Sometimes I think that performance skills may be what I really learned in college. We referred to class performance as the ability to *bullshit*: to manipulate elements of a text into a reading that sounded convincing—or at least made it sound as if we knew the material. This description sounds hollow, and many of our class discussions were. We all could, on occasion, take part in a discussion without having read the assignment. We were performing for one another and for the teacher, but mostly for the grade. I cared about the books, as I suspect many of my classmates did, but a cynical gloss covered this love, a gloss born of our anxiety to succeed in a grade economy.

It is a grade economy because grades are the currency, and like money they skew everything. In my early teaching experiences, in a conventional system in which I was working with well-prepared students, every time I gave a writing assignment one student would raise a hand after I had explained the task and ask, "But what do *you* want?" How in good faith could I answer "I want you to think for yourself," when, indeed, I would be grading their assignments? At those moments, I felt as if the system were laid bare: to be a successful student one learns how to read the teacher, not the text. These students were only doing what the system had trained them to do; it was far more efficient than figuring out what they wanted for themselves. How often do students feed the teacher the interpretations they believe the teacher wants rather than engage with their own reading?

The right-answer discourse affects teachers, too, possibly even more than it affects students. We show students only the polished results of our engagement with a text, not the creative process of trial and error that marks our own reading. Gordon Pradl distinguishes between kinds of reading: "primary acts of reading," when a reader is still messing around and working a way through a text, and "secondary acts of reading," when a reader reports on the results of the primary act (1994, 234). Because teachers are locked in a right-answer discourse, we are reluctant to reveal to students the mistakes we have made, the ways we sense a text's coherence, or the questions we ask. We'd rather the students make the mistakes. But what are the goals of our teaching? To foster dependence or self-reliance? Pradl argues for a kind of apprenticeship in which the practiced reader models reading strategies, with all the errors and reconsiderations made visible: "primary acts of reading should serve more openly as the source for our pedagogy" (1994, 238).

Much of our education directs us to read for comprehension, and this also forms a discourse. Remember SRA cards? Each color-coded card contains a passage and a set of multiple-choice questions. If you answer enough of the questions right, you move to the next card and then to the next color. The SRA cards are at best a challenge, and at worst a humiliation. I relished them because I could work at my own pace for once and went at them like learning to read was a race up a mountain. The text, however, became the recalcitrant block of sentences and facts in which I described clues to the right answers. Aside from those clues, the rest of the text did not matter. I learned to pay a certain kind of attention, but was not learning to engage with my own imagination, to take in and question new ideas, to play with words and sounds. (I also remember being encouraged to put a pencil in my mouth to stop me from mouthing the words, so that I would read more quickly.) I read the passages, answered the questions, and moved to the next card. This form of instruction conveyed its own corollary lesson: there is no practical reason to engage with the words on the page, since "meaning" is carried away to be used in framing the right answer for discussions, tests, and papers.[5] For reading comprehension we need to be able to carry meanings away and use them, but this ill-equips students for reading literature.

When we carry a meaning—a message, a claim, an idea infused with a certain feeling—away from a poem, we leave the poem itself behind. In *Fifty Contemporary Poets: The Creative Process*, Alberta Turner asked the contributing poets to answer a series of questions about writing and revising a particular poem. She asked if the poem could be paraphrased and, if so, how. Many refused even to try. They had said what they had to say as clearly as they could in the poem. How else to say it? Marvin Bell comments, with increasing irritation:

Of course, the paraphrase also leaves out the music, the language, the organization, and the pacing of line and phrase and stanza. Used improperly, the paraphrase allows us to avoid the poem altogether. In fact, this is the most common use of paraphrase. The paraphrase kit comes with thick gloves, a blindfold, a gag, and four corks (Turner 1977, 44).

Poetry often begins when the usual resources of the language no longer suffice. Only the full package—the phenomenon of the poem with its music, language, organization, and pacing of line and phrase and stanza, with its elisions and allusions, its euphony and its discord, in other words, with all of its effects—can "say" what the poet wants to say. Poems, then, do not just say what they mean, they act it out. Reading comprehension—or paraphrase—asks the student to set aside the phenomenon of the poem, along with one's experience of it, in order to seek the central idea.

Probably the most powerful literary discourse is that of realism. Its power can be attributed more to the culture at large than to the teaching in English classrooms. We read for realism and for veracity, as if the text opened a window from our world onto the action in another parallel world. Can we project ourselves into the scene and follow the action? Can we make the movie in our minds? Do we suspend our disbelief?

Again, the reader tends to set aside the phenomenon of the text in order to perceive the action. Alison Lee describes the effect of this way of thinking: "Readers are invited to read *through* the poem, as if gazing more or less directly into its presented world. . . . In realist response discourses, there is an effacement—or at least a subordination—of the textuality of the poem, and its metaphorical character" (1994, 103). Most readers have grown accustomed to reading for the imagined scene, the characters, and the action; for the movie in their minds; for the forward momentum of a plot; for being swept away from the mundane world into a vivid dramatic world for a few hours. I do not want to downplay these pleasures of reading, but if we read only the real, we can miss a lot. For example, many books use an unreliable narrator. Fixed on the realism of the scene as it unfolds in the narrator's vision, readers fail to be skeptical and miss the narrator's biases and bad judgments, and hence their own.

Add the realist discourse to the right-answer and reading-comprehension discourses and the poem virtually ceases to exist as a phenomenon, as a made thing to be experienced and appreciated by a reader. "Meaning" can be separated from the poem and the reader's experience of reading.[6] No wonder students seem incapable of paying attention both to what is on the page and what is happening inside them.

A related problem is that students are taught literature as a field of knowledge, a subject matter to know about, rather than as a vital aesthetic experience of a living art. Even though many college English teachers consider it problematic, our educational model remains in many ways a transmission model, what Paolo Freire dubbed the "banking" approach to education. In contrast to the radical nature of many literary theories, much of the pedagogical theory operating in English classrooms remains quite conservative because the pedagogy and the assumptions about teaching literature *as a field* remain in force institutionally through the curriculum and degree criteria.[7] Literature is a field of knowledge with a rich history, but *reading* is an aesthetic experience. The field will not meaningfully open to study until a student has become a practitioner—

an active, engaged reader and meaning maker. Instead, we subject beginning and intermediate students to survey courses in which they cover two hundred years of literary history in fourteen weeks. It all blurs. No wonder they stop reading.

Aesthetic Experience and Reading

What is aesthetic experience? I will start with the definition offered by Louise Rosenblatt, who applied practical criticism, experiential learning theory, pragmatic philosophy, and transactional psychology to reading. Her first major study of the reading experience, *Literature as Exploration*, was published in 1938, the same year John Dewey published *Experience and Education* and the same year Goddard College was founded.[8] Her second major study, *The Reader, the Text, the Poem*, was published forty years later. During the interim (and since), she steadfastly advocated progressive reforms in the teaching of literature. She defines the aesthetic experience of reading as follows:

A novel or poem or play remains merely inkspots on paper until a reader transforms them into a set of meaningful symbols. The literary work exists in the live circuit set up between reader and text: the reader infuses intellectual and emotional meanings into the pattern of verbal symbols, and those symbols channel his thoughts and feelings. Out of this complex process emerges a more or less organized imaginative experience. When the reader refers to a poem, say, *Byzantium*, he is designating such an experience in relation to a text (1976, 25). She stresses that this experience "provides a *living-through*, not simply *knowledge about* . . ." (1976, 38). Above all, aesthetic experience is active; reading is "a continuing, constructive, 'shaping' activity (1978, 53). This is *not* to say that anything goes:

Because the text is organized and self-contained, it concentrates the reader's attention and regulates what will enter into his consciousness. His business for the moment is to apprehend as fully as possible these images and concepts in relation to one another. (1976, 33).

What distinguishes Rosenblatt's theory from most theories of reader response is her characterization of the relationship between the text and the reader as transactional.[9] Meaning is located neither in the text nor in the reader but is made in the "live circuit" of the transaction between the two. Text and reader shape and are shaped by each other: "What the organism selects out and seeks to organize according to already acquired habits, assumptions, and expectations becomes the environment to which it also responds" (1978, 17). As we read, "we are living in the world of the work which we have created" (1978, 67–68). Reading is creative, imaginative, and adventuresome; readers make choices, try, discard, shape. Yet much also goes on below the surface. We are rarely conscious of all the choices we make, the assumptions we carry, the predilections we have. Rosenblatt accounts for social context, for a reader's relative competence, for the power of discourse communities, for personal concerns, for literary conventions—for the many influences that work on us as we make meaning.[10]

Rosenblatt's transactional theory of reading and its emphasis on aesthetic experience leads to experiential learning theory, which defines learning in general in similar terms. I was first introduced to the theories of David Kolb through work that the Goddard faculty did on curricular design starting in 1992. It always takes me time to come to grips with theory, because I like to know how the abstract works out on the concrete, practical level. I was exposed to many kinds of literary and linguistic theory in graduate school but to no educational theory. If I learned anything in graduate school, however, it was that theory matters; even if they remain unspoken or unexamined, philosophical assumptions work through all kinds of literature and criticism. This understanding, however, rarely extended to our own practice as teachers. Perhaps because I was already engaged in teaching in 1992, experiential learning theory quickly made sense. It was as if I finally had the right concepts and words to describe what I experienced in the classroom. Specifically, it helped me to understand some of the ways students struggle as they read literature, and especially poetry.[11] It also made me question basic assumptions underlying my practice. In what follows I will try to distill the essence of experiential learning theory as synthesized and presented by Kolb and apply it to reading literature.

Learning, the primary means of human adaptation, results from the resolution of conflicts, an ongoing dialectical process, among different learning modes within an individual and between the individual's personal knowledge and the society's knowledge system. Kolb defines certain terms more closely, specifically *learning, knowledge,* and *transaction. "Learning is the process whereby knowledge is created through the transformation of experience"* (1984, 38). Experience generates ideas, or to turn this the other way around for the moment, we test new ideas out in experience. At the same time, all individuals have more or less well-defined ideas about any given topic, or a "theory-in-use" (1984, 27), and new experiences and ideas must be integrated within these theories-in-use. This leads to the definition of knowledge itself: *"Knowledge is the result of the transaction between social knowledge and personal knowledge"* (1984, 36). Kolb's definition of this transaction is much like Rosenblatt's, and both are rooted in John Dewey's and Charles Peirce's work and also stand in contrast to a simpler idea of interaction: *"The concept of transaction implies a more fluid, interpenetrating relationship between objective conditions and subjective experience, such that once they become related, both are essentially changed"* (1984, 36).

Knowledge, then, is created in two ways: the transformation of experience and the transaction between personal and social knowledge. What are the natures of these two processes, transformation and transaction?

Transformation and Transaction

"Learning is the process whereby knowledge is created through the transformation of experience" (1984, 38). When we transform experience we

must resolve the conflicts among our four different learning modes, *concrete experience, reflective observation, abstract conceptualization,* and *active experimentation.* In these learning modes, there are also two different adaptive orientations: prehension, or grasping, and transformation. In order to create knowledge we must both grasp and transform experience (1984, 41). We grasp experience in two ways, by apprehension and comprehension, and transform it in two ways, by intention, or internal reflection, and by extension, or external manipulation. In other words, to create knowledge we must apprehend, reflect, comprehend, and act. Here is a visual grounding:

apprehension
of
concrete experience

transformation by   transformation by
external manipulation   internal reflection

comprehension
through
abstract conceptualization

We read a poem and apprehend what is on the page (concrete experience), we reflect on what we perceive and connect this poem to other poems we have read and to other experiences we have had (reflective observation), we conceptualize and think about poetry in general (abstract conceptualization), and we experiment by writing similar poems (active experimentation) and come full circle to the concrete experience of a poem on the page. According to Kolb's theory, knowledge is created through both grasping and transforming experience, and engaging all four learning modes makes this possible.

Literary education in my experience stresses reflection and comprehension. In creative writing workshops, generally reserved for writers and seen as special or extra, three of the modes—reflection, comprehension, and experimentation—come into play. Apprehension, however, remains largely ignored. We associate apprehension, and rightly, with the barely articulate preference—*I like it,* or resistance—*I hate it.* When we overlook and even discount apprehension in the classroom, however, we do our students and ourselves a great disservice; we erode the ground of experience on which their reading must be based.

Students are not adept apprehenders. I used the noun *students* advisedly; by virtue of being students—because they are in a classroom rather than in a living room—they do not call upon certain faculties. School rewards them for their comprehension skills and, as a result, they leap into the comprehension mode before they have fully apprehended what is even on the page. This is a learned adaptation, as I hope the earlier discussion makes clear. Every teacher of literature has encountered the rigid conceptual response, the imposition of an idea on a poem that seems to ignore almost all available evidence. The student has recognized something—an image, a phrase, a character—and connected it with earlier literature classes, or with a current obsession or prejudice.[12] The poem itself seems to dissolve on the page before this onslaught. The student, however, is trying to meet the expectations of school and be a good student.

What gets left at the classroom door? A few years ago, in a women's literature course I taught Marilynne Robinson's coming-of-age novel, *Housekeeping*. I love this book. The first time I picked it up I couldn't finish it because I was so envious that I hadn't written it. Part of the class loved it, part hated it. Rather, the students who hated it were thoroughly baffled and needed to account for their bafflement. We tried an exercise. I selected a paragraph almost at random and asked everyone to spend fifteen minutes reading slowly and recording their reactions, feelings, and experiences of the passage. The responses, in particular from those students who claimed *not* to get the book, were astonishing. One said that she felt that the action was happening on the other side of a gauze curtain. Another that she was in the room with a person who was telling the story of her life, and though she, the student, was interested and following the speaker, the story did not make sense. Another that the characters felt untouchable, distant, and cold. Another that the book's narrator reminded her of a former employer who was old-fashioned, almost Victorian, smart, and excessively fussy. Each of these responses to the book is true in astute and interesting ways. I am especially struck by the metaphors and analogies they used. Nevertheless, the students were discounting their own experiences of reading and their own feelings about the characters and the narrator. They had no idea how right their experiences were, and were only willing to bring these experiences into their "academic" considerations of the novel when pressed to do so. Worse than that, they were not using these responses to enhance their own reading process.

To speak of what *Housekeeping* means, you must consider the narrator Ruthie's voice: how it's oddly distant from the experience she describes, how she sounds fussy and old-fashioned, how she talks and talks about her life and still fails to comprehend it, about how lonely she sounds. In other words, you need to describe what the voice does as well as what it says. The students were all onto something.

They got tangled in contradictory responses. They sensed certain things about the narrator and the book, but what they sensed was largely intuitive, emotional, personal, global. They did not feel free to bring this response into their academic reading process. Blocked in this way, these students all responded by judging the book. They hated it; they did not want to read it.

At that time, I did not know how to move past this exercise and these observations. I acted as a cheerleader, let them know just how astute their impressions were, and encouraged them to bring this kind of knowledge into the classroom with them. They remained resistant to the book, however, and I was unable to help them establish a relationship with it. Since then, I have stressed that feelings are useful in reading; they provide information about a poem or a story. (Now, I would work from their intuitive responses and design some dramatic exercise so that students could enter the characters' experience.)

Experiential learning theory sets a higher value on knowing by apprehension than schools traditionally have:

The interactionism of experiential learning theory places knowing by apprehension on an equal footing with knowing by comprehension, resulting in a stronger interactionist position, really a transactionalism, in which knowledge emerges from the dialectical relationship between the two forms of knowing (Kolb 1984, 101). These two ways of grasping do not coexist comfortably; the conflict between them must be resolved as one learns. Apprehension is registrative, affective, sensory, engaged, intuitive, appreciative, subjective, personal, timeless, global, tacit. Comprehension, on the other hand, is interpretive, cognitive, conceptual, distanced, reflective, critical, objective, social, linear, analytical, articulate. For emphasis, I'll list these adjectives in juxtaposition:

registrative	interpretative
affective	cognitive
sensory	conceptual
engaged	distanced
intuitive	reflective
appreciative	critical
subjective	objective
personal	social
timeless	linear
global	analytic
tacit	articulate

Although they are not neatly opposed, these two sets of processes clearly exist in tension.

In poetry classes, I have encountered the be-here-now approach. *Why do we have to talk about poems? Why can't we just read them?* Sometimes, these students are resisting analysis and critical thinking and respond out of their fear of the unfamiliar, of not knowing, of challenging their likes and dislikes. But I have failed to recognize that the resistance to criticism also has a legitimate base. I have rushed them: "Appreciation involves attending to and being interested in our apprehensions of the world around us. Such attention deepens and extends the apprehended experience" (Kolb 1984, 104). Criticism and interpretation distance us from the immediacy of the apprehended experience; comprehension crowds out apprehension. Students know that once we start to talk about the poem—ordering raw experience, reflecting, and analyzing—they will in some senses stop experiencing it. As Kolb notes: "Appreciation of immediate experience is an act of attention, valuing, and affirmation, whereas critical comprehension of symbols is based on objectivity, . . . dispassionate analysis, and skepticism" (1984, 105).

Earlier, however, I noted that students are not adept apprehenders. Even those students who resist criticism seem impatient to go on to the next poem. They rarely know how to pay attention in a deep, sustained way.

Television, advertising, and our fast-paced media teach us to gloss over language—to consume words quickly without really noticing substance. Is this merely a result of sloppiness or are we being encouraged not to think? Frederic Jameson, a Marxist cultural and literary critic, poses this question:

What if, in this period of the over-production of printed matter and the proliferation of methods of quick reading, they were intended to speed the reader across a sentence in such a way that he can salute a ready-made idea effortlessly in   passing, without suspecting that real thought demands a descent into the materiality of language and a consent to time itself in the form of the sentence (1971, xiii) ? As we are sped across the surface of a sentence, the *only* means of grasping the experience is apprehension; we register it globally, immediately, through feeling and intuition, through our senses. But we do not engage our attention deeply, nor do we extend and cultivate our interest. There is simply not time, because advertisers and politicians do not want us to have the time to test the truth value of their outrageous claims.

Literature, by contrast, moves slowly; it invites us to consent to time. Poetry, in particular, tries to slow time down by concentrating meaning, feeling, music, and other effects so that the reader cannot speed across the surface but must sink into the material stuff that is language. Poetry is thick; there is a great deal on the page to apprehend. Without the global, intuitive, timeless grasp of apprehensive processes the resonant unity of all those different effects—the texture of the affective experience—is lost; poetry does not exist. In a speeding world, fewer and fewer people are able to slow down enough to engage with poetry.

At the same time, we need our skepticism. We should no more readily accept the truth claims of a poem than we should those of a beer commercial. We need the distanced, reflective, critical, and analytic approaches to help us bridge the gap between what is out there and what is in here, between what we know and what others know. "Knowledge is the result of the transaction between social knowledge and personal knowledge" (Kolb 1984, 36). Social knowledge is here defined as a socially and culturally transmitted network of comprehensions, and personal knowledge as our apprehensions and socially acquired means of explaining and interpreting those apprehensions (Kolb 1984, 105). Social knowledge makes personal knowledge possible. At the same time, personal knowledge, based in our powers of apprehension, enables us to maintain our individuality: "Because we can still learn from our *own experience*, because we can subject the abstract symbols of the social-knowledge system to the rigors of our own inquiry about these symbols and our personal experience with them, we are free" (Kolb 1984, 109).

Poems and Democratic Education

Louise Rosenblatt formulated a liberal, democratic, anti-fascist literary pedagogy in response to events abroad and at home. In 1938, she developed her program in *Literature as Exploration*. Demagoguery scared her: "Unprepared to think independently, the young man and woman seek to return to the infantile state in which there is no responsibility to make decisions; they are thus willing to blindly follow some 'leader' whose tools and prey they become" (1976, 129). Although fascism may not pose a significant threat at home, all sorts of homegrown prejudices do: "It would be fatuous to ignore the crude, oversimplified, and false pictures of human behavior and motivation presented by the mass media and the drugstore paperbacks" (93). In literature she sees an antidote to these prejudices and easy simplifications: "the very essence of literature is a rejection of such stereotyped, superficial, and unshaded reactions to the mere outlines of situations or to the appeal of vague and generalized concepts" (104). The teacher can help "the student to develop conscious resistance" (93) to prejudice and easy reactions, by encouraging the student's "ability to enter vicariously into the experience of others" (187) through deep and life-enhancing engagement with complex and demanding literature, our literary heritage. In the classroom, the means must correspond with the ends; the teacher must respect the individuality of the student and recognize that every aesthetic experience is unique, and the student must respect the integrity of the text and meet it on its own terms as much as possible. Through thoughtful teaching, Rosenblatt believed, literary art could be used to nurture independent, skeptical, imaginative, and empathetic citizens who are qualified to undertake the ongoing work of a democratic society.

Sixty years after the publication of *Literature as Exploration*, teachers still encourage students to resist being passive, unquestioning "consumers of unambiguous ideologies" (Corcoran 1994, 7). Instead of drugstore paperbacks, we speak of an array of popular books, movies, magazine articles, advertisements, and television shows. The context has changed, but our hopes seem to have remained much the same. Instead of worrying about the rise of international fascism, we worry about the economic power and cultural influence of global corporations. Instead of the demagogue, we picture the corporate raider, the tobacco lobbyist, the advertising executive, the political spin doctor, or the Hollywood executive. Teachers hope that by helping students examine the ways they make meaning of literature, they can also help them to be more self-possessed and more self-conscious of the ways that the "unambiguous ideologies" might influence them.

In the place of a liberal and scientific vocabulary, our vocabulary is poststructural. The reader is a textually constructed subject, the text a site of competing discourses, the teacher a provider of opportunities to appropriate or to resist those discourses, and the struggle is about power: "Readers construct readings, not as originators of meaning, but as human subjects positioned through social, political, and economic discursive practices that remain the location of a constant struggle over power" (Patterson, Mellor, and O'Neill 1994, 66). Although I am often tempted to parody poststructural language, these points seem valid to me. We have learned many ways to make meaning, from high school classes, from our grandmothers, from the girls we grew up with, from a religious teacher, from television and movies, and from our siblings. Those voices, all shaped by social, political, and economic dialects, shape us; we are spoken by our culture. In making meaning of a novel, I draw on different kinds of language and different possible interpretations. But where is my own voice in this chorus? Can I have my own experience of *Age of Innocence* or *Their Eyes Were Watching God*?

In experiential learning theory the focus shifts from making meaning to learning. David Kolb also seems concerned with cultivating conscious resistance to the dominant abstract symbols of the social knowledge system. He identifies two kinds of social pressure on the learner that limit full individual development. First is the domination of social knowledge, what he refers to as "the command feedback loops of the increasingly computerized social-knowledge system" (1984, 109). This dominance fosters the illusion that knowledge exists independently of the learner, "out there" in a system of symbols. Second is the pressure to specialize, *to be our function* and therefore to repress nondominant learning modes and to fail to integrate all four learning modes. Creativity, independent thought, and innovation are only possible when one is free to create knowledge. With access to all our learning modes—the affective as well the cognitive—resistance to the command feedback loops seems guaranteed. Learning from our own experience helps us remain skeptical: "the knowledge of comprehension is held provisionally to be tested against apprehension, and vice versa" (Kolb 1984, 109).

As I have thought about teaching poetry and about making democratic values come to life in the classroom, I have thought a lot about the power of apprehension and about the affective domains. Not only is apprehension a source of individual freedom, but it is also the ground of experience that is usually neglected in literary study. How to develop experiences of poetry that nurture more than the cognitive? I have reflected on my own experiences of poetry. How do I experience poems? How do I make meaning? What kinds of intelligence do I bring to reading?

I have also thought a lot about the experience of my friends as they learned about poetry outside of the school setting. The metaphor of relationships is helpful in the classroom. How can I even out the power imbalances and authorize the student? How to do this and not succumb to whatever-you-experience-is-your-truth relativism?

Georgia O'Keeffe, not surprisingly, was wise: "Nobody sees a flower, really—it is so small—we haven't time, and to see takes time, like to have a friend takes time." Time and give and take: a relationship. Students need to slow down and spend time with poems, take liberties with them, play with them, find unusual approaches to the material, shape and reshape them, and then come back to honor the integrity of the poem—the other. They need to bring their whole selves to this give and take, just as they bring their whole selves to friendships. This full engagement, I believe, forms the basis for independent thought.

Experiences of Poetry

In the fall of 1997, I offered "Experiences of Poetry" to undergraduates, second-semester sophomores and above, in Goddard's residential program. The catalogue description of the course directly echoes my writing in this essay:

> Television, advertising, and our fast-paced media teach us to gloss over language—to consume words quickly and to move on without noticing substance. Literature by contrast moves slowly, demanding engagement, response, solitary reflection, imaginative play—everything that our larger culture seems to deaden. Books invite us to stop and to commit our time. Poetry, in particular, tries to slow time down by concentrating language, music, image, and other effects so that a reader

cannot speed across the surface but must sink into the material stuff that is language. Powerful poems register not just in thought and feeling but in the being and the matrix of the body. Poems do not just *say* what they mean but *do* what they mean.

This will be a course concerned with perception as well as with reading and creative writing. I offer this group study for students who are serious about poetry. There are two challenges: to read and to experience poetry in profound ways, and to use that reading experience to enhance your own writing. I will structure a series of experiences, both playful and serious, in both reading and writing. Around and in relation to those structured experiences, we will read the work of several poets and use writing workshops to develop writing skills and revision strategies. This was followed, Goddard-style, by a list of the possible readings, though in fact I ended up making all the selections (usually, I make the first few and then let the students choose from a set of select texts).

A more concrete description appeared in the evaluations I wrote of students at the end of the semester:

This course was designed for students who already had some familiarity with poetry and wished to pursue further knowledge. The work consisted of doing reading, reading exercises, and writing exercises; submitting two poems, two essays, and a portfolio of selected work; and making a final presentation of a "poem construction" in which the students took their poems off the page and made something. Students tried a series of reading exercises based in different intelligences, musical, visual, spatial, kinesthetic, and emotional (loosely grounded in Gardner's categories), along with writing exercises. There were two rounds of poetry workshops and two rounds of essay workshops. Students compiled portfolios of selected work from the class and exchanged this work with partners. In this process they also exchanged letters, one describing their work and the other responding to their partner's work, and met in conference with the facilitator. The books were Mark Doty's *My Alexandria*, Linda Hogan's *Book of Medicines*, Tony Hoagland's *Sweet Ruin*, and Li-young Lee's *Rose*. In addition, we used handouts for particular exercises, and at one point students brought in lists of their favorite poetic resources, which included books, poems, paintings, and songs.

I came to this course after a year's hiatus from classroom teaching. During that time, I had done much of the background reading for this essay and had been evaluating the effectiveness of my own teaching. As I designed this course, I set some goals for myself and decided to experiment more radically than I had before: first, to emphasize the active nature of both poem and reader; second, to stress apprehension as heavily as comprehension; third, to keep the relationship among the learning modes as described by David Kolb active and alive; fourth, to bolster the effective reading practices that Harold Vine and Mark Faust had identified in their brilliant reading study, *Situating Readers*; and, fifth, to create a community of readers and writers in the classroom. I used *conversation* as a paradigm for the class because of its familiarity, informality, and active give and take.

Rather than elaborating on each of these goals, I will describe the structure of the course and particular exercises, keeping my goals and assumptions in view and assessing the experiences of the students. The course was organized around these activities:

1) reading the assigned texts and doing a series of reading and writing exercises directed at certain kinds of intelligence

2) writing poetry and participating in two sets of writing workshops

3) drafting and revising two essays, designed around the principle of dialogue with a poem, and working with other students on drafts of these essays

4) assembling a portfolio of work from the class and reflecting about one's learning

5) constructing a "poem," possibly in another medium or in mixed media, as a final project and presenting it to the class

In the syllabus I named the kinds of intelligence I hoped would frame our work: thinking through the body, thinking through space, thinking through things, thinking through feeling, and thinking through time. (I had named some other forms, such as thinking through transformation and thinking through thinking about thinking, but we ran out of time.)

I was working loosely with some of the intelligences named by Howard Gardner, specifically musical, kinesthetic, visual/spatial, and emotional intelligences, and saw them as starting places. They offer entries into apprehension—ways to know before comprehension kicks in and ways to slow students down and get them to dwell in the experience of the poems rather than immediately interpreting, analyzing, and criticizing. I was also working from a poet's point of view. The poem is a phenomenon, a made thing, with physical as well as intellectual properties. Poetry is the art of language itself (not of story, dramatic action, or discourse), and poets consciously focus upon the literary resources of language, so that a poem creates or discovers a form that the reader's imagination can enter and inhabit, even if only for a few minutes. As Robert Hass puts it, the point of a poem is not its understanding but "the shape of its understanding" (1984, 58). The shape of understanding cannot be understood; it must be felt *and* understood.

I sought to create exercises that would stress the phenomenology of the poem—its physical properties (sound, rhythm, looks), what it evokes sensually in the reader, its structure, its unfolding movement through time, its emotional associations—and then asked students to reflect on their experiences and how experiences led to meanings.

Thinking Through the Body

We started with the senses. When you are listening to or reading a poem, what do you see, hear, smell, taste, and feel? What sensual world is evoked in the poem?

Hearing. For the second class, a few volunteers brought in favorite poems and read them aloud. I asked the rest of the class to close their eyes, to listen, and to suspend their desire to make sense of the poems. Leaving content aside, what did they hear? They were tentative at first, and a few hadn't a clue how just to listen, but some began to notice the prevalence of certain sounds, the rhythms, the movements of the language. The volunteers read their poems again after a few students had made observations, and everyone listened together—a little more attentively—and started to connect sound to content and to effect.

We also did a silly exercise together, adapted slightly from Christopher Davis's exercise "Chanting the Flowers Off the Wall" in *The Practice of Poetry* (1992, 20). I asked each person to choose a word they liked the sound and feel of, and then for several minutes everyone said their word over and over. Of course, everyone felt self-conscious for awhile, but this exercise stresses the physicality of the word—how it feels in the saying, each nuance of its sound, its cadence, its absurdity.

For the rest of the course we made sure to read everything aloud, to give each poem's music its due. I also kept referring students back to the music and to their own listening. In retrospect, I wish I had used this more extensively and stopped at various points during the semester to do the listening exercises again, to help students tune their ear and notice how their ability to hear was sharpening. This would have meant naming certain skills that make one a more acute reader of poetry. In the future, I plan to use children's rhymes, with their wild play in sound, and to combine reading them aloud with writing original rhymes. All of this, I hope, would move the class into nonsense and into the textures and physical pleasures of language.

Seeing. In the next class we moved into the other senses. I read Mark Doty's poem "Night Ferry" aloud and instructed them to let their senses loose, to listen, taste, smell, see, and feel, and to notice their emotional responses as I read to them. Then, I handed out copies of the poem, set out a box of materials, including sketch pads, markers, pencils, cloth and textured paper, glue, scissors, etc., and the following instructions:

> After you have listened to the poem, read the text again silently.
> Sketch out images that come to mind. Does an image in the poem remind you of another image? Draw that. Draw the movements of the poem. Sketch the shape of the whole. Try maps or diagrams.
> Let all your senses work. What do you feel, smell, see, hear, taste? Note the particular parts of the poem that connect with your sensory responses.

Free associate. If a word suggests another word or phrase, write that
down. Does the poem remind you of things? Relate anecdotes. Follow
threads of memory.
Revisit the text and your sketches and diagrams and notes. Remember
the feelings of the poem's music. Now, start to think about the poem.
What is it doing? How do your doodles, drawings, and notes help you
to read the poem? In looking back and forth between the text of the
poem and what you have put on paper, what more do you learn?

After a few minutes of silence, students got up, found materials they wished
to use, and settled to work. A few appeared dumbfounded and unable even to
start the assignment; others started wild sketches around the poem, or on larger
sheets of paper.

After they had worked for half an hour or so, we reconvened as a group.
Though I had not intended to focus only on sight and visual intelligence, this was
largely what happened. Students discussed their responses to the exercise,
showed their work, and talked about what they had learned about the poem. Two
admitted defeat. They could not enter the poem through visual images and
stopped the exercise at that point rather than moving into another kind of
activity. Their lack of competence in this area, when others around them were
busy drawing and mapping, clearly troubled them. I reassured them, as I had
earlier, that everyone would experience such moments, that no one would have
an equal measure of competence in all areas, and that if they felt weak in one
area, they would likely feel strong in another. Indeed, both of these students were
able writers and one turned out to be the strongest poet in the class—to the point
that all the students in the class felt a little intimidated by him despite his
intellectual generosity; both students had other strengths. Other students,
however, felt energized and empowered by this visual work. One student
observed that she had never thought she could use drawing to think about poetry
and that this opened up a host of new possibilities for her. Using her visual
intelligence and skills—her drawing was intricate and beautiful—made poetry
more accessible; she was thrilled. Later in the semester, I noticed that the pages
in her poetry books were covered with drawings. As I observed then and later,
however, it was difficult for her to articulate her discoveries for others because
she tended to travel away from the poem into her visual imagination and not to
return to the linguistic mode.

In *Situating Readers*, Harold Vine and Mark Faust identify both the
practices that disempower readers as meaning makers and the practices that
empower them. The disempowering practices include: *reading critically* and so
being unable to imagine another's point of view; *being immersed* and unable to
distinguish between one's own perceptions and the author's; and *abstracting a
theme statement* through contrast or isolation. The empowering practices
include: *deductively explaining*, starting with a hypothesis and attending to the
supporting details, analysis, and categories; *inductively explaining*, starting with
a tentative sense of the situation and attending to the supporting details, analysis,
and categories, while remaining willing to try a new hypothesis; *deductively
imagining*, starting with a hypothesis and then visualizing, hearing, feeling,

synthesizing, and portraying the situation; *inductively imagining*, starting with a tentative sense of the situation and then imagining while remaining open to change; and finally, *inductively imagining and explaining*. To paraphrase the passage from Corinthians, all these empowering practices are great, but the greatest of these is inductively imagining and explaining. Furthermore, Vine and Faust observed that effective readers were aware of three things: *the poem's unfolding in time* (1993, 113), *their own abiding concerns* (116), *and the relationship between self-awareness and other-awareness* (118). Vine and Faust characterize powerful reading further:

> readers engage in a continuous dialogue between what is socially shared and personally significant as they inductively imagine and explain their sense of the situation. In this way, these readers produce readings that are plausible and, at the same time, bear the stamp of individual concerns (111).

These observations about reading practices overlap with experiential learning theory in intriguing ways. Vine and Faust distinguish between deductive and inductive approaches. The deductive is rooted in comprehension, because the reader starts with a hypothesis and explores the text through its framework. The inductive is rooted more in apprehension, because the reader uses a hypothesis but pays closer attention to the experience of reading the text. The authors also distinguish between imagining and explaining, and again these activities can be identified with the learning modes of apprehension and comprehension. By naming inductive imagining and explaining as the strongest approach to reading, they corroborate Kolb's notion of transaction among learning modes, and between personal and social knowledge.

In this exercise, I saw examples of both disempowering and empowering practices. One student isolated one element of "Night Ferry" and illustrated it. Even though he was working in a nonlinguistic, visual mode, he was doing what "good" students do and engaging in the right-answer discourse: abstracting a theme statement and fitting his reading of the poem to that abstraction. This limited his ability to experience and to engage with the poem; his reflections on the visual exercise and what it taught him about the poem were tidy and strictly to the point. Because he was seeking the right answer, he did not seem able to experience the poem outside of this narrow range. In other exercises, he continued to isolate and abstract elements of poems, even when the exercises were designed to draw on intelligence beyond the cognitive. When he was not being a "good" student, he used reactive strategies that closed him down in other ways, either reading very critically and bringing so much of his own agenda to the reading that he was unable to find a way into another person's point of view, or being so immersed that he was unable to distinguish between his perceptions and the author's. During the semester, he tended to veer between the "good" and the "bad" student roles. His best learning came in an extracurricular assignment, a short story he handed in for critique. In our discussion of how his story could work better as a whole and of how writing raises a reader's expectations and must meet or dash them in a thoughtful way, light bulbs were going off. He began to see how all the elements of a piece of writing contributed to an effect in the reader's experience.

The student who was so excited to use her visual intelligence was imagining inductively. She started with a tentative sense of the poem and then visualized her way further into it. As I noted above, however, she was somewhat limited in her ability to explain herself. Several things may have been going on. First, she felt liberated by the exercise, because she was allowed to bring her powerful visual intelligence into an academic classroom; and so she simply got carried away. She tends to focus intently on her art and, by her own description, gets "lost" in it. Second, her focus on the visual in this exercise may have blocked her access to some other resources of the imagination, to her other senses, and to her ability to synthesize. Nevertheless, this was a powerful exercise for her and may have changed her relationship to poetry in significant ways for the better.

Thinking Through Space
In this exercise, I deliberately set out to tap visual intelligence: the ability to think globally and to imagine in spatial relationships. Again, we used a poem by Mark Doty, "Brilliance". This time, I will reproduce the poem:

> Maggie's taking care of a man
> who's dying; he's attended to everything,
> said goodbye to his parents,
>
> paid off his credit card.
> She says, *Why don't you just*
> *run it up to the limit?*
>
> but he wants everything
> squared away, no balance owed,
> though he misses the pets
>
> he's already found a home for
> —he can't be around dogs or cats,
> too much risk. He says,
>
> *I can't have anything.*
> She says, *A bowl of goldfish?*
> He says, he doesn't want to start
>
> with anything and then describes
> the kind he'd maybe like,
> how their tails would fan
>
> to a gold flaring. They talk
> about hot jewel tones,
> gold lacquer, say maybe

they'll go pick some out
though he can't go much of anywhere and then
abruptly he says *I can't love*

anything I can't finish.
He says it like he's had enough
of the whole scintillant world,

though what he means is
he'll never be satisfied and therefore
has established this discipline,

a kind of severe rehearsal.
That's where they leave it,
him looking out the window,

her knitting as she does because
she needs to do something.
Later he leaves a message:

Yes to the bowl of goldfish.
Meaning: let me go, if I have to,
in brilliance. In a story I read,

a Zen master who'd perfected
his detachment from the things of the world
remembered, at the moment of dying,

a deer he used to feed in the park,
and wondered who might care for it,
and at that instant was reborn

in the stunned flesh of a fawn.
So, Maggie's friend—
is he going out

into the last loved object
of his attention?
Fanning the veined translucence

of an opulent tail,
undulant in some uncapturable curve,
is he bronze chrysanthemums,

copper leaf, hurried, darting,
doubloons, icon-colored fins
troubling the water?   (1993, 65–67)

The assignment was to read the poem and to design a representation or three-dimensional analogue of the *whole* poem. Each student had a packet of pipe cleaners.

When we met for the next class, all the students had constructed something. We broke into small groups of three or four, so students could present their models in a small setting and reflect on their thinking with others, and then talked as a whole class. This established a practice we used regularly: creative work, followed by reflection and explanation, either spoken or written. Through this I was hoping to stress and to give them practice imagining and explaining, using both their powers of appreciative apprehension and critical comprehension. We also worked in both smaller and larger settings throughout the semester, so that the students could form an intellectual community for one another without my presence and so that shyer students would feel more comfortable presenting their materials (or at least be pushed to take responsibility for how their small groups worked). I joined different groups, and would present my work alongside theirs. In the whole-class setting I posed questions designed to encourage the students to develop their thinking further and to notice their accomplishments.

Two students chose to work conceptually, constructing a model of brilliance. At first, I feared that this was another way to isolate and abstract a theme, especially because one of these students was the one who had isolated a visual element in the previous exercise, but their approach turned out to work much more effectively than that. The concept of brilliance is large and open enough that their models helped them conceptualize the whole poem. One constructed an open box with a number of pipe cleaners running through the interior in different directions. As he explained, brilliance appeared to have a smooth surface (we were to imagine the sides of the box closed) while internally it was active, dynamic, restless. He associated this with the emotional state of the man in the poem.

Wonderfully, other students added an element to these constructions I had not anticipated: movement. Through movement, they also imagined the poem as process, as something that unfolds and changes. Two of the other kinds of intelligence—thinking through time and thinking through things—had already entered our work.

Kristen Lougheed's construction moved a bit like a see-saw. Since it is too visually complex to describe and was hard to photograph, here is a sketch of the model:

She arrived at this model *in the doing* and realized that doing something with her hands while thinking about a poem enabled her to think in new and exciting ways. Through movement, her own movement in making the model and the movement of the seesaw as representation, she found her way into the poem. She thought of the back-and-forth motion in relation to the man's decision: does he want to close down or open? Finish everything tidily or start something he will be unable to finish? The loop that spreads out beneath the stand represents the Zen master's story, opening out beneath the story in the present. In her understanding, the man (and the poem's speaker) balances his questions and then finds a resolution in the closing, the loop representing the parable.

Kristen, a dancer, describes her relationship with words as painful and problematic. She is dyslexic and spent time at Landmark College before coming to Goddard. She was scared to take a poetry course, scared to engage in the critical analysis, and scared to write the papers, yet determined to try. She is also wonderfully self-reflective and conscious of how she learns and had done an independent study on Gardner's multiple intelligences before beginning this course. Consistently, she was able to reflect on what she had done, made, or written and explain herself clearly to the group. Although the spatial and global thinking of this exercise gave her access to the poem, the kinesthetic element of making was clearly even more important. Once she was able to sense the movement of any poem, she was able to imagine her way into it and explain what she found there (even in writing, with extra effort), often through metaphors of movement, change, or process. What made her so successful? What can I learn from her learning?

Thinking Through Things

"No ideas/ but in things," William Carlos Williams declares in "A Sort of a Song," "through metaphor to reconcile/ the people and the stones." Although Williams was referring to images, I also take this quite literally. Poets are notoriously concrete thinkers; we often think not in concepts but in objects—concepts embodied. Objects inspire us; objects carry our poems forward; objects root us to the earth. In this two-part exercise, I was moving away from the intelligences I had read about and trying to explore one I experience. What do I know in my fingers, in touch—not just through manipulating objects but through connection to the concrete?

In the first part of the exercise, I asked students to choose a poem from Linda Hogan's *The Book of Medicines*, to read it aloud and to feel their way into it, and then to find a small collection of objects that corresponded with different parts of the poem, holding each object as they read through the corresponding part of the poem in order to get the feel of it into their hands. Using these objects as mnemonic devices, they were to memorize the poem. They then brought the objects to class and, using them, recited the poems in small groups. My goals were double: to encourage them to connect their poems with the feel of objects and to get the feel of the language into their bodies through memorization.

They got a little lost. They tried to find the *right* objects to resonate with the poem (no one chose symbolic objects); they tried to find an object to match each major image and got frustrated; and they were scared by the challenge of memorization and so some could not, or would not, do it. Others, however, had fun collecting the objects and did memorize their poems. Their recitations had a different feel than ordinary reading, as they turned inward toward memory and focused. One student who could not memorize the poem nevertheless made a pageant of his presentation and through the drama connected with the work.

In the second part of the assignment, I asked students to use their objects as writing prompts, to hold them and to look at them, and then to follow their memories and associations into language and into other memories and associations. The poems that resulted often loosely modelled the Hogan poems, and a number of them were quite striking. The students clearly felt more at ease with writing than with memorizing.

Later in the semester, I used another exercise with objects and making in relation to a poem's unfolding in time. I handed out a selection of poems by James Wright, William Carlos Williams, and Alberto Ríos, gave the students modelling clay, and asked them to sculpt small objects to represent different moments in the poem, and while doing this, to think about each small sculpture separately and in relation to the others. I was trying still to emphasize concrete intelligence.

Two students chose "The Jewel" by James Wright, a short lyric:

> There is this cave
> In the air behind my body
> That nobody is going to touch:
> A cloister, a silence
> Closing around a blossom of fire.
> When I stand upright in the wind,
> My bones turn to dark emeralds   (1990, 122)

Their sculptures were quite similar; each had a tall, fluid figure to represent the self in this poem, vulnerable yet graceful. One, however, also supplied props for the figure and set them out for us to see in a set sequence: cave, blossom of fire, figure. Again, this was Kristen, who in making the figures, felt the poem's elements and its unfolding process.

Others struggled with this exercise as they had with the Hogan exercise because they sought to make the "right" representational figures. The selection of poems included Williams's "To a Poor Old Woman":

> munching a plum on
> the street a paper bag
> of them in her hand
>
> They taste good to her
> They taste good
> to her. They taste
> good to her

You can see it by
the way she gives herself
to the one half
sucked out in her hand

Comforted
a solace of ripe plums
seeming to fill the air
They taste good to her   (1985, 97)

Students sculpted the woman, a bag, plums; they could not find ways to represent the extended pleasure of eating plums in abstract shapes. Only one, in protest, used abstraction and brought in four cubes, an identical cube for each stanza.

I still believe that this exercise can be productive. The instructions may have to be changed or a better context provided. Possibly, representation has to be prohibited; by throwing the students into the abstract realm, they may discover other ways to imagine the relationship between shape, idea, and feeling.

Dialogic Essays

I assigned no conventional analytical essays in this class, but structured two as dialogues. In the first, I asked students to choose a poem from the reading and to create a response to it, using or adapting one of the methods we had already tried. They were then to reflect on and use the creative response as a way to think further about the poem and to answer three questions. *What does the poem do? What do you learn about the poem from your creative work? What meanings do you construct from this poem?* The final instruction was to write a description or narrative of the ways they made meaning of or from the poem. A draft was due in class. We would break into small groups and review the essays in preparation for revision.

On the day this draft was due, there was general uproar in the classroom. The students were baffled, flummoxed, irritated. One student volunteered to be the guinea pig and describe what he had done so far and the problems that he had encountered. He had written a poem of several lines that condensed elements from a three-page poem by Mark Doty, "Becoming a Meadow," but he was unsure how to take this further into an engagement with or an analysis of the poem itself. We used the student's poem as the basis for discussion of Doty's poem. What did the student's poem capture? He was able to articulate what interested him in Doty's poem: the transitions, the ways one element blended into another (a meadow becomes the sea, a person becomes a meadow), the breakdown of boundaries between things. The class talked about how the student's poem achieved this effect and then went on to talk about how Doty's poem achieved it. From there, the discussion widened. Students posed questions. Other students or I answered. By the time we were done, the student had a good idea of how to write the essay—as did others.

This was a good lesson for me. The assignment was complex, multi-layered: read a poem, create a response, use your creative response to write about the poem. It wasn't bad that the students got flummoxed, since we were able to discuss their confusions and work from there. In future, however, I will break the assignment down into parts. Choose a poem, create a response, come to class. In class we can discuss the responses and start to think together about how we individually make meaning of the poems in light of the creative responses. Then, they can write the essays.

The second essay was more straightforward, though still open-ended. They could choose freely, but it had to be a poem that they wanted to explore further. Here are the instructions:

> Set this essay up as a kind of dialogue or exchange—between you and the poet or speaker, between you and different parts of the poem, or between different aspects of yourself, of your understanding, or of your experience. The challenge here is to meet the poem halfway, bringing your own experiences and concerns to meet the experiences and concerns of the speaker. Do not feel obliged to reach conclusions. Explore the nature of your own questions. You will need to find the right form for your essay.

Possibly because they had had practice with the first essay, students were readier to meet this challenge. Several students chose to hand in more conventional analytic essays that explored more than one point of view: maybe this, and maybe that, too. In other contexts, I would have been thrilled to receive such essays, but in this context I thought these students were being cautious.

The most daring and interesting essay came from Kristen. She set up a coffeeshop conversation among three people, a kind of interpretative drama. In doing this, she inhabited three distinct viewpoints with three distinct reading strategies. Amazingly, these strategies might have been drawn from Vine and Faust's list. One of her characters read critically, another deductively explained (and tended toward theme statements), and the third imagined inductively and explained and served as the mediator between the other two points of view. In class she remarked that she felt convinced by each speaker as she wrote out their parts. I was also impressed—and believed in her belief in the viewpoints—because Kristen's writing smoothed out in this paper. As she indicated from the start of the semester, she struggles with writing and argument; here, the written arguments were clear. Possibly by inhabiting imagined characters and points of view and believing in them, she was able to write more easily and capably. In my experience, students write better when they are writing something they believe in; the grammar improves, the sentences flow more smoothly. When they write away from themselves and try to inhabit some poorly understood "academic" other-self, the writing suffers. Though her conviction shows, because each speaker has a point, there is one voice that I identified with Kristen, a mediating voice, that of the synthesizer and mediator.

The dramatic element in her paper may be key and is what I wish to preserve in future assignments. Make it creative, playful, human. Through a small drama, students can explore their own "abiding concerns" (Vine and Faust 1993, 116) and "the relationships between self-awareness and other-awareness"

(118). This is also a way to ease students into writing analytically; analysis will not feel so foreign in the setting of a conversation.

Poem Constructions

The final project in the class was the most amorphous: make a poem construction and present it to the group. I gave minimal instructions:

> These will take a wild variety of forms. I have seen poems made from rocks and sticks and leaves, sandblasted in glass, cut in foam core and suspended as a mobile from the ceiling, constructed from logs and installed in a basement. What does a poem *do*? How can you make the action concrete?

This assignment is adapted from one used by Katherine Haake, as she describes it in "Teaching Creative Writing If the Shoe Fits" (1994, 93–94). It is a fun way to end a course. It may take you out of the classroom. I have used it twice now with some remarkable results.

Jeff Tonn showed up in a business suit, something we rarely see on the Goddard campus. Talking a mile a minute like some pitchman and telling us about the sources of poems, he began pulling slips of paper out of pockets and cuffs and off the bottom of his dress shoes, gradually making his way around the room to hand each of us our slip, a line from an original poem. Then he read the poem to us:

> If a boat were
>
> If a boat were
> in the fold
> of your brow
>
> your body
> canvas stretched
> between wooded frames
>
> of everything I hold
> rigidity and the
> ability to change
>
> the most rigid
> things I
> don't know anymore
>
> wait for that brisk
> rush of air.

Alexia Chamberas took us to the art studio where she had set up her poem in a stairwell. Hanging horizontally from a pipe was a stick, across the top of which she had waxed a row of candles, thus creating a large, natural candelabra. Hanging from the stick was an old satin slip, a dead rose, and a card inscribed with a poem. Suspended in the half-dark stairwell, this construction was ghostly. Appropriately, the poem flickers in the moment and contemplates dangers of beauty:

> I am afraid of beauty
> reflections of death
> the sorrow of peace.
>
> A shadow of breath,
> I'm tired, trembling
> on the ceiling
>
> Candles burning out
> like cheap wine,
> like America dying.
>
> A room filled for a
> moment, with contradictions
> three women crying
>
> for the death
> of memory
> swim away into
>
> darkness, Ophelia is
> dead. Beside me lays
> the gift of dreams
>
> too heavy for sleep
> like a child hidden
> in my weakness.

These two powerful poems reassure me that individuals will continue to read and take to writing poetry because it helps them wrestle with the simplest and hardest question: how do I live?

The beauty of this exercise is that it takes the poem off the page, incarnates it, and makes it walk and talk. Students find ways to make a poem real, and their meaning cannot be separated from form; words take tangible shapes and so embody thought and feeling. What's more, constructing a poem defies their good-student habits. In this aesthetic experience, students can find poetry.

Last Thoughts

Was this class successful? The students became more engaged readers and tried all sorts of new approaches. I doubt that they will ever think of poetry in quite the same way. They are all still talking to me, and a few came back for a more conventional seminar on poetic innovations the next semester. One of those who came back then had an exciting breakthrough semester with both his creative and his critical work. Another had a smaller breakthrough (or I may have just seen less of it) with her own poetry.

I am happy with many of the parts of "Experiences of Poetry" but not quite satisfied with the whole. Some wonderful learning went on in this class. These students engaged with poems in meaningful—and silly—ways, and poetry was demystified for them; they have begun a meaningful relationship with poetry. The exercises were most successful with the visual and kinesthetic learners, because they provided them new routes of access to language. But there were moments during the fall semester when I wondered. The energy of the group crashed at times. The portfolios included very few of the creations (sculptures or models or drawings) from class exercises and focused almost exclusively on the poetry of the students. Students crankily resisted some of the exercises (the four clay cubes).

A year and a half ago, I heard a presentation on portfolio assessment in the composition classroom. The teacher had asked business students to assemble portfolios of written work from the class and to write self-reflective assessments of this work. A number of the students resisted, one vociferously. He had mastered certain forms of writing for business and was angry that he was being asked to write in this new way. The presenter discussed her exchange with this student and ended up questioning her own right as a teacher to push this student out of his zone of competence into an unfamiliar zone. He was at school for practical, business training, and through the portfolio assessment process she had undermined his confidence.

I was quite shocked because she seemed to conclude that self-reflection might not be the business of college. My shock was certainly situational, and it brought home to me how different Goddard is. At Goddard, self-knowledge is one of the named literacies, written self-reflection one of the skills students must practice to graduate. So my students were well-prepared for self-reflection, but the verbal learners were not well-prepared to draw and sculpt and listen for rhythms and patterns of sound. In teaching "Experiences of Poetry" I was pushing students out of their zones of competence frequently, and requiring them to use kinds of intelligence that were unusual in an English classroom—unusual in school, period. These cognitive and noncognitive muscles had not gotten much, if any, exercise. They balked sometimes, and I, like the conference presenter, sometimes acceded to their resistance. But mostly I pushed them—playfully, when I could. Dared them, cajoled them, nudged and teased and encouraged them.

To push students out of the familiar poses a problem in a "democratic" classroom: it is easy to stay in the students' zone of competence or zone of comfort. Similarly, this poses a problem in a "democratic" institution. Paradoxically, in our experimental institution, students are often the conservative block that resists experimentation. With no required courses, Goddard students are not used to the idea of trying a subject that is unfamiliar or uncomfortable. They come to Goddard in order to have a greater degree of control over their education, and this can translate into timidity. To resist the resistance may require sharing less of the power over a class, or so I thought. I was far more structured in teaching this class than I usually am, and this structure may have been bossy. There was little opportunity for students to help shape the course, since I had my agenda and my syllabus. The syllabus was amended, but that was mostly a matter of timing when it was clear we needed to move more slowly. Sometimes, I was clearly too structured and hence controlling. Students let me know after the fact that they wanted more options in approaching some of the exercises, but at the time I was charging ahead with my plans.

Did I undermine my own democratic values while trying to teach independent thinking? That's a conundrum. Possibly, I did.

I am not convinced that democratic values preclude structure in the classroom. Structure is always there; it may just become more obvious and more uncomfortable when it is out of the ordinary and when the expectations shift. The means and the ends must match, however, and so I think it important that I find more ways to involve students in shaping a class even when the material and the practices will be wildly unfamiliar. As I learn more about these techniques, the challenge will be for me to present my thinking about poetry in such a way that students can choose the areas of inquiry that most intrigue them. Then I can invite them into a series of experiments in reading and writing and using new muscles.

Endnotes

1. In her important 1938 book *Literature as Exploration*, Louise Rosenblatt referred to the drugstore paperback as an "easy relaxing drug" that encouraged readers to think of human life in the simplest, stereotyped ways (1976, 103).

2. Rosenblatt emphasizes the aesthetic experience as a "vital personal experience" (1976, 59) that leads a student to a "zestful sense of literature as a living art" (1976, 66).

3. Harold Vine and Mark Faust studied how two-hundred-eighty-eight readers, ranging from middle school students to graduate students, made meaning from a poem. In *Situating Readers* they identify three reading strategies that consistently hamper readers: one, reading critically, or bringing so much of one's own agenda to the reading that one is unable to imagine a way into the other person's point of view; two, being immersed, so that one is unable to distinguish one's own perceptions from the author's; three, abstracting a theme statement either through contrast or isolation, even when this statement fails to correspond with much that is on the page (1993, 97–99). Readers struggle most when they "ignore or fail to attend to a sense of the situation" (1993, 106). Students who abstract a theme statement are doing their best to be "good" students; they are doing what they think they should. These three reading strategies correspond to what I have observed in classes, but in the light of experiential learning theories I have some different understandings of what is going on. Further discussion will follow.

4. Jonathan Culler (1980) also discusses the power of schooling to shape readers' responses in "Literary Competence," an essay included in J. P. Tompkins, ed., *Reader-Response Criticism: From Formalism to Post-Structuralism* (Baltimore: Johns Hopkins University Press), 101–117.

5. In her 1978 study *The Reader, the Text, the Poem*, Louise Rosenblatt referred to this kind of reading as "efferent" and opposed it to the "aesthetic" reading necessary for experiencing literature fully.

6. Critical theorists have opened debates about the "location" of a poem's meaning. New Criticism locates meaning in the text itself; reader-response criticism locates it in the reader; poststructuralism dislocates literary meaning altogether and defines it as plural, contextual, shifting. (These are sweeping generalizations.) Experiential learning theory bridges these three positions. In a school system with grades, however, power issues grow vexed and liberating theories may be so many pretty words, as the structure builds up power imbalances that the individual classroom teacher and her or his students try to break down.

7. Louise Rosenblatt declared in 1976 in the face of back-to-basics reactionary pressures that we need a clearly articulated philosophy of teaching literature: When literature is rescued from its diminished status as a body of subject matter and is offered as a mode of personal life-experience, all other kinds of relevant knowledge and skills can be added to it. Then we can explain that the "basic skills"—whether of beginning reading or sophisticated

interpretation—will be learned within a meaningful context: the only reliable mode of learning. (1976, x)

8. This was also the year of Cleanth Brooks and Robert Penn Warren's *Understanding Poetry*, which is seen as the first New Critical book of criticism. Although Rosenblatt's progressive emphasis on the reader and on democratic education was welcomed by many teachers, her work was largely ignored by the academy until the 1960s. I first encountered reader-response theories through the collection edited by Jane Tompkins (1980). This was one of the most exciting books I encountered in graduate school, because reader-response theories, after I got over my initial resistance, resonated with my experience as a writer and a reader and had applications in the classroom. Louise Rosenblatt, however, was not represented in this collection and was only mentioned in passing in the introduction. I came away with the impression that Wolfgang Iser and Stanly Fish were the originators of the approach. I only came upon her work after I started teaching as I continued to explore reader-response theories in relation to experiential learning. In her 1976 preface to the 1938 book, she registers the long neglect and writes of her rediscovery in the '60s: "In many ways it seemed to me that the college and university faculty were discovering what the schools had known all along—a responsibility to the student as well as to the discipline" (1976, ix). It seems, however, that she keeps getting rediscovered. I wonder if college and university faculty can keep sight of the responsibility to students given intense professional pressures. See Carolyn Allen, "Louise Rosenblatt and Theories of Reader Response," for another story of discovering Rosenblatt (1991, 15–22).

9. In "Democratic Practice, Pragmatic Vistas: Louise Rosenblatt and the Reader's Response" (1991), Ann E. Berthoff sets Rosenblatt apart from most reader-response theorists by exploring the philosophical roots of the different approaches.

10. I find her theory of reading wonderfully expansive and the most flexible that I have encountered. Earlier, I noted that it bridged the New Critical, reader-response, and poststructuralist positions on the location of literary meaning. It does this through the concept of transaction. She rejects the simpler and more usual notion that reader and text interact to make meaning, because that implies separate, already defined entities that act upon each other like "billiard balls colliding." Transaction "designates, then, an ongoing process in which the elements or factors are, one might say, aspects of a total situation, each conditioned by and conditioning each other" (1978, 17). For this theory she drew upon the work of John Dewey, Arthur F. Bentley, William James, and Charles Sanders Peirce.

11. David Kolb's *Experiential Learning: Experience as the Source of Learning and Development* (1984), synthesizes the work of educational philosophers, psychologists, radical educators, neurologists, management theorists, and others. As a synthesizer, he draws grand conclusions about how we learn.

12. This observation was made by I.A. Richards in *Practical Criticism* (1929). Criticism took two routes in response to Richards, toward the emphasis on

the text as a way to overcome such misreadings and toward the emphasis on the reader as a way to work through the process of reading. Rosenblatt comments that Richards's work reinforced her interest in the "subjectivity of perception" (1976, viii).

References

Allen, C. 1991. "Louise Rosenblatt and Theories of Reader Response." In *The Experience of Reading: Louise Rosenblatt and Reader-Response Theory*, edited by J. Clifford. Portsmouth, New Hampshire: Boynton/Cook.

Berthoff, A.E. 1991. "Democratic Practice, Pragmatic Vistas: Louise Rosenblatt and the Reader's Response." In *The Experience of Reading: Louise Rosenblatt and Reader-Response Theory*, edited by J. Clifford. Portsmouth, New Hampshire: Boynton/Cook.

Brand, A.G. and R.L. Graves, eds. 1994. *Presence of Mind: Writing and the Domain Beyond the Cognitive*. Portsmouth, New Hampshire: Boynton/Cook.

Clifford, J., ed. 1991. *The Experience of Reading: Louise Rosenblatt and Reader-Response Theory*. Portsmouth, New Hampshire: Boynton/Cook.

Corcoran, B. 1994. "Balancing Reader Response and Cultural Theory and Practice." In *Knowledge in the Making: Challenging the Text in the Classroom*, edited by B. Corcoran, M. Hayhoe, and G. Pradl. Portsmouth, New Hampshire: Boynton/Cook.

Corcoran, B., M. Hayhoe, and G. Pradl, eds. 1994. *Knowledge in the Making: Challenging the Text in the Classroom*. Portsmouth, New Hampshire: Boynton/Cook.

Culler, J. 1980. "Literary Competence." In *Reader-Response Criticism: From Formalism to Post-Structuralism*, edited by J. Tompkins. Baltimore: Johns Hopkins University Press.

Davis, C. 1992. "Chanting the Flowers off the Wall." In *The Practice of Poetry: Writing Exercises from Poets who Teach*, edited by R. Behn and C. Twichell. New York: Harper Perennial.

Dewey, J. 1938. *Experience and Education.* New York: Collier Books.

Doty, M. 1993. *My Alexandria*. Urbana: University of Illinois Press.

Haake, K. 1994. "Teaching Creative Writing If the Shoe Fits." In *Colors of a Different Horse: Rethinking Creative Writing, Theory and Pedagogy*, edited by W. Bishop and H. Ostrom. Urbana, Illinois: National Council of Teachers of English.

Hass, R. 1984. *Twentieth-Century Pleasures: Prose on Poetry*. New York: Ecco Press.

Hoagland, T. 1992. *Sweet Ruin*. Madison, Wisconsin: University of Wisconsin Press.

Hogan, L. 1993. *The Book of Medicines*. Minneapolis: Coffee House Press.

Hunt, R.A. 1991. "Modes of Reading, and Modes of Reading Swift." In *The Experience of Reading: Louise Rosenblatt and Reader-Response Theory*, edited by J. Clifford. Portsmouth, New Hampshire: Boynton/Cook.

Jameson, F. 1971. *Marxism and Form: Twentieth-Century Dialectical Theories of Literature*. Princeton, New Jersey: Princeton University Press.

Kolb, D.A. 1984. *Experiential Learning: Experience as the Source of Learning and Development*. Englewood Cliffs, New Jersey: Prentice-Hall.

Lee, A. 1994. "Unfixing Meaning: Challenges of Poststructuralist Theory for Classroom Study." In *Knowledge in the Making: Challenging the Text in the Classroom*, edited by B. Corcoran, M. Hayhoe, and G. Pradl. Portsmouth, New Hampshire: Boynton/Cook.

Lee, L. 1986. *Rose*. Brockport, NY: BOA Editions.

Patterson, A., B. Mellor, and M. O'Neill. 1994. "Beyond Comprehension: Poststructuralist Readings in the English Classroom." In *Knowledge in the Making: Challenging the Text in the Classroom*, edited by B. Corcoran, M. Hayhoe, and G. Pradl. Portsmouth, New Hampshire: Boynton/Cook.

Pradl, G. 1994. "Imaginary Literature at the Point of Utterance." In *Knowledge in the Making: Challenging the Text in the Classroom*, edited by B. Corcoran, M. Hayhoe, and G. Pradl. Portsmouth, New Hampshire: Boynton/Cook.

Ríos, A. 1990. *Teodoro Luna's Two Kisses*. New York: W.W. Norton.

Rosenblatt, L. 1976. *Literature as Exploration* 4th ed. New York: Modern Language Association.

Rosenblatt, L. 1978. *The Reader, the Text, the Poem: The Transactional Theory of the Literary Work*. Carbondale, Illinois: Southern Illinois University Press.

Rukeyser, M. 1996. *The Life of Poetry*. Ashfield, Massachusetts: Paris Press.

Tompkins, J.P., ed. 1980. *Reader-Response Criticism: From Formalism to Post-Structuralism*. Baltimore: Johns Hopkins University Press, 1980.

Turner, A., ed. 1977. *Fifty Contemporary Poets: The Creative Process*. New York: Longman.

Vine, H.A. and M.A. Faust. 1993. *Situating Readers: Students Making Meaning of Literature*. Urbana, Illinois: National Council of Teachers of English.

Vinz, R. 1994. "Entering the Discourse: Learning the Languages of Literature." In *Knowledge in the Making: Challenging the Text in the Classroom*, edited by B. Corcoran, M. Hayhoe, and G. Pradl. Portsmouth, New Hampshire: Boynton/Cook.

Williams, W.C. 1985. *Selected Poems* 2d ed. C. Tomlinson, ed. New York: New Directions.

Winterson, J. 1996. *Art (Objects)*. New York: Alfred A. Knopf.

Wright, J. 1992. *Above the River: The Complete Poems*. New York: Noonday Press.

SEVEN

Investigating Spiritual Experience: Progressive Pedagogy and the Nonrational

Kathleen Kesson

There is an intimate and necessary relation between the processes of actual experience and education.

Spirit indwells within the body, and manifesting itself, realizing its own nature, it makes that body its own organ and servant. It thus makes the spiritual body.
—John Dewey

A meaningful education, according to most progressive educators, begins with the interests of the students, interests that have emerged from prior learning experiences. Such emergent interests are often thought of as problems-to-be-solved. Paramount in progressive educational philosophy is the centrality of *experience* as an organizing principle. Experiences are not externally imposed, however, as in traditional schools. Instead, the goals of learning and the experiences that are chosen to facilitate this learning must come from the deeply felt, inner impulses, or "needs" of the students. As one might assume, teasing out these needs and differentiating them from mere "wants" is an important part of the advising/teaching function at Goddard. Currently, many students express deeply felt interests in various aspects of spirituality, and although these interests are sometimes reflected in standard surveys of religion and religious history, they are more often located on the fringes of the academically respectable: parapsychology, goddess worship, holistic healing, cakra balancing, cross-species communication, channeling, or some combination of topics, the intersection of esoteric spirituality and art being a favorite.

This prevalence of interest in the spiritual, even the supernatural, presents progressive educators with a number of contradictions, our own problems-to-be-solved. In certain ways, the foundational ideas of progressive pedagogy provide a useful method for the exploration of *any* idea or experience. The primary method of inquiry developed by Dewey and continued by most progressive educators is an observation/hypothesis/action/reflection model. It is an eminently practical method of inquiry, one geared toward pragmatic ends. It is primarily an empirical model of investigation, and does not readily account for factors we usually think of as "nonrational," including the unconscious mind, intuition, subtle phenomenological experiences, and mystical states of consciousness. So, in some ways, the method of investigation utilized by progressive educators may be so inconsistent with emergent interests in the "nonrational" as to render the method itself suspect, if not invalid. To get to the heart of these contradictions, it is necessary to revisit the sociohistorical context of progressivism.

The theory and practice of progressive education arose in a particular historical moment and was shaped by a specific set of circumstances. It developed in a period of nascent U.S. capitalism, at a time when the development of science, modern industrial technology, and socioscientific management principles seemed to herald the continuous improvement of material conditions. Dewey, the acknowledged father of progressive education, saw it as his task to advance a mode of inquiry, grounded in a scientific approach to problem-solving, that would be in tune with the general direction of modernism. Modernism, for Dewey, was characterized by a shift from reliance on traditional forms of authoritative knowledge (such as religion or scholasticism) to a scientific, empirical approach to problem solving. He was most concerned with the elaboration of the conceptual foundations of modernity and attempting to overturn older, established forms of authority in the prevailing religious and philosophical systems. His notion that authority could be located in the experimental approach to inquiry was truly radical at the time. The traditional disciplines of knowledge played a role in Dewey's developing theory of education, not as ends in themselves nor as mental training as in older classical traditions, but as conceptual tools that might inform the inquiry processes related to scientific problem-solving.

The current postmodern period presents us with a very different set of circumstances from those in which Dewey wrote and taught. Modernism itself is under assault, and many of its guiding principles, such as reason, progress, individualism, development, science, and technology have been implicated in the enormous global problems that we now face (Kesson, 1999). The foundations on which modern knowledge rested have been shaken, the canon that sustained modern academic institutions has been quite thoroughly deconstructed, knowledge has been relativized as a variety of stories have replaced the grand cultural narratives, subjectivity has been valorized, objectivity has been challenged, and empiricism and the "scientific" method have come to be understood as hopelessly political. There are ways in which Dewey's philosophical project has been accomplished (as in the overturning of traditional philosophical systems) and ways in which these postmodern currents challenge his own cherished assumptions (note, for example, his uncritical acceptance of the objectivity of the scientific method and his association with positivism). One of the characteristics of this postmodern period is the recovery of submerged histories and forms of knowledge, as well as a sense of the personal empowerment and political potency that is released when marginal discourses are evoked.

The many forms of spirituality that our students are interested in certainly qualify as marginal discourses. Often located outside the boundaries of mainstream science (as in holistic healing or parapsychology) and of established religion (as in the interest in neo-Pagan and Earth-centered spiritualities), these ideas radically conflict with the basic tenets, both secular and sacred, of modernism. The differences between these emergent forms of knowledge and the forms of knowledge valued under modernism are *paradigmatic* differences. That is, the epistemological assumptions, conceptual categories, and value bases of the forms constitute fundamentally distinct worldviews. So, at the heart of the issue under consideration is the question of whether a particular mode of inquiry that is rooted in a specific set of historical circumstances is adequate to the changing circumstances and worldview of a new era.

Dewey's theory of learning embodies a deliberative rational process in which problems are posed based on the emergent interests of the student. Once problems are identified, the student sets about to plan a solution, whether the problem is social, environmental, or artistic. To solve problems, one first observes the relevant conditions, then forms hypotheses about possible solutions. In this process, the comparative values of differing choices are assessed and determinations are made about potential ways to reach desired ends. The order or sequence of activity is planned, the student takes action, and then evaluates the success or failure of the action, at which point the learning cycle may begin again, sparked by whatever new problems arose from the preceding cycle. It is an inquiry process distinctly related to explicit knowledge and to the creation of concrete products and outcomes. This process is a tidy, conceptually sound, linear model of how one comes to know something. The question I am concerned with relevant to this paper is: *How effective is this pedagogical model, this deliberative, rational process, when student interest is in the exploration of what is essentially nonrational, or mystical, and when the desired outcomes relate to internal states of consciousness and meaning-making?*

Dewey's notion of spirituality was a naturalistic one; we might today call it an organic spirituality. Although he was critical of a religiosity that might posit a supernatural force or intelligence over and above human experience and intelligence, he did not discount the religious function in human beings, the striving toward ideal ends that required a kind of practical faith in human growth and development. He believed that the dependence upon supernatural forces as explanatory principles inhibited the development of a genuine social intelligence that might enable human beings to both identify the sources or material causes of their suffering and to carry out the kind of intelligent problem-solving that might create better material conditions. Supernaturalism, he declared,

> stands in the way of an effective realization of the sweep and depth of the implications of natural human relations. It stands in the way of using the means that are in our power to make radical changes in these relations (quoted in McDermott 1981, 708).

As a philosopher, Dewey strove to establish a nondualistic set of relations between body and soul, though what he called the "soul" might more rightly be called the "psyche," for he attributed no *transpersonal* dimension to it. He was critical of an idealist perspective that understood matter and flesh to be but the servant of a separate spirit:

> [T]he body is not an external instrument which the soul has happened upon, and consequently uses, as a musician might happen upon a piano. The body is the organ of the soul because by the body the soul expresses and realizes its own nature. It is the outward form and living manifestation of the soul (Dewey 1970, 117).

He was equally critical of the mechanistic, materialist position that human purpose is somehow inherent in the functions of the cells and fibers of the nervous system. He notes, in the essay "Soul and Body," that if we claim the function of "purpose" for matter beyond the basic material principles of cause and effect, we actually dematerialize matter, thus creating a teleology. His naturalistic spirituality, rather, assumed the "immanence of the psychical in the physical" (1970, 104), thus reconciling the idealist and the materialist contradiction. We can assume that although he would likely have been critical of the supernaturalism in some New Age ideas, he might well have supported efforts such as are found in the broad area of holistic health and healing to reconcile mind and body.

I have a particular interest in the topic of spirituality, and am a sympathetic facilitator of student inquiry in these areas. My own spiritual journey has been a lifelong quest to understand the many complex dimensions of the idea of "spirit." As an adolescent, I was intrigued with the Big Questions: *Why is there something instead of nothing? What is the meaning of life? How do we discover our purpose? Are we all there is, or is there some other, divine intelligence guiding our affairs?* Howard Gardner, in his newest conceptualization of multiple intelligences theory defines this proclivity to ask the big questions as the "existential intelligence." As a young adult, I continued to develop this intelligence, taking a minor in Comparative Religion and Philosophy as an undergraduate student, undertaking the practice of meditation that I continue to this day, trying out different spiritual paths, and weighing carefully the truth claims of various spiritualities. I sincerely believed at one time that one of the spiritual paths must be true, and that if I studied hard, and kept an open mind, I would discover the Truth that would perhaps enlighten me.

Fortunately, this conviction was a passing one, and my investigations led me increasingly more toward philosophy than religion, and the examination of the very nature of belief. In terms of my own beliefs, I acknowledge that there is something extraordinarily mysterious about the very fact of our existence, and that consciousness, or the capacity to reflect upon our thinking and our existence, itself is indeed magical. I think it is eminently practical to think of all of creation as Divine, if that epistemology leads us to treat the natural world as sacred, and worth conserving. I believe that it is worthwhile to consider all human beings children of one spiritual (gender-neutral!) parent if it causes us to treat everyone as brother and sister. I think that my spirituality is, like Dewey's, very much an embodied one, and although I agree in principle with him that the dependence on the supernatural as explanatory is mostly a diversion from the more concrete task of making the world a better place, I don't discount the new paradigm that is emerging from the confluence of "new science," ecology, feminism, and the wisdom traditions (Spretnak 1991) that some thinkers have called the "re-enchantment" of the world (Berman 1984; Griffin 1988). I am not ready to close the door on the supposition that there is some form of overarching intelligence that we have not yet fully understood.

Whether we come to understand this intelligence as David Bohm's (1983) "implicate order," Carl Jung's (1968) "collective unconscious," Karl Pribram's "holographic" model of consciousness (in Wilber 1985), or the physics-related "field theory" of Fritjof Capra (1977) remains to be seen. What is clear is that when one begins to explore the mysteries of consciousness, one necessarily trespasses into the realm of speculative metaphysics, and it is this realm of inquiry, traceable in the West from Plato to Hegel, that the "scientific" method of intelligence, including Dewey's theories of learning, supposedly displaced. This contradiction between scientific inquiry and speculative metaphysics is one of the issues at the heart of our investigations into the study of spiritual pedagogy in progressive institutions.

In a traditional institution, one might study spiritual topics, but the studies would be carried out in a context of supposed neutrality or objectivity. In a progressive context, which honors the experiential basis of learning, one doesn't just study "about" topics—one immerses oneself in an *experience* and draws the learning from that experience. According to Dewey's theory of experience, intelligence develops in a hierarchical manner—that is, experiences generate reflection, which then sparks increasingly complex problem posing, action, and problem solving. It is an eminently rational process, though not a process divorced from emotion:

> "Reason" at its height cannot attain complete grasp and a self-contained assurance. It must fall back upon imagination—upon the embodiment of ideas in emotionally charged sense (Dewey 1980/1934, 33).

Intelligence for Dewey is intimately connected to action, action fueled by imagination and passionate interest or desire. Such action has an internal and external continuity and culminates in a "true termination" or sense of completion. And this sense of termination is essentially an emotional as well as an intellectual experience. In a very real sense, it is *holistic*, integrating mind, body, emotion, and what Dewey might have called the human spirit. When a student seeks to explore spiritual ideas or incorporate spiritual practice into their learning plan, many of the questions we might pose to them are identical to questions we pose in relation to any learning situation: Is the desire to learn related to a deeply felt need? Does it emerge from prior learning experiences?

Does it encompass the entire spectrum of consciousness—reason, imagination, emotion? Is there a natural progression toward further learning? Is there a sense of fulfillment, of completion—perhaps a gestalt-like experience—when all of the pieces of learning fall into place?

Many of the students who come to Goddard, although not necessarily acquainted with the sophisticated theories of postmodernism, nevertheless embody some of its primary commitments. They have, as noted above, more than a passing interest in esoteric, or spiritual, discourses and practices. They often resist "patriarchal" constructions, to the point of refusing to read male authors. They often reject "linear" thought, logic, and rationality, referring to these as the "tools of the master", and exhibit what Belenky calls subjectivist knowing, in which the knowledge most valued is "personal, private, and subjectively known or intuited" (Belenky, et al. 1986, 54). Many of them are skeptical of the claims of science and "objective" knowledge, because of the affiliation of science with power elites, and are more trusting of their own inner knowing or intuition.

Although most faculty at Goddard celebrate the kind of critical consciousness exhibited by students who question and challenge the status quo in these ways, we are often stymied by the issues raised by these positions: What *does* constitute knowing? What is the appropriate relationship between reason and intuition? Who should decide this? What methods of study are relevant to intuitive studies? How should we deal with student dependence on revealed (for example, scriptural) knowledge? *Can* one use the "tools of the master" to deconstruct the master's house? What are the new standards, if any, of legitimate knowledge? Who gets to decide this? What is the role of the disciplines in learning that seeks to blur the boundaries of the disciplines?

Progressive educational theory, although seemingly able to accommodate postmodernist strains of thinking, remains perplexingly rooted in its own modernist assumptions. Many of us still value logical and critical thinking, we understand the disciplines as foundational to *interdisciplinary* or *transdisciplinary* study, we believe in the importance of expository writing and carefully constructed arguments, and we still believe that empirical investigations are perhaps the most generative of truth claims. At the same time, we are open to well-formulated critiques of these positions and encourage students to develop such critical perspectives. Our interdisciplinary faculty is methodologically eclectic, and we welcome the advent of qualitative, narrative, autobiographical, hermeneutic and other strains of inquiry. We celebrate students who propose to demonstrate their learning in visual and expressive ways; through art, dance and movement, poetry, film, and song. We have no particular academic canon to uphold; in fact, Goddard is known for students and faculty who regularly burst through the boundaries of *knowing, doing, and being.* But we do get nervous when students want to engage in spiritual practice as the experiential basis of their learning, and are currently engaged in discussions about how best to facilitate and assess such learning.

It is clear to me, from a careful reading of contemporary culture, that interest in spirituality is flourishing, and I predict that in the years approaching and following the millennium we will witness every sort of religious fervor conceivable. Modern people, emerging from a rather extended period of materialism and skepticism, have a fair degree of naiveté when it comes to spiritual matters. Our students are hungry for spiritual knowledge. In this time of spiritual profusion and confusion, charlatans and frauds abound, and they often exploit the innocent. I believe that it is in the best interests of us all to be as thoughtful and critically reflective about spiritual knowledge as we can be. So how should we respond when students approach us with an interest in spirituality? What sort of teaching practice is appropriate? How can we honor their desire for genuine spiritual experience, *and* engender the kind of thoughtful, critical reflection that is the hallmark of progressive pedagogy? In order to delve into these thorny pedagogical questions, I chose to employ a "Deweyan" method of self-study as I took on a facilitative role with a group of students who were carrying out a self-designed study in spirituality. I tape-recorded our conversations during advisory meetings and then analyzed the kinds of questions I posed. I tried to uncover the tacit assumptions and predispositions I brought to the task, and I documented my phenomenological responses to their statements. Reflecting upon all of this, I then tried to tease out my pedagogical goals and methods, and I record some of them here in the interest of furthering our conversations about "investigating spirituality." I have noted some of my own struggles and contradictions as I try to understand this complex issue, and conclude the paper by noting what I believe are some ethical and pedagogical dilemmas we face when we engage in this kind of holistic teaching.

One Case: The Study of Wicca

In the spring of 1997, a group of female students approached me about supervising a "group independent" in Wicca studies. A "group independent" differs from a "group study," in that students themselves design and carry out the study independently, in consultation with an advisor. A "group study," in contrast, is usually planned by a facilitator, or planned collaboratively with students. Students and faculty in a group study meet weekly, whereas in the group independent, students only meet with faculty five or so times during the semester to check in about the progress of the study. The faculty advisor of a group independent has oversight over the study plan and over the evaluative function.

These students were seeking to design an "experience" in Wiccan practices that would clarify and extend their own personally held beliefs. They chose me for an advisor because of my stated interest in comparative religion and emergent forms of spirituality. They also invited a library staff person, Kaye, herself a practicing witch for thirty years, to co-facilitate the study. Kaye was an active participant in the study, and provided readings for the students, worked with them to develop and carry out rituals, and had dialogues with them about various aspects of Wicca. Kaye considers herself a "kitchen witch"; practiced in the lore and the craft of the tradition, she lives close to the land in northern Vermont and makes her own artifacts such as incense, oils, and herbal potions from local natural materials. She rejects the commodified form of her spirituality that is represented in New Age catalogs and stores. Although Kaye would be directly involved in their study, my regularly scheduled meetings with the group would focus more on the analysis and interpretation of their experiences.

Celeste, Elena, and Mari, and Kaye (not their actual names) created an ambitious plan of study, which included the design and performance of rituals; readings about the history, mythology, and practice of witchcraft; the making of oils and incense for the rituals; the sharing of feelings and thoughts about their experiences; and discussions with me about their learning. I approved their plan of study, with the request that our meetings be devoted to exploring the assumptions and beliefs that lay underneath their investigations as well as their reflections on what they were learning. I was forthcoming with them about my research interests, and they were willing participants.

Wicca, or modern witchcraft, is a broadly defined system of beliefs, rooted in but not identical to, neo-Paganism, which is, according to the Institute for the Study of American Religion, the "fastest growing religion in the United States" (Thorn 1993, 101). Practitioners of Wicca adhere to ancient pre-Christian religious beliefs and adapt them to modern life. Some of the core principles and practices include a reverence and respect for all life forms, acknowledgment of a divinity that is both immanent and transcendent, feminist consciousness, rituals and observations grounded in seasonal and lunar cycles, and the practice of "magick" (attempts to influence or control phenomena through the use of spells, incantations, or divination). The practice of Wicca is, at its heart, an attempt to align oneself with the natural energies of the planet—seasons, climate, plants, lunar cycles, tides—and beyond this, to use the energy of these natural forces to exert control over the forces of one's life. The origin of the word "Wicca," according to some scholars, is from the Indo-European words *wic* and *weik* (to bend or shape) signifying, according to Manfred (1996), "someone skilled at bending or shaping reality (84). She quotes renowned contemporary witch Starhawk at length:

Magic, the art of sensing and shaping the subtle forces that flow through the world, of awakening deeper levels of consciousness beyond the rational, is an element common to all traditions of witchcraft. Craft rituals are magical rites; they stimulate an awareness of the hidden side of reality, and awaken long-forgotten powers of the human mind (84).

Other aspects of Wicca might include meditation, ritual drama, healing, herbalism, creative mythology, and more (Thorn 1993, 102). Many Wiccans worship or revere the "Goddess" of antiquity in one or more of her many forms, and some Wiccans recognize a divine male entity or energy as well.

At the initial meeting of the group of three students, Kaye, the co-facilitator, and I hoped to have them articulate the past experiences out of which this interest in the study of Wicca had emerged. Celeste, perhaps the most experienced in the group, defined herself as a practicing pagan, whose "destiny is clear from my astrological chart." She said that she had always been interested in the paranormal, and remembers writing a paper in the third grade on ghosts. She also remembers "always believing in birthday wishes!" When a close friend abandoned their friendship to become a born-again Christian, she felt a need to explore and articulate her own belief system, and she began an inquiry that led her to research witchcraft. At last she discovered a worldview that she identified with—"Wicca was acceptable—it didn't go against my beliefs."

Elena discovered Wicca when she researched a paper for an anthropology class at another college. Originally from the Bahamas, she found herself depressed when she moved to the mainland U.S.—"I had never been more than a ten-minute walk from the ocean, and my blood and psyche run with the tides." Elena was experiencing "the most stressful year of my life" and her "self-esteem was at an all-time low." Her parents had recently become divorced. At this point in her life, the "Goddess" became the answer to all her confusion. She tested her newfound faith with a "love spell," which, though apparently successful, backfired (the lover she had attracted turned out to be not so attractive!). It was at this point that she recognized the need for further study: "I learned to not mess with it without knowledge."

Mari was sort of an outsider in the group from the start—she was interested in the history of witchcraft, and considered herself an apathetic agnostic. She quickly dropped out of the group after the first few planning meetings with Celeste, Elena, and Kaye. Later conversations with the group suggested that she was dealing with too many emotional issues in her life to undertake this intense sort of experiential study.

In our very first meeting, I wanted to explore their motivations for undertaking this particular study. One of my initial assumptions about the reasons that people turn to the supernatural was that they do so when they do not feel in control of the forces that govern their lives. When people feel vulnerable, I assumed, they turn to a greater power to sustain them. Celeste felt rejected and abandoned by a close friend and began to question her own belief system. Elena was suffering from the divorce of her parents and her move to a new culture, and she indeed confirmed my understanding that there was a correlation between her "life getting bad" and her attraction to Wicca. In this respect, these students were no different than other people who turn to mainstream religion for comfort and strength. But there was clearly more to their interest than this. When they sought spiritual sustenance, they turned to a religious practice that was consistent with their own beliefs and assumptions about nature, ecology, and "women's way of knowing." Wicca, as a worldview and as a spiritual practice, was more closely attuned to their politics than the more established religions, and seemed to speak to their evolving identities as "womyn-centered womyn." So, although this study was clearly undertaken in response to psychological and spiritual need, the interest in this topic in particular emerged from a synthesis of other studies they had pursued.

In subsequent conversations, we discussed the experiences they had designed for themselves. They did a lot of work preparing for rituals, reading about traditional ritual forms, and then adding their own creative ideas to the event. This creative, improvisational approach to ritual is consistent with contemporary Wiccan practice. Lynda L. Warwick (1995), in her paper on a feminist Wicca, notes that

> The Wiccan community is highly creative. Rituals tend to be written or improvised for each celebration and may include aspects of theater, dance, art, poetry, singing, and creative ways of interacting among group members (123).

When I reviewed my notes and the tape-recordings of subsequent group discussions, I began to understand my pedagogical approach as a multifaceted one. I classified my instructional strategies into five categories: phenomenology, perspective taking, meta-cognition, theory building, and axiology. These were not rigid categories, but fluid ones—information easily flowed over from one category to another. Using the categories as an analytic device, I discuss below some of the topics that came up in our dialogues, and try to make explicit my line of questioning the students. Following this, I will clarify what emerged as my own epistemological position, and then discuss some of the ethical and pedagogical dilemmas that emerged for me in this experience.

Phenomenology
    In the Wiccan paradigm, thoughts are energy forms, and the projection of thoughts through the use of the will is considered to have effects, negative or positive, on both the emotional and the material levels of experience. Inherent in this idea of thought projection is the notion of the "boomerang effect"—the idea that thoughts wrongly projected can come back to you and create difficulties. This, coupled with the notion that other's thoughts are either being directed towards oneself, or that one might become a victim of randomly circulating "negative energy," gives rise to the notion of the importance of "protection." Protection is created or enhanced through the medium of spells, charms, and affirmations. Central to this discussion are the related notions of "auras" and "fields of energy" that are thought to surround people and other material objects.
    Although some parapsychologists (people who study phenomena such as ESP, psychokinesis, and clairvoyance) have attempted to do empirical studies on auras and energy fields, conclusive data remains elusive. Because claims about thought projection are usually couched in the language of *energy* or *affect*, I thought it might be useful for these students to explore their phenomenological experiences. So I asked them to describe their sensations and their perceptions, and worked with them to separate these two related categories of experience. For example, when they talked about auras, I asked them to describe their perceptions, and they reported both sensory and perceptual data: "I feel it in my chest"...I sometimes see it (sensory)...it's a kind of emotion that a person brings

out in you" (perceptual). We worked to differentiate sensory (more or less "raw" data such as colors in the visual field or tightness in the chest), from perceptual data, which I am defining as a more holistic phenomena that is shaped by a prior conception, such as a rainbow or a feeling of anxiety. At the root of this approach is an epistemological concern: how do you *know* what you *know*? And beyond this, how might what you *see* be shaped by what you *think* or *expect*? My assumption here, based on my own earlier experiences with spiritual exploration, was that when people encounter a compelling new worldview or belief system, there is a strong desire to fit all data into that framework. So, for example, if one is convinced of the existence of spirits or ghosts, then curtains rustling or shadows in the woods could signify the presence of supernatural beings. But these events could also signify other, more mundane phenomena such as wind interfacing with mental phenomena in a synchronistic manner. Articulating the data sources makes them more available for analysis and discrimination. My goal was to encourage them to articulate what seemed to be vague sensations ("energy," blips in the peripheral vision, increased heartbeat) to heighten their awareness of the data that they were utilizing to build their conceptual framework.

Perspective Taking
At every opportunity, I encouraged these students to explore multiple explanations for their sensations, perceptions, and concepts. They are very interested in this notion of "protection." I want to know "from what?" They have many ideas about this: "little spirit friends...people floating around between lives...they may not be human, they may not ever be human...there are a wide variety of beings on the 'other side'...guardian angels...spirit guides." They go on to explain, "When you're consciously using energy it creates a beacon on the spiritual plane like this big ball of light that attracts entities." I want them to explore some psychological explanations for their assumptions, and I tentatively ask them if the protection they seek might not be from aspects of their own unconscious. They readily concur: "Protection is not just from outside forces, but from your own subconscious as well...most things you encounter on the spiritual plane that give you problems are generally just aspects of yourself...sometimes when I talk about eerie subjects the room fills up with eerie energy—it's all about myself...that's really something I need to learn to recognize as well...what is my own paranoia and what is something else."

Contrary to usual methods of religious instruction, which tend to be doctrinaire, perspective taking requires us to examine the idea under consideration using analytic tools that are not necessarily inherent in the tradition that is being studied. Or it requires us to try to imagine what an idea or a phenomenon might look like from a different positionality (gender, culture, etc.). In this case, I wanted them to try to understand their experiences from a disciplinary perspective, psychology. I might have asked them to engage with their ideas from a differing cultural perspective. (How, for example, might a Christian fundamentalist think about this idea of protection?) Perspective taking is an important way to help students think outside of their conceptual frames. I expected these students to resist exploring multiple explanations for the phenomena they described (these *are* new ideas after all, and probably fragile), but they seemed eager to examine their experience in this way. Some people are more ready to do it than others. These particular students demonstrated an interesting mix of open-mindedness (in their willingness to explore psychological explanations) and doctrinaire ideas (guardian angels, spirit guides).

Metacognition

In many instances, I would reframe, or restate, some of the students' statements in more analytic terms, with the intention of moving them toward more metacognitive stances, that is, toward becoming astute observers of their own thinking processes. For example, they talked a lot about "drawing energy from things, and refocusing the energy...every living thing is an extension of ourselves." I was extremely curious about the assumptions that lie underneath this proposition, and I wanted them to articulate these assumptions for themselves. So I restated their assertion by saying "So, the act of attunement, of connecting emotionally with objects allows you to draw energy from these objects and then utilize it in some act of exerting your will?" I thought that by hearing their proposition re-stated, they would come to question the assumptions that underlie it. On the contrary—one of the women said "I couldn't have said it better."

To me, this set of ideas represented a clear instance of paradigmatic conflict. Within a rationalist paradigm, the notion that one can draw energy from objects and use it in thought projection makes no sense—it seems absurd. There is no empirical foundation for such a claim. But in a paradigm of interconnection, such as that explicated in deep ecology or in a quantum mechanics paradigm in which the borders between apparently separate objects are fuzzier than in a Newtonian universe, the notion of subtle energy exchanges becomes more plausible, if speculative. Rather than accept these possibilities so matter-of-factly, however, I wanted these students to struggle with the enormity of the paradigmatic differences that I was so acutely aware of.   In this dialogue, our generational differences were perhaps evident. Celeste and Elena had grown up in postmodern times and clearly took for granted some of the explanations of the world that seemed so novel, so esoteric, and so far-fetched to us "pre–paradigm shift" elders!

Metacognition is, essentially, "thinking about thinking." It involves, for me, trying to tease out the underlying assumptions, preconceived notions, and biases in any given thought or thought pattern. It assumes a genealogy of thought, and asks that we attempt to trace the sources of our ideas. It asks that we notice how our thoughts connect with each other. It is an act of intellectual labor. Reframing and restating students' assertions in ways that push them to think about their thinking embodies a certain kind of pedagogical authority. My intention in doing this is to encourage students to examine the ways in which their thinking has been constructed—by experiences with peers and elders, by print and visual media, and by material culture (such as architectural space and artifacts). In understanding something about the social construction of our ideas, we learn about the limitations of our own thinking. When we become aware of the limited nature of our thinking, our horizons are broadened, and new possibilities open up for our consideration. We become capable of wondering how our thinking might be qualitatively different had we had different life experiences. When we study spirituality, the understanding of how our beliefs have been constructed through our experiences and exposure to ideas can help us be more discriminating about our relationship to "revealed" or "authoritative" knowledge, such as that found in scripture or in myth. Aside from wanting the students to look at how their belief systems had developed, I wanted to help them relate their personal experience to more abstract concepts, principles, and generalizations. I wanted them to know that *all* knowledge is paradigmatic, and to understand and articulate how the knowledge they are constructing fits into a particular paradigm. This aspect of meta-cognition overlaps with the next category—theory building.

Theory building
I am interested in the learning that can occur when students attempt to develop a theoretical framework for their tacit or explicit set of beliefs. Phenomenology asks students to describe their experiences as accurately as possible. Perspective taking asks students to look at things from different angles. Meta-cognition asks them to think about their own thinking, analyze their assumptions, and trace out the connections and constructions of their thoughts. Building a theoretical framework requires all of this, and more—it asks students to generate an intellectual context for their ideas and to articulate a story as a container for their ideas. It requires them to expand their subjectivities and draw upon the ideas of other people for explanatory frameworks. It requires them to weigh evidence, assess truth claims, and evaluate competing explanations. It often nudges students into disciplinary studies that held no prior fascination for them. I know this from very personal experience. In my own high school and undergraduate experience I had been steadfastly uninterested in science of any sort. Instead, I immersed myself in literature, the arts, philosophy, and Asian spirituality. In the 1970s, I came across Fritjof Capra's book *The Tao of Physics*. I was at that time much more attracted to the notion of the Tao than the study of physics, but Capra's suggestion that there might be a conceptual link between the worldviews of physicists and mystics captivated me, and proved to be the catalyst for a serious study of the philosophy of science in graduate school. My own experience serves as a continuous reminder to me that students find their own unique ways into disciplinary knowledge, and I want to stay alert such openings as they present themselves.

Throughout the course of this study, these students began to articulate an understanding of the context of their beliefs that drew upon the Gaia hypothesis (the notion that the earth itself is a giant, interconnected organism) and popular understandings of quantum mechanics: "Science," they say with confidence, "is headed toward understanding the web of life." A genuine understanding, however, of the relationship between physics, ecology, and consciousness was far beyond the scope of their study. They did situate their studies historically, with the readings they did on the history of the Wiccan tradition. They were open to multiple explanations for their sensations and perceptions, as demonstrated by their willingness to entertain psychological explanations for their experiences. Ultimately, I asked them the same fundamental questions that I ask students engaged in theory building in any area of study: What intellectual problems or dilemmas did you encounter? How did you solve these? What contradictions made themselves apparent? How did you resolve these? How have you changed as a result of this study? What new questions do you have? What new areas of study opened up for you as a result of this study? What have you done or will you do with your knowledge that will make the world a better place? This last question, concerning the moral dimension of the study, finds its expression in the last category, that of axiology.

Axiology

I want to explore with these students the source of value for their decisions. If we take seriously the notion that thoughts can have material effects and influence events (and many people in many cultures, past and present, do take this notion very seriously), then the issue of how one uses one's power has a moral dimension. I ask them, How do you make moral decisions about your intentions? How do you decide when it is appropriate to interfere? What is the source of your moral decision making?

They answer that they follow the standard moral code of Wicca: "Do no harm." Traditional Wiccan lore also states this value as "An' it harm none, do what ye will." According to some scholars, this stringent moral code and the belief that any thought projection returns to the sender threefold provides the moral checks and balances in a system of magic, spells, and charms. Accepting the statement of value as a given within the system they are studying, I pursue this moral dimension diligently: How do you know that you do no harm? How can you predict the course that events might take if you interfere? Who are you to decide what is best for someone? What about the unknown variables? They tell me that they think about things for a long time, that they try to "think of the good of the whole," and that they ask for guidance through divination. Kaye adds that Wicca is about asking "energy forces" to guide you. I want to explore this notion of divination: When you are asking for guidance, or divination, how do you assess the information you get? Celeste eloquently describes this intuitional process:

> You call on your own higher self. Some tools make it easier to access information, such as Tarot *(a set of archetypal cards used for divination)* and Runes *(letters of an ancient Germanic alphabet that were used to cast spells and work magic, and are currently used as divination tools)*. It's difficult to describe how the answers come to you;

they come from the unconscious, through intuition. Divination is an initial tool—the development leads toward an intimate relationship between nature and intuition. You get to a place where certain objects create "moments of stillness" that suspend conscious thought. These are opportunities to remember something.

This dialogue showed me that these students, although they are engaging in what modern people might call "magical thinking," understand it in the context of psychological development. The process they described is an "integrative" one—that of bringing the ego and the unconscious into attunement. They seem to view their spiritual practice as a process of self-awareness, of coming to know themselves as whole human beings. There is also a *transpersonal* aspect to their practice in that they seek knowledge and value that transcends the self, that has sources in nature and the cosmos.

This problem of the source of values was addressed by James Macdonald, an eminent curriculum theorist, in his groundbreaking paper "A Transcendental Developmental Ideology of Education" (1974). In this paper, he suggested that this problem of the source of values was not adequately addressed in any of our dominant paradigms (he called them "ideologies") of education, neither in the *traditional* paradigm, in which values are picked up culturally by association, or conditioned in us behavioristically; nor in the *romantic* paradigm, in which they are emergent from our biological nature; nor in the *progressive* paradigm, in which they are derived from cognitive reflection upon experience, nor in the *radical* paradigm, in which they are weighed against abstract principles of equity and social justice. Values, he suggested, are ultimately personal, and must develop from a "dual dialectical" process, in which the person engages in reflective transactions not just with the environment (as Dewey suggested), but with their own inner depths, or the unconscious mind (Macdonald seemed to accept Jung's notion of the collective unconscious as well). Attunement with this ontological ground, says Macdonald, coupled with critical, reflective engagement with the world, is the only adequate source of value. He called this new paradigm of education the *transcendental developmental* ideology.

The Wiccan tradition meets these dual requirements of attunement and critical engagement. As witches such as Starhawk have stated, there is a definite political dimension to the practice of Wicca (Starhawk 1989). Wiccans are active in the struggles for the health and safety of the environment, for women's rights, and for peace and justice. The students in the Wicca study clearly reflected an ontological grounding, and a commitment to the development of intuitive judgments about ethics and values. Although they were not explicitly political as part of this study, they often articulated the connections between a political position and a Wiccan belief.

Some Dilemmas

Throughout the course of this reflective inquiry, I became more clear about my own pedagogical commitments, especially as they relate to the study of spirituality. My own commitments in this area are inextricably twined with my own spiritual history, which I articulated earlier in this paper. Therefore, they could hardly be generalized beyond personal pedagogical principles. I have come to understand how important it is for facilitators of spiritual studies to undertake their own spiritual autobiographies. We need to be clear about how we have come to know what we know, to believe what we believe, and to value what we value if we hope to help students do the same. And, despite my own rather extensive archaeology of personal beliefs and values, I do not hold my pedagogical commitments unambiguously, as will be clear when I raise some ethical dilemmas that I am struggling with. So it is probably not something we can do once and be done with, but rather something that must be part of our on-going personal and professional development.

First, I believe that our interpretations of our experiences depend largely upon our beliefs about the world, or worldview. It follows from this that a serious reflection on experience requires that we come to a deep understanding of our beliefs. Exploring our beliefs in a systematic manner reveals that they are largely constructed through our experiences. The way that experience shapes beliefs and beliefs shape experiences is a complex dialectical process. If our beliefs are socially constructed through our experiences, then all beliefs must be contingent. They depend, after all, upon the various experiences we have had, and we are all unique in our combinations of experiences. It is clear to me that the social conditioning of our beliefs inhibits an unmediated experience of the world. *Everything* is experienced through the lens of a socially constructed worldview. In this way, belief would seem to work against true spiritual and intellectual freedom. If the liberation of thought, the development of a mind free of conditioning is the ultimate aim of education, and I believe that it is, it follows that the "deconstruction" of belief, through awareness, analysis, and unconcealing, is an essential pedagogical strategy. We need to decide for ourselves whether this liberation of thought is indeed our most valued aim of education. If it is, there are questions we can ask ourselves as students engage in the study of spirituality. Is the study leading toward greater freedom of thought? Is the student clinging to the comfortable and the reassuring, or is she taking the great leap into the unknown and the uncharted? Does the discourse of spirituality that is under investigation empower and enlighten or does it repress and subdue? Does the student understand the dynamic differences between these forces?

I think that this set of commitments embodies a postmodern spiritual pedagogy—it acknowledges the contingency of beliefs and ideas, seeks to reveal what is hidden in the texts of experience and belief, and deconstructs tacit and explicit assumptions about the world. Its intention is to "uncondition" the mind of the student, so that they might come closer to an unmediated experiencing of the world (not that this is easy, or entirely possible). "Deconditioning" as a pedagogical method is consistent with certain spiritual pedagogies, notably that of the Indian philosopher Krishnamurti, and with Buddhist practices. It raises some interesting theoretical and practical dilemmas, however. First of all, beliefs are fragile and uncertain states of mind at best. People construct beliefs about the world for a variety of reasons: beliefs and myths bring certainty in a highly uncertain world, comfort and consolation in the face of pain and loss, explanations for the impossible sufferings that people endure, and meaning to a sometimes incoherent world. "Worldviews," says Huston Smith (1989), "obscure life's precariousness and contingency, the ways in which we dangle by threads over seventy thousand fathoms" (21). We tamper with people's beliefs at great risk, for the loss of belief and the resulting uncertainties can lead to nihilism and despair. This can certainly be witnessed in people who have been colonized, invaded, dislocated, or otherwise shaken out of their familiar ways of thinking and living. In a paradoxical way, undercutting belief is consistent with the modernist project of disenchanting the world. We need to acknowledge our complicity in this, even as we suppose that we engage in a postmodern project of "re-enchanting" the world. In this particular study, students said in their evaluations that they came to understand some crucial differences between Pagan and Wiccan beliefs, and that they feel more competent now to make informed choices about which spiritual path (if any) they would follow. In this instance, the course of study helped them to clarify their beliefs. It did not leave them adrift.

From an evolutionary perspective, it seems to me that some beliefs have an "adaptive" quality. Wicca, for example, as explored in this study, fosters interdependence, connectedness, eco-sensibility, and the stricture to "do no harm." From where I sit, these qualities and principles seem to have more survival value than the modern capitalist principles of competition, aggressiveness, domination, and accumulation. When we seek to do away with belief we undermine some of the important foundations of moral behavior. Are we prepared to provide substitutes? Do we know how to both deconstruct taken-for-granted beliefs *and* lead students to a deeper understanding about the ontological ground that might provide a more significant source of value than the socially constructed set of beliefs they may have acquired along their life path? Otherwise, we risk leading students into nihilism and despair.

When we teach and learn spirituality, we cannot do so from a position of disengagement. The very subject matter requires a genuine reciprocity. The usual categories of "mature" and "immature" learner (Dewey 1938, 21), teacher and student, become less relevant than an attitude of respect and mutuality. We must become vulnerable, open our hearts to the wisdom and insight that might come from our students and foster our own spiritual development. James Macdonald asserts that spiritual pedagogy is not inconsistent with progressive pedagogy. The main difference is that the teacher herself is also "in process...immersed in the process of centering from her own point of view" (1995, 94). We must, as Macdonald said, engage in the process of locating one's center in relation to the other: to "see" ones self and the other in relation to the centers of our being; to touch and be touched in another in terms of something fundamental to our shared existence (95).

With the cultivation of such a deeply felt internal ethic and thoughtful attention to the dynamics of the teaching and learning situation, I believe that we can assume the risks inherent in spiritual pedagogy. Progressive education, as formulated by Dewey and others, provides us with necessary but not sufficient tools for investigating spirituality. We need to further explore and articulate methods that might encompass the nonrational, that might help students deal with the explosion of contemporary spiritual ideas, and that will assist them in finding their own ontological ground and source of value. To be effective at this, we must be willing to walk the road of spiritual autobiography with our students, to seek our own centers, and to engage in on going learning processes that lead to our own liberation of thought. We must learn *together* to investigate spiritual experience.

References

Belenky, M.F., Clinchy, B.M., Goldberger, N.R., & Tarule, J.M.1986. *Women's Ways of Knowing.* New York: Basic Books.

Berman, M. 1984. *The Reenchantment of the World.* New York: Basic Books.

Bohm, D. 1983. *Wholeness and the Implicate Order.* New York: Ark Paperbacks.

Capra, F. 1977. *The Tao of Physics.* New York: Bantam Books.

Dewey, J. 1980/1934. *Art as Experience.* New York: Perigee Books.

Dewey, J. 1938. *Experience and Education.* NewYork: Macmillan.

Dewey, J. 1970. "Soul and Body." In *The Philosophy of the Body*, edited by Stuart F. Spicker. Chicago: Quadrangle Books.

Griffin, D. R., ed. 1988. *The Reenchantment of Science.* Albany: SUNY Press.

Jung, C.G. 1968. *The Archetypes and the Collective Unconscious.* Princeton, New Jersey: Princeton University Press.

Kesson, K. 1999. "'Thinking Against' from Within: Reconstituting the University as a Democratic Space." *The Vermont Connection* 20.

Macdonald, J. 1974. "A Transcendental Developmental Ideology of Education." In *Heightened Consciousness, Cultural Revolution, and Curriculum Theory,* edited by W. Pinar. Berkeley, California: McCutchen.

Manfred, E. 1996. "A Return to the Circle." *New Age Journal.* (September/ October).

McDermott, J. J. 1981. *The Philosophy of John Dewey.* Chicago: The University of Chicago Press.

Smith, H. 1989. *Beyond the Postmodern Mind.* Wheaton, Illinois: The Theosophical Publishing House.

Spretnak, C. 1991. *States of Grace.* San Francisco: Harper.

Starhawk. 1989. "Ritual as Bonding: Action as Ritual." In *Weaving the Visions:Patterns in Feminist Spirituality,* edited by J. Plaskow and C.P. Christ. San Francisco: Harper & Row.

Thorn, M. 1993. "A Portrait of Wicca." In *A Sourcebook for the Community of Religions,* edited by Joel Beversluis. Chicago: The Council for a Parliament of the World's Religions.

Warwick, L.L. 1995. "Feminist Wicca: Paths to Empowerment." In *Women's Spirituality, Women's Lives,* edited by J. Ochshorn, J. & C. Cole. The Haworth Press, Inc.

Wilber, K. ed. 1985. *The Holographic Paradigm and Other Paradoxes.* London: Shambhala.

EIGHT

Between Individual and Society: An Essential Dialectic in Progressive Teaching and Learning

Katherine L. Jelly

If democracy has a moral and ideal meaning, it is that a social return be demanded from all and that opportunity for development of distinctive capacities be afforded all.

—John Dewey

The individual and social aims of education are not only both essential but are also each necessary to the other. Only through the actions of competent, ethical, creative individuals can a society be sustained and improved. Only through the systems and ethos of a humane and supportive society can an individual thrive and reach his or her fullest potential. Further, it is only through working in the social realm—with and for others—that the self can develop. Thus, education must foster not just the individual's growth and accomplishment but also social justice, appreciation of diversity, and attention to the greater good. Each of these aims is essential. Each needs to function in constant interaction with the other.

The problem, however, that the educator faces in the design of pedagogy is how best to serve both these aims—and their inherent relationship—in one's teaching. That is, how does one, through both pedagogy and curriculum, work with the creative tension between the individual's and the group's needs in the teaching and learning process? How does one use the *how*, pedagogy, and the *what*, curriculum, of education to reflect and work toward the *why*, the fundamentally related individual and social aims of education?

In what follows, I try to address these questions through a discussion of two group studies, "The Self and Others: Unraveling Human Relations" and "Alternatives in Education in Theory and Practice," which I led at Goddard College and which grapple with the role of pedagogy and curriculum that support both the social and individual aims of education. In my discussion of each of these studies I hope not only to explain how each worked, through process and content, toward both individual and social ends but also to demonstrate how each study constituted a pedagogical reflection of a fundamental philosophical tension in education. That is, I hope to discover what can be effective means to worthwhile ends, and also to demonstrate the necessary and integral relationship of these aims.

As both group studies drew heavily on several basic tenets of Dewey's thinking and of progressive education, before discussing the studies themselves, I will outline briefly some of those underlying tenets.

Tenets of Progressive Education

In my understanding of progressive education, in which individual and social aims provide the foundation, education ought to be student-centered and problem-focused. The content of education should arise from the student's own context and interests, work toward the student's goals, and meet the student's needs in relation to the world we live in. It is through a student's interests that real questions emerge. It is through attention to the broader context that the student can gain the knowledge and skill necessary to competent and rewarding functioning in the world. And it is through attention to both that the student's growth is spurred from within and without and that the issues that arise have both personal and wider meaning. Thus, curriculum should derive from and focus on real questions, questions of import to the individual and to society.

And thus teaching and learning ought necessarily to be experiential. That is, they should draw on the whole of the student's experience—past and present, as well as future—to deepen understanding, inform thinking, and frame questions. Teaching and learning ought to use past and present experiences to engage the learner, to expand awareness, and to broach real questions. And they should work toward the ongoing and constructive reshaping of experience through the constant interaction of action and reflection.

Fundamental then to progressive education and to education that supports democracy is, as Schapiro puts it in his introduction to this volume, democracy *in* education. In order to foster real understanding of the issues involved and skill necessary to working with others toward a common goal, the student must experience the dilemmas, conflicts, and diverse views *within* the group study (or course or other educational experience at hand). At Goddard, studies that are undertaken are called group studies precisely because a group of individual students comes together to pursue a particular topic, each bringing to that topic his or her own interests and goals and each needing to negotiate with others in the group to frame the questions, develop the curriculum, select the readings, and design the activities that will constitute a *group* study, that is, a fundamentally social enterprise that will meet the needs of both the individual and the group.

Also essential, in my view, to democracy in education and to education for democracy is a pervasively critical approach both to experience and to theory. In using the term *critical* here, I intend its meaning in relation both to critical thinking, which should include analysis, synthesis, and evaluation of the ideas at hand, and to critical theory, which, in relation to education, examines curriculum, pedagogy, and school organization as these aspects of schooling are embedded in a political, economic, and cultural context. Each of these uses, it seems to me, is essential to informed, thoughtful, active citizenship. Critical thinking is necessary to questioning that which is and to moving constructively and creatively forward to more humane and effective systems, while using the lenses of critical theory gives us the tools to "problematize" the context which one takes for granted and to take constructive action to both address and reshape that context.

Further, critical theory gives an additional framework for understanding, appreciating, and working with diversity. Knowledge of and respect for individual differences and diversity of race, class, gender, culture, and modes of knowing and learning are essential not just to effective education but also to a just and open society.

Related to each of these tenets ought to be a dual emphasis on theory and practice and on the integration of theory and practice. We should not lose sight of implications for practice or forego involvement in actual practice for the sake of emphasis on theory; nor should we forsake theoretical inquiry or knowledge of theoretical foundations as we re-examine problems in practice. Each is essential to and informs the other.

Thus, as theory informs and moves into practice, not simply through direct translation but rather through praxis, through the constant and essential interplay between theory and practice, so too are both the individual and social aims of education served. For, related to each of the principles and approaches noted above, that is, to education that is student-centered, problem-focused, experiential, and critical, and that emphasizes the integration of theory and practice, are the goals of fostering the individual's development and of increasing the individual's capacity for and commitment to constructive action in the world.

Moving these ideas to action myself, I turn now to two group studies that I recently led at Goddard College. The explicit agenda of one, "The Self and Others: Unraveling Human Relations," related both to individual and social aims, that is, both to personal growth and to human interaction. The agenda of the other, "Alternatives in Education in Theory and Practice," related to a fundamentally social enterprise. For both studies, I will describe the goals, the teaching and learning processes, the topics of inquiry, and the learning outcomes for students and then discuss these studies in relation to the tenets of progressive education outlined above and to the fundamentally dialectical relationship between the individual and social aims of education.

"The Self and Others: Unraveling Human Relations"

The published description of this group study read:

> This study will look at the self and the self and other in interaction; at different kinds of relationships (including family, friends, lovers, and

groups); at psychological, social, and political factors affecting relationships; at our own relationships and patterns in them; at additional questions of individual interest; and at approaches to building and maintaining stronger, more satisfying relationships. Drawing from both our own experience and pertinent literature, using the group itself as a laboratory, we will examine human relations in both theory and practice.

First, in terms of process, it is important to note that this description was published after three earlier stages in the curriculum formation process, the first in which I, the faculty member, "floated" an idea for a study in human relations at an organized curriculum fair and discussed possible topics of inquiry with interested students, the second in which I asked students who enrolled in the group to brainstorm all the questions—whether about themselves or theories of interaction or interpersonal skill—that they brought to the study. I then organized and placed these questions in a conceptual framework for the students' approval. Each of these steps involved a degree of negotiation and accommodation of diverse interests and goals among the group that elected to work together in this area of inquiry. To lay bare this process, I include here the full list of questions and topics of interest, as they phrased them, that students brought to the study:

> conflict resolution in close friendship
> relationships/communication through the arts (e.g., music)
> what we carry with us from family and early beginnings
> sustaining long-term relationships—keeping them alive
> nonconfrontational communication
> being assertive
> not feeling trapped by people
> why people get so weird; why so much other "stuff" comes in; why we
>   can't just just be
> why we're one way with some, another way with others
> why we're afraid to be ourselves
> why we're drawn to certain people, repelled by other people; what is
>   chemistry?
> the role of the spiritual, the unknown, the unconscious in human
>   relations
> what we are supposed to talk about and why in different circles (norms,
>   taboos)
> levels of disclosure
> shame, self-blame
> internalizing stigma
> what to do about others' shame
> the extent to which we create our relationships, the extent to which they
>   create us

how the culture conveys "not-okayness" to all of us
other cultures' ways where morality comes in
judgment
different meanings of morality
revision of norms
how we change—for good or ill
why I think some things are my fault; why I do some of the things I do
why we make certain choices; how we deal with consequences
difference between who we want to be and who we are
how to let go of someone
co-dependency
how we have a relationship with ourselves
learning to be by ourselves
learning to be with others
communication styles: culture, gender, age
getting family to let you become an adult
how to identify/deal with irrationality
how to acknowledge you're a good person
conflict between interior belief and exterior feedback
projection of others' expectations onto self (internalizing)
how to value self, define self-worth
acknowledging one's own strengths
listening well—how listening opens or blocks expression
how stable, vulnerable self-perception is

What then emerged from these questions was the following tentative outline of topics:

    I. The self: What's inside us?
    A. Needs
    B. Motives
     Identity
     Childhood/family experiences
     Personal patterns
     Self blame and shame
     Self-acceptance and self-esteem
     Choices we make
     Potential for change
    II. The self and others
    A. What's between us?
    Facades
    Roles
    Internalization, projection, attribution
    Systems
    Codependency
    Judgment, questions of morality

Potential for change
B. What's beyond us?
  The unconscious and irrational
  Chemistry/attraction
  Spiritual realm
  Social norms
  Cultural messages
  Political factors
  Potential for change
C. Kinds of relationships
  Families
  Friendships
  Intimate relationships
  Groups
III. Interpersonal effectiveness
  A. Communication
    Self-disclosure
    Expressing oneself (including assertiveness)
    Hearing the other (listening)
    Different languages (including gender, culture, and age; verbal and
        non-verbal; the arts)
    Different levels
  B. Conflict resolution
  C. Helping
  D. Entering, maintaining, and letting go

What this outline represented, through its conceptual framework and prioritization of the students' questions and interests, was at this point a proposal, a proposal that balanced in a particular way questions individuals were bringing to the study and topics of general interest. And as such it presented to students the problem of negotiating the needs of individuals and the group in an attempt to carve out the most effective and satisfying means to the accomplishment of our shared and individual goals. Clearly, such a process provides valuable experience in and of itself in the balancing of one's own and others' needs, in striving toward the "greatest good for the greatest number."

While in some group studies this tentative outline might change as a result of the negotiation, in this group study, the proposal was accepted as presented. In relation to these topics, we agreed to a core reading list to be completed by all participants and to do additional readings of particular interest to individual students; to keep a journal recording personal responses to readings and discussion; to write three short reflection papers regarding experiences that related to our topics of inquiry; to do a longer paper drawing on both theoretical understanding and personal experience in order to examine in greater depth a question of particular importance to the individual student; and to participate fully in all group discussions and activities.

The group study was designed to encompass both theoretical and experiential exploration of our topics of inquiry and to examine theory and experience in relation to one another; that is to say, while we read, discussed, and wrote about theories of human interaction, group dynamics, intimacy, etc., we also participated in structured exercises that were designed to help us to examine our own past and present experience and to develop interpersonal skill. Thus our group sessions served as both seminar and laboratory in our exploration of human relations.

In regard to content and to the conceptual framework for the study, as the outline of topics indicates, we began with a focus on the self, then moved to thinking about relationships and to exploring questions such as how and to what extent the self creates the relationship and how and to what extent the relationship creates the self. We looked at theorists who emphasize subjectivity, such as Carl Rogers (1961), and theorists who emphasize the power of relationship, such as R.D. Laing (1969), or the power of the broader social and political context, such as Russell Jacoby (1975). We examined the dialectic between self and others, probed questions related to free will and determinism, and worked to understand and assess the potential for change within the individual and/or the relationship.

As they talked about Jacoby, for example, whose scathing critique of humanistic psychology pushed students to question the subjectivist vision of Rogers, students confronted directly the question of the relative autonomy and sociality of the individual. Having, in the main, appreciated and embraced the propositions of Carl Rogers regarding "becoming a person," they then had to face Jacoby's argument that "With barely a glance toward objective reality, a blinkered and constricted view of 'self,' 'becoming,' 'authenticity' is promoted. That to be or to become, in a society whose being is one of mass administration and blatant violence, is hardly acknowledged as a problem. . . .The subject abstracted from the social context decays into a thing—the very ill existentialism was to cure" (Jacoby, 1975, 63). Then they interpreted Helen Lynd in *Shame and the Search for Identity* (1958) to be saying that self-realization occurs in and through relations with others; students explored, in a sense, the question of whether and how one can achieve Rogers' vision in Jacoby's world.

Reading Laing's *Self & Others*, as we pushed further in our theoretical, conceptual explorations, we also brought these questions directly into our experience. In group discussion, for example, students analyzed and evaluated Laing's conceptualizations of attribution and of complementarity in human relations, but they also, in a brief reflective paper, identified a relationship in their own lives that characterized to some extent one of these dynamics. They used the concept to articulate and examine just what goes on in the relationship and were also asked to consider if they could and how they might interrupt and change the dynamic. These kinds of explorations students found to be invaluable, both to their understanding and to their personal awareness.

Coming even closer to home in terms of the group's shared experiences, we took time to explore a conflict that had arisen in the group concerning one student's use of a term that had offended another. In basic terms, while one person felt deeply offended by the expression, the other student felt "shut down" in being asked not to use it. In a microcosm, our group was grappling with a profound and challenging question in a democratic society, namely the reasonable and just line to draw between the individual's right to speak, even the most hurtful words, and society's interest in humane and civil norms of discourse; or, put differently, the line between freedom of expression and freedom from offense. We wrestled with this question on several levels and in different realms as we examined the actual incident in the group, explored further through role plays, and used our theoretical understanding to this point to gain understanding and push our thinking further.

Later examining individual histories in our families of origin and personal patterns in past and current relationships with others, again we used examination of both theory and experience to raise once previously unidentified dynamics and patterns to consciousness in order to question, evaluate, and, perhaps even to interrupt and change them. And we used our experience in, and of, the group itself to gain understanding of ourselves and of others and to probe what goes on in human interaction. What does the other (here used to refer to *any* other— friends, family, the community, society as a whole) do that helps me to be who I want to be and do what I can do? What does the other do to hinder me from developing to my fullest potential? What do I do that helps others to become who they hope to become? What do I do that hinders them? If I see destructive dynamics in which we/I am caught, can I/how can I interrupt those dynamics? In all cases, for all questions, we moved in and out of theory, in and out of experience in various kinds of relationships, using each to test and inform the other.

With no questions answered but rather with all questions deepened, with awareness heightened, and with self-knowledge increased, we moved to more practical work; that is, we turned to skill building in the interpersonal realm. Drawing on the insights we gained from our explorations of theory and experience, we used structured exercises to work directly on communication (including expression and listening), on helping, and on conflict resolution and to focus directly on increasing interpersonal effectiveness.

In talking about their learning from this study, students speak of enhanced self-knowledge, of greater insight into others and into human interaction, and of increased interpersonal effectiveness. One student, who had hoped to gain from the study "understanding of [her] own feelings and actions in relationships," reports that her work in the study "has made me more comfortable with myself and with sharing who I am with others." Another student, also referring to her personal goals for the study, says: "I learned important aspects of myself that I need to work on such as patience and understanding." Another writes: "I have gained a lot of insight into myself and [into] what ways my experiences have made me who I am." Referring to the broader context in identity formation, another states: "I have learned a great deal about friendships and patterns in family experiences and their relation to the development of identity."

As she talks about gaining insight into others, one student says she gained a sense of "how scarred, lost, and confused people really are." Another talks of her discovery of unexpected commonality of experiences: "I have begun to realize my similarities with others." Several students talk of the importance of having examined human relations in the broader social, political, and economic context. Says one: "I have been able to move beyond how they [relationships] just apply to me and to examine them in terms of race, class, and sexual orientation."

In addition, students describe the role of the study in developing their interpersonal skills: "I can take what I've learned about myself and relationships and use this knowledge in relationships right now. I can also use the skills I have gained to better relate to people and to analyze myself and my relationships." And finally, one student for whom a central goal in the study was to gain understanding of himself in relation to his music and, through his music, to his audience, states that through his work in this study he was able to gain confidence in his music and to trust in his individuality as a musician. In this connection but more generally, he writes:

I learned that trusting and being honest with yourself, although difficult, [are] key to relating successfully to others. . . . I am more conscious about what constitutes a good, successful, strong relationship. . . . Through the readings and my careful selection of valuable knowledge gained from them, I feel I have been able to relate to people a little better and to myself a lot better. Learning to have completely successful interaction with someone on all levels is a never-ending process, so to say that I have successfully applied and reaped all the benefits of the learning gained from this study would be very untrue. I am, however, conscious of actions, words, and general characteristics involved in healthy relationships, so it's a good base or root to my beginning to relate on a level I'm more happy with. I believe that one must understand oneself first, though. I feel I have an obligation to myself to figure out who I am, and what I am capable of, and this study has opened many doors for me in this way.

What students report, then, is a greater understanding of self and of others and of many facets and dynamics of human interaction, as well as increased interpersonal skill—understanding and skill that have served them already in their work to build and maintain stronger, more satisfying relationships, and that they will continue to build on, having gained the tools to examine ideas and their own experiences critically as they strive for continued growth.

Before going into a discussion of this group study in terms of its individual and social aims and implications, I turn now to a description of the goals, teaching and learning processes, topics of inquiry, and results of the group study, "Alternatives in Education in Theory and Practice."

"Alternatives in Education in Theory and Practice"

This study began with a student's idea for a study in "Alternative Education." Several other students were interested in this topic, and so, again going through Goddard's structured curriculum formation process in which ideas for studies can be "floated" by either students or faculty, the study was born. Right at the outset, however, I posed a problem to the students, questioning what they meant by alternative education. Alternative to what? Traditional education. What did they mean by traditional education? We quickly arrived at a new title "Alternatives in Education" and a more broadly conceived topic of inquiry, including, for example, so-called traditional approaches to education.

Similarly, when students articulated the questions they brought to the study such as, "How do alternative schools function? How can we create 'good' schools and change 'bad' schools? How do good schools go 'bad'? What gets in the way of their good intentions? What alternatives 'work'? What alternatives do not 'work'?" we saw immediately the need to probe all the questions these terms raised: What do we (each) mean by good? What do we (each) mean by bad? What do we (each) mean by effective, by ineffective? On what basis do we hold these ideas?

What emerged, then, from our initial curriculum formation process for this study was the group's decision to get at their initial questions, first by addressing the list of questions raised by their evaluative terms through inquiry into both philosophies of education and their experience of education; then by reading about a range of alternatives in education, including, for example, the Romantic school of thought, progressive education, deschooling, Friends schools, and Waldorf education; by visiting schools; and, finally, by attempting to design a school down to the last detail ourselves as a way of addressing directly the issues, questions, and problems raised along the way.

Thus the following group study description emerged:

> In this group study, we will explore various alternatives in education in theory and practice. Through reading, discussion, and examination of our own experience, visits to schools, and papers, we will attempt to broaden our knowledge of alternatives; to understand better the purposes, practices, and effectiveness of these approaches; and to examine and develop our own views regarding the aims and possibilities of education.

Essential of course to this inquiry was that we examine critically all the theories, experiences, and practices that we encountered. Necessary at the outset to this critical inquiry had been the shift in our title from "Alternative Education" to "Alternatives in Education," which called into question possible assumptions about our area of inquiry. Beyond this initial shift, however, students also needed to make explicit and thus expose to critical examination as many of their preconceived ideas and assumptions as possible. In a context such as Goddard, which many students have chosen to attend for its progressive philosophy and alternative approach to education, the rejection of traditional education's values and approaches is a commonly held stance. Indeed, as students shared and listened to one another's experiences of school, they voiced not only rejection of but deep anger about their traditional school experiences. Thus, in this study, as in others at Goddard, it was important—essential—to students' critical analysis of all the ideas and approaches under our microscope to help students to move past merely absorbing the critique of public education put forth in many of their readings. That is, they needed as well to critique the critique and, throughout the study, to subject all ideas to the same careful scrutiny. I urged them, for example, for all readings they did, for all practices they observed, for all experiences they shared, both to problematize what they might assume to be "good" and "effective," that is, to look at what a seemingly effective approach leaves out or at the problem to which it gives rise or at other questions it raises, and to look for possible justification or value in what they might have rejected.

We embarked then on an exploration of theory, individual experience, and practice in order first to address the question for ourselves of what schools *should* do and to begin to articulate, even if only tentatively, a developing philosophy of education. Only then could we move on to questions of effectiveness, for only then could we talk about effectiveness toward a given end. Once we arrived at these tentatively and individually held ideas of ends, we were able to examine and evaluate in a context and by criteria made explicit, the means to these ends. And thus, predictably enough, what we found was that our backtracking to the previous questions that our initially framed topic of inquiry raised had become much of the semester's agenda as students used these questions to gain knowledge and push their thinking about education further.

In fact, while we did look at several schools of thought, including cultural transmission and the Romantic and progressive schools, through examination of our experience and of theory in the limited time that remained we managed to interview only one educator and did not get to the school visits that we had originally intended. In addition, though in this case due not to lack of time but rather to a shift in the group's interest, we decided not to undertake the originally intended design of a school but rather to turn our attention to Goddard. Excited by the ideas they'd been engaging and by discussions of the philosophical tenets underlying Goddard College's approach to education, instead of designing a school, the students wanted to put Goddard under the same critical lens they had been using to examine other approaches.

Bringing to this stage of their study the categories they had developed earlier in the semester for examining schooling, the group looked at Goddard in the areas of philosophy, organization, curriculum, and pedagogy. Their goals were to understand what the college attempts, how it goes about this, and why; to evaluate both its goals and its effectiveness in relation to these goals; and to consider possible avenues to increasing its effectiveness. This focus on Goddard students found fascinating and important as they were now exploring not only their former but also their own current experiences in education and as they shifted their attention from the hypothetical design of an "ideal" school to the critical examination and possible improvement of their own real educational setting.

And to this segment of our inquiry, students brought as well the questions they had been developing and engaging over the course of the semester concerning ideas such as the individual and social aims of education, freedom and authority in schooling, the individual and community, and the locus of evaluation and accountability—all issues that we had encountered not only in our examination of the readings and of our former experiences in schools, but also in the actual functioning of our group study.

What, for example, did students view to be the ideal relationship between individual and community and why? How close did Goddard come to reaching that ideal? What structures—whether of organization, of teaching and learning, or of living—played what roles in supporting the individual or the community? How might those structures or norms be changed to achieve stronger support of both and of their sustaining of one another? How—and how well—were we in our group study fostering the growth of the individual and the development of our community? Which elements of our study had served what ends and how? Where did the tensions lie, and to what extent were those tensions perceived to be creative and rich, yielding learning and enhanced understanding, and to what extent were they perceived to be obstacles and distractions to achieving our shared and individual purposes? All of these questions we raised as we looked both at the college as a whole and at our group study.

Once again, though, we were confronted with how huge a task we had set for ourselves—each question seemed to lead to another and we developed a clear sense that we had only barely begun to get to the originally stated goals of some students of examining the effectiveness of various approaches and of exploring a wide range of approaches to get at these questions. While we had explored several approaches and had looked at Goddard—in theory and practice—we had not gotten as far as we had hoped in our examination of Goddard; nor, as mentioned earlier, had we visited many schools.

And so, arising directly out of the questions and goals of our first semester together, "Alternatives in Education II" began. First, of course, we needed to clarify our multifaceted agenda, which proved to be a challenging undertaking, as we decided on what topics we would undertake together and what topics individuals would take responsibility for, identified the schools we hoped to visit, and clarified expectations regarding reading and writing for the study. For this semester's work the description we agreed to was:

> In this group study, we will continue to explore various alternatives in education in theory and practice. Through reading, discussion, and visits to schools, we will attempt to broaden our knowledge of alternatives; to understand better the purposes, practices and effectiveness of these approaches, and to examine and develop further our own views regarding the aims and possibilities of education.

Placing more emphasis this semester on individual research and on school observation, we intend to approach our work in a problem-solving mode; that is, through bringing to this research specific questions regarding, for example, goals, organization, curriculum, and teaching processes, we hope to glean approaches, ideas, solutions, which are helpful both to our ongoing examination of Goddard College and to the development of our ideas regarding meaningful and effective education.

While we would, again, share a core reading list or topics of general interest and while we would decide on and visit schools as a group, most of the particular approaches to schooling we left to individuals to explore in greater depth and to present to the group. Thus, Montessori schools, Waldorf schools, magnet schools, deschooling, and home schooling all remained as topics that individuals pursued. Even with this careful negotiation of shared and individual topics of inquiry and learning activities, we found that we frequently needed to return to this negotiation to navigate most effectively among the study's components, both to achieve coherence and depth of inquiry and to accommodate the diversity of interests within the group. For me, the main organizer of all our goals and activities, balancing individual and group topics as well as readings and trips to schools, remained challenging right to the end of the semester.

To recapture a tiny piece of one of the first semester's goals, as well as to raise and re-raise some of the questions we would bring to this semester's inquiry, I asked the group in our first class session to break into two groups and, drawing on the work of our first semester, to design a public K–12 school. With attention to philosophy (which they were asked to articulate at the outset), organization, curriculum, and pedagogy (the teaching and learning process), and remaining mindful of questions related to individual and community, freedom and authority, heterogeneity, and evaluation, they were to discuss and attempt to reach agreement on a particular design. Each group was then asked to present its design, along with its underlying philosophical foundation and practical rationale, to the other and to defend or reconsider that design in light of the other group's questions. Although of course such an exercise could not allow the participants to plumb the questions that arose in any real depth, it surely did serve both to spark and re-spark important questions and to remind the students emphatically of the diversity in the room and of the extraordinary complexity of undertaking public education in a democracy.

Emphasizing in particular our problem-focused mode this semester, first we considered our own ongoing negotiations about our learning activities as demonstrations of the teaching and learning laboratory within which we were working. Throughout our work, we remained self-conscious, and took time at various intervals to examine and work toward improving our teaching and learning processes. We needed, for example, at the outset of this new semester, to wrestle again with the question of evaluation, to decide for ourselves within this group study what the appropriate role of the facilitator was to be in evaluation of students. We pushed and probed, heard the concerns of students who felt "stifled" by external evaluation and faced the realities dictated by earning credit toward a degree for one's work.

Further, we repeatedly encountered—in both our reading and our observation of schools in practice—questions related to diversity and uniformity that called directly for our problem-focused approach. We live in a diverse society; students bring diverse interests, needs, and ways of knowing; parents bring diverse perspectives and even demands regarding their child's schooling. Educators in public schools in the United States today are constantly confronted with diversity. How does one deal with this diversity in regard to the curriculum? In regard to methods? In regard to evaluation? In regard to discipline? Neither in the readings nor in the schools did students find easy answers to these questions.

When we turned our problem-focused lens toward Goddard we faced similar conundrums. If, as students concluded after some discussion, Goddard erred in the direction of fostering individualism at the expense of the community and on the side of freedom at the expense of the social order, how could the community's interests be served while still providing for individual freedom? Asking "What aspects of Goddard undermine the development of social responsibility?" students tried to look at possible structures and processes for fostering responsible social involvement and for building community.

As she talks about the results of this freedom, one student writes in a paper that she wonders whether Goddard offers so much freedom that it falls short in stimulating some of its students; elsewhere, she laments the loss to everyone when students came to studies unprepared. Yet unwilling to shift the focus of responsibility from the individual, most students perceived this problem to be a necessary evil in the process of students taking responsibility for their actions, a positive outcome.

In the simplest of examples, whether the issue is about having pets on campus or noise at night or a discipline system for infraction of rules, again and again students came up against these questions. In one conversation, a student argued that one has no right to question anyone else's behavior, to which another responded that he expected others to let him know if he was out of bounds. Another said that social responsibility seems to be defined by the individual. Related to this question of where does/should control lie, one student suggested that re-examined and shared goals within the Goddard community would foster freedom. But to this another replied that while shared goals would foster community, Goddard students do not have a shared purpose.

Out of all these conversations, we began to see as well the links between and among the questions we were exploring. As we confronted and explored diversity in education, for example, we looked now at how to provide for diversity *and* community and for diversity *and* equality.

Or in several other conversations in which we confronted the complex problems posed by evaluation of their own learning, students grappled first with their own views about the most appropriate locus of evaluation, then with the purposes of evaluation, with the role of accountability to others, and more. As she wrestles with the concept of freedom in relation to evaluation, one student writes: "Is there a way to be free from that feeling of someone else looking at my thoughts and deciding that they may be eloquent but they don't fit the requirements for the class?. . . .How free was I really when I had to think about how it [her paper] would be received?" Problem-solving throughout—whether in relation to an approach or view we had just read about or in relation to how our own group study would conduct evaluation—we kept coming up against tough questions, against imperfections. If, for example, the student views the ideal locus of evaluation to be the self, how does self-evaluation satisfy the legitimate public interest in the verification of one's knowledge? Self-evaluation fosters ownership, engagement, and accountability, yet lacks external verification. External evaluation provides the outside feedback and assessment but can hinder the development of individual creativity and responsibility. As when we had wrestled with questions surrounding individual freedom and social respon- sibility, though brought directly into our own small environment, these questions and problems still proved large and difficult. There were no easy answers or solutions, only creative—and illuminating—tensions.

Indeed, in students' evaluations of their learning from both the first and second semesters of the study, it is evident that they had discovered and confronted new questions as they worked toward their originally stated goals for the study. Clearly students had gained a sense of the host of possible alternatives in education. One writes: "I have learned of so many alternatives, more than I would have believed existed." Talking about our look at the way that schools, including Goddard, function, one student writes, "Seeing some of the problems other small alternative schools have faced and what they've done about them has helped me to begin developing ideas about what could be done here." And another says of our attempt "to make Goddard come closer to that ideal [its stated philosophy], . . . I'm not sure that we arrived at any conclusions, but I feel like I have an understanding of the complexity of the problems facing an educational community beyond any I would have imagined." Also about Goddard, another says: "I began to realize that in studying and discussing problems at Goddard, in planning strategies for solving these problems, and in trying to implement these strategies lay a golden opportunity for me to not only make my school a more effective place to learn but to also learn a great deal about how to effect change in general."

Students also understood use of an experiential approach in the group study. One student writes:

In this group study we focused not only on EDUCATION, the abstract, but also EDUCATION, the personal, and I think this is a large part of what made this group so important to me. We looked at the general question of evaluating a student's work and then we looked inward at the process we knew we would take at the end of our semester. And we were not afraid to question the validity of [our] process and to open our minds to alternatives beyond our own experiences. Perhaps we should all evaluate each other was one thought, or maybe we should each choose one other group member to evaluate our progress. Why should all of the responsibility/power be given to Kathy who has functioned all semester as a group member much more than T-eacher, as [Holt uses the term, Holt 1976]? These are such wonderful questions and I wonder why it is that it has taken us this many years to reach the point to ask them?"

Describing our dual emphasis on theory and practice and our use of the group as its own teaching and learning laboratory, one student writes,

I found the learning in this group happened on several levels. There was the more direct learning from the readings/written work/discussion portion of the group. There was the hands-on reality of the classroom from the school visits and administrative interview sessions. There was all that, but then there was the actual forum in which the group was held. We were able to see the idea of cooperative education happening in our own classroom. The content matched the context. This is a powerful environment in which to learn.

Another says: "I think a major part of our learning as a group. . . was building community and social responsibility inside of the group study. . . . I am now able to see just how important one person can be to a community."

Referring to the widely divergent perspectives within the group, one talks of her learnings from working with our diversity this way: "Even this situation became a learning experience. In any community there will be people who perceive their role differently [than I do]. I need to learn how to continue to communicate with this person either through or around this discrepancy."

And finally, in regard to the importance of the study to him personally, one student writes: "This study has affected who I am. I feel more directed now; my resolve to work in education is firmer. I also feel that I understand myself and others more fully as a result of studying education."

Certainly students did gain a sense of the complexity of the issues and of the variety of approaches involved in education. With both broader and deeper understanding of purposes and practices in schooling, they did address their goal of learning about and evaluating various educational alternatives and of considering ways of improving this social institution. And they did, as well, enhance their self-awareness both as learners and as community members, thus enhancing their ability as individuals to play a more informed and constructive role in their own education and their community.

Between Individual and Society: Two Studies

How then did these two studies work toward both individual and social aims in education? What can we learn from the ways these group studies progressed, from the questions they wrestled with, and from the learning that resulted? What questions are we left with? And, finally, in what ways do these two studies reflect the fundamental and necessary relationship between education's individual and social aims?

That these two group studies embraced both the individual and social aims of education is clear. In the case of "The Self and Others," personal development was explicitly and directly an aim and outcome of the study. Yet stating explicitly its goals not just of enhancing self-awareness, but also of understanding human interaction and increasing interpersonal effectiveness, its social purposes and, later, outcomes were also evident. And while such a study could have remained primarily personal, or even interpersonal, while ignoring larger social aims and societal contexts for inquiry, we delved into the social, political, and cultural context of human interaction. Our study explored and eventually confirmed the centrality of that context to the development of the individual just as it explored and demonstrated the centrality of the individual to the development of the relationship, of the community, and of society. Thus, as they examined the broader societal—including cultural, political, and economic—context that profoundly affects the development of the individual, participants gained understanding of self, other, *and* society. And as we examined our families of origin, relationships in our lives, and personal patterns, we developed our capacity to bring individual understanding and awareness into our functioning in and contributing to the community.

In the case of "Alternatives in Education, I and II," gaining understanding of the means to improving a social institution was explicitly and directly our aim— and an outcome—of the study. Yet the focus on the individual was also clear as students gained understanding of their own experience in education, of themselves as learners, and of their role in shaping education. And we used that focus on individual experience to make real and gain insight into the questions at hand. In studies that could have remained almost solely externally focused, that could have been limited to the philosophical, historical, political, and social contexts, these studies brought in personal experience and used that experience to examine, critique, and reconnect to the public enterprise. As well, participants used their increased understanding of views and approaches in education and of their own experience in education to further their development as students, through more conscious and informed attention to their own learning and to their learning environment. Thus, students gained understanding of their experience in education, of themselves as learners, and of their role in shaping education. And from both studies, clearly, these individual and social purposes were fundamentally and intrinsically related. Each both supported and derived from the other.

Important in working toward these ends were the progressive means outlined earlier, namely the student-centered, problem-focused, experiential, critical, and integrative approaches that attended to diversity and democracy within the studies. I noted earlier the processes through which the curriculum of each of these studies was formed. Both studies were fundamentally student-centered, as they arose from the students' questions and worked toward their learning goals, and the studies were consistently problem-focused, as they addressed questions of import in their lives and the world, used a variety of lenses to probe these questions, and worked toward increased effectiveness—whether in the realm of human relations or of education.

In talking about the questions that emerge in student-centered and problem-focused approaches to teaching and learning, I should emphasize here that I refer to *real* questions, to questions that have meaning and import for the student and in the world. So in saying that students brought their own real questions to the study, I am talking about questions to which the student does not know the answers, questions that *matter* to the student. And in saying that we addressed real issues and problems in our lives and in society, I am saying that we dealt not with the issues that one might have presumed to be the topic but rather with the actual puzzles, views, and challenges that arose through our inquiry.

Key here, in regard to both student-centered and problem-focused approaches to teaching and learning, is the concept of significance. The questions that we pursued in these group studies were questions of significance to the participating individuals and in the world. And in that sense, the dual emphasis on student-centered and problem-focused education in these studies could be viewed as not only directly supporting but also directly replicating their dual emphasis on individual development and social reconstruction. The means here reflect precisely the ends.

Interestingly enough, in light of the present discussion, significance itself can be viewed in either an individual or a social context. William James characterized the notion of significance as the result of the individual struggle to achieve one's ideals (1950). As such, his vision of significance was fundamentally individualistic. In George Herbert Meade's thought, however, a gesture holds significance only as one knows its meaning to the *other* (1934). And, as such, in his schema, significance was a fundamentally social concept. But whether individually or socially derived, what I am arguing here is that significance—both to the individual and to the world—is essential to real inquiry; that is, inquiry that springs from questions of genuine interest, and to real learning; that is, learning that one has taken into one's experience and understanding and through which one achieves greater capacity for action in the world.

Our studies also took an experiential approach as students tapped their own experience and the experience of others to gain knowledge of themselves and of social systems, and as they experienced *within* the studies the very questions we were addressing as the topics of the study. Thus, as students attested to in their evaluations, in "The Self and Others," for example, students gained self-awareness and insight into human interaction as they turned the lens onto the dynamics and interactions within the group. Similarly, in "Alternatives in Education," through wrestling with the dilemmas, conflicts, and challenges arising from an ongoing negotiation of both content and processes and through conscious reflection on these processes, students confronted and experienced directly not only the gains and losses of any given choice but also the challenges involved in accommodating our own diverse interests and goals.

So, not just wrestling with issues in human relations or in democracy in education (both theoretically and practically) *outside* of our own enterprise, we were also working directly with the relation and balancing of individual and group purposes *within* the groups, with the goal of achieving the "greatest good for the greatest number." And, I would argue, through striving toward democracy in our own education, we were working as well to learn about and to create education *for* democracy.

In theory and practice, the questions these students were confronting dealt with the complexities, conundrums, and challenges presented by the ongoing, integral relationship between the individual and society. In "The Self and Others" that object of study involved examining the ways in which the self contributes to and creates the relationship—whether one on one, in a family, as a member of a group, or as a part of community—and the ways in which the relationship (again ranging from two persons to all of society) contributes to the formation of the self. In "Alternatives in Education" that object of study involved examining the individual and social aims of education, the potential for competing emphases, and their relationship to one another. Thus not only our process but also our content frequently reflected directly the individual and social aims of the studies.

And, through our ongoing integration of theory and practice (and here I include experience in the category of practice) students gained both a stronger sense of self *and* knowledge of interpersonal and societal structures, each of which spurred them to examine and question not just social systems but also themselves, their views, and all the ideas and practices we were encountering.

Finally, in regard to our topics of inquiry, I would like to underline here the value of education and of human relations as objects of study for our students. Schooling—in whatever form—has had a profound and lasting impact on their lives. Education has extraordinary powers to help or to hurt, to open up or close down, to stimulate or to stifle. For our students to gain insight into that power—both in their own lives and in society—can make a real difference, again both to them and to society.

For through examining their own education, both former and current, students gain understanding of its impact on them and of their own role in their learning: the study of education enhances self-knowledge. And, too, it fosters the development of students who can not only make better use of their learning environment but also take steps to shape and improve that environment. Precisely these claims can be made for the study of human relations.

In these studies, it seems clear that the why, the how, and the what of our educational enterprise were all addressing the same question—how to achieve the most effective, that is, just and fruitful, relationship between the individual and society. And in so doing, these studies both reflected directly the philosophical tension underlying their design and demonstrated emphatically the profound and mutually supportive relationship between individual and social development.

It is of course no accident, as I reflect on the directions these studies took, on the processes we adopted and on the questions we pursued, that although I have little question about the ways in which the individual development of students will serve to promote the social good and about the ways in which their experience and inquiry in relation to community, social responsibility, and social reconstruction will contribute to their individual development, I am however, as a facilitator, left with the perennial question of how best to navigate and to balance needs and interests of the group and of individuals and how best to tap the mutually supportive relationship of the individual and the group. I ponder still, for example, the gains and losses of providing in the second semester of "Alternatives in Education" for more individual exploration and presentation of topics of interest, a decision that the group made that did support individuals' pursuit of their own interests and that did, through presentations, broaden the group's exposure to various schools of thought and approaches to education but that also, inevitably, cut into the group's shared work. To my mind, this remains a central tension in effective and meaningful teaching and learning. It is a tension that never goes away. The good news, though, is that in making that tension visible, in making explicit how it plays out—in the processes, content, and outcomes of the study—we do advance our understanding.

Again, it all comes around. Education must foster individual development. Education must promote a just society and the ongoing reconstruction of that society. And, in both theory and practice, education must strive toward understanding and support of the integral relationship of those aims. Each is necessary to the other and each fosters the development of the other.

References

Dewey, J. 1916, 1966. *Democracy and Education*. New York: Macmillan Publishing Company, Inc.

Dewey, J. 1938. *Experience and Education*. London: Collier-Macmillan.

Holt, J. 1976. *Instead of Education*. Boston: Holt Associates.

Jacoby, R. 1975. *Social Amnesia*. Boston: Beacon Press.

James, W. 1950. *Principles of Psychology*. New York: Dover Publications.

Laing, R.D. 1971. *Self and Others*. Baltimore: Penguin Books.

Lynd, H.M. 1958. *On Shame and the Search for Identity*. New York: John Wiley and Sons, Inc.

Meade, G.H. 1934. *Mind, Self, and Society*. Chicago: University of Chicago Press.

Rogers, C. 1961. *On Becoming a Person*. Boston: Houghton Mifflin Company.

NINE

Learning to Teach as We Were Not Taught: Democratic Teacher Education at Goddard College

Kenneth L. Bergstrom

Introduction

Democracy is a great word, whose history I suppose remains unwritten because that history is yet to be enacted.

—Walt Whitman

During a brief exchange a few years ago with my thirteen-year-old daughter about possible career choices, I asked if she would ever consider teaching. She responded, "Probably not, but I think about it sometimes." Ever the keen teacher inquirer, I saw an opportunity here to learn more and I pursued the obvious question. "When do you consider it?" I asked. She replied, "When I see teachers doing things to kids that are not okay and I think to myself, 'I could do better than that.'" I was a bit surprised, but I should not have been. Teaching at a college that nurtures and builds upon the resistance of students to much of their earlier educational experience, I have seen this phenomenon frequently: A strong desire to teach better than one has been taught. This notion of resistance— an inclination to trust one's inner self at some level, even when challenged with accepted practice, is embedded within every good teacher I know and is a gateway to the democratic reform of teacher education. How do we transform schools from control-centered institutions to places that cultivate liberating experience required for democratic living? Our schools will not change until our teaching changes; teaching will not change until teachers confront the challenge of learning to teach as we were not taught.

We often describe our teacher education program at Goddard as "learning to teach as we were not taught." By that we mean we intend to help our students go back into their own educational experiences and "mine" them, not only for the lessons of how they may have been taught ineffectively, but also for a critical foundation of how they might do it differently. Most of our students come to Goddard to actively seek an alternative form of education, often because they were so poorly served by their own schooling. They experienced a form of education in which teaching did not correspond well to their mode of learning. Those who decide to teach have at least the beginnings of a critique of what is not okay in education today. Some already have a strong vision of how to do it better. Very few have yet cultivated the set of skills, knowledge, and dispositions that could help us to move from our current system to a more democratic one.

If, as suggested in the introductory chapter to this book, democracy is both a means with instrumental value and a moral ideal that stretches beyond clear definition, then what is the task of democratic teacher education? How does Goddard College attempt to structure its teacher education program to mold democratic educators who can educate for democracy?

In light of Whitman's epigraph at the beginning of this chapter, this question seems more pertinent than ever. What should be the goals and processes of democratic teacher education at this time? A primary part of our program design focuses on the role of the teacher—the one closest to the learners. It is the human beings who practice and reshape their concept of teaching that must be at the heart of this conversation.

This essay intends to examine the multilayered role of teacher as described in Goddard College's teacher education program philosophy statement (italicized text) within the greater context of democratic education. With these articulations of reconstructed domains of teacherhood, and the examples I offer, I hope to provoke some thought, stimulate some discussion, generate some reactions, and perhaps reinvigorate the debate about democratic teacher education. The discussion will proceed to coincide with the figure (see Figure 1, p. 226) that was developed in 1992 in our most recent reconceptualization of the program and that is prominently displayed in our teacher education handbook. This discussion will not describe in detail the program's structure; it will focus primarily on the teacher-focused conceptual underpinnings which are used to guide it. In closing I will look at some of the problems and dilemmas we still encounter in our program and that still remain to be addressed.

Teacher as Person

We teach who we are. Children learn from what we do, not from what we say. Research on the prerequisites of an effective helping relationship, one that can lead to self-directed growth on the part of the learner, indicates that authenticity and congruence on the part of the teacher are essential ingredients (Hunt, 1971; Ginott, 1976, 1993; Rogers, 1978; Carkhuff, 1983). Teaching is a helping relationship that requires that teachers know themselves, their strengths and weaknesses, their values and dispositions, and that they act in ways that are consistent with those values and beliefs. They must be aware of their biases and prejudices and work to not let those attitudes affect their work with their students (Nieto, 1992). Teachers must be clear about the needs they are filling through teaching, and be careful to maintain clear boundaries between their needs and the needs of those in their care. Teachers should be people of integrity and fine moral character, with high self-esteem and deep self-knowledge (Jersild, 1955; Hunt, 1987, 1992; Lickona, 1992). For all these reasons, ongoing introspection, reflection, and personal growth are essential components of any teacher education program.

Teacher as person is one of the two primary pillars of Goddard's teacher education program. Before they are accepted into the program, students are questioned about their "calling" to teach. We look for a certain expressed passion related in a story or an anecdote that tells us that a student has come to this vocation for reasons that can be found within, not just because the student desires a socially acceptable role. Once they are admitted, we encourage students to examine those qualities that make a good teacher and to develop them in a way that is consistent with who they are. This is learning to teach from the inside out. Too many teachers "burn out" from trying to teach in a way that is incongruent with who they are personally. Progressive education is based, in part, on a strong relationship between the teacher and the student; education is, at its core, people business. To be the most human, one must first be oneself, not some iteration of what others think a teacher needs to be.

Beyond what we teach and how we teach it, kids always learn who we are and what we believe. In this age of uncertainty, kids are looking for more than algebra and the causes of the War of 1812; they are seeking who they are and where they fit in the world. Teachers who are not intimately familiar with themselves and their core beliefs are not equipped to help students struggle appropriately with their concerns. We ask our teachers to use narrative and autobiography to search for the roots of their calling to teach and to come to a deeper understanding of those events and critical incidents that have led them to this work.

We are not suggesting that all teachers commit to intense psychotherapy or that we immediately disclose our life histories in the classroom. We do think that one way to improve our teaching is to recognize the unspoken lessons that kids learn from us and begin an intense examination of how we teach who we are. Teacher educators need to provide for teachers to critique their own schooling, to become reacquainted with their reasons for this career choice, to explore these more elusive dimensions of teaching, and to consolidate their practice into a pedagogy based in personal beliefs.

I spoke a few years ago with the assistant principal of a school to which one of my off campus students had applied to student teach. He told me that he was familiar with students from other alternative teacher preparation programs like ours. He said, "They don't always have the technical skills to begin in the classroom, and they often struggle for the first couple of years. But in the long run, they are clear about why they are teaching and they eventually make better teachers." Helping teachers to understand the moral dimensions of their work is paramount if we are to change practice. The call to teach has an ethical aspect. It is not merely a reaction to one's own schooling, but also a commitment to discover how to do it better.

Through a guided process of introspection, students seek input from others––mentors, supervisors, parents, advisors, and students—on who they are as teachers, inside and outside of the classroom. They are asked to reflect on this feedback in a written form that is usually a personal philosophy of education, a self-assessment of one's teaching qualities. Just as personal integrity is one of the fundamental concepts of democratic living, so also knowing oneself is one of the basic tasks of the democratic teacher. To listen to the "rhythm within" is to stay whole and human among the cacophony of superficial trends of educational reform and to remember the reason one was called to teach.

Teacher as Inquirer

Increasingly, the focus of teacher education is moving away from a "technocratic" orientation, with its emphasis on techniques and methods (Kliebard, 1975) toward an interest in helping pre-service teachers become "reflective practitioners." This movement recognizes the complexities of the teaching profession, and the importance of educating (as opposed to training) teachers to be critical thinkers and knowledgeable problem-solvers (Elliot & Ebbutt, 1986; Valli, 1992). A inquiry-based approach to teacher education acknowledge John Dewey's notion of reflective practice as well as the more contemporary ideas of theorists such as Donald Schon (1983, 1987), with his interest in the artistry of teaching and context-specific knowledge.

As professional researchers acknowledge the practical wisdom of practicing classroom teachers, teachers are increasingly urged to engage in collaborative research toward the improvement of school curriculum, instruction and governance (Nixon, 1981; Hopkins, 1985; Elliot, 1988; Goswami & Stillman, 1987; Clift & Pugach, 1990). This expanded view of teaching requires teachers who understand the context and content of the social realities of teaching, the complexities of the culture of the school, and the problematic nature of the school change process (Lieberman, 1992).

At Goddard, we believe that the construction of "teacher knowledge" occurs within the larger framework of a broad liberal arts education, in which pre-service teachers are encouraged to research questions of personal significance, think critically about a wide range of contemporary social issues, and to develop the interest in, and skills relevant to lifelong learning.

Teachers must have a broad range of knowledge that they can share with their students, but most important, they must know how to learn. They must have experiences as active learners who know how to ask questions and to find answers using a variety of methods and forms of inquiry. It is teachers who are active, curious and excited learners who can best help students to become engaged in the learning process. In that sense, studies in the liberal arts at Goddard are not seen as separate from studies in teacher education but as an integral part of those studies.

There is certainly a trend in teacher education that suggests that teachers who know something—those who have majored in the liberal arts or in the sciences—are better teachers. Although this may or may not be the case, it is not a safe assumption unless we ask our students to show how their learning in other areas improves their teaching practice. Although we do not have "majors" at Goddard, students here are encouraged to develop depth and breadth in their studies. In the teacher education program, students are required to show the State of Vermont 30 credit hours of study that is equivalent to 30 credit hours of study in a major field. However, we go further; we ask our students to present this area of concentration, to label it as they understand it, and then to speak to how this "major" has prepared them for what they will teach in terms of content, and more intriguingly, how this "way of knowing" contributes to the process of teaching and learning they will facilitate in the classroom.

A few examples could help illustrate this dimension of the teacher as inquirer. Students have construed areas of concentration that befit their teaching practice in a number of ways. Brian's concentration of "conflict studies" was an appropriately articulated match for his teaching of secondary social studies. Mary's focus on "women and art" extrapolated the importance of nurturing relationships for creative self-expression as a sound foundation for teaching at the elementary level. One of our students, disconcerted by the state requirement of a liberal arts or science major, had a degree in landscape architecture from a prestigious university. While she could find a number of art and ecology courses within that degree to satisfy the requirement, she also chose to argue how the process of learning in that program itself, and its content focus on ecological design, was a very appropriate preparation for teaching elementary-aged children.

So it is not the isolated learning in other areas that makes a teacher competent—not the discipline itself—but rather how teachers conceptualize this "way of learning" to enhance their teaching practice. In this way, our students are expected to bring their own interests and passion for learning into the classroom as enthusiastic inquirers. If we want our children to expand upon their natural curiosities, we must model how one continues to do this throughout his or her life. We need teachers who are learners first and foremost.

To this end, we emphasize constant reflection upon one's preparation to teach and upon one's ultimate practice. It is not enough to think about what one is doing; one must also consider why it needs to be done. The zoom lens analogy is useful here. A good teacher must develop the ability to be in the moment and out of it at the same time—reflection in action and reflection on action. The learning within a particular situation also needs to be seen and considered from a distance. It is through this dual focus that one really becomes conscious of the depth of learning and one's role in it. Students are asked to journal in a detailed way about one incident per day—the most prominent event in they recall—in a way that objectively describes what happened, interprets possible motivations of those involved and other possible perceptions, and finally evaluates the learning for what is to be added to one's teaching persona. At the end of a practicum, students who trust this process find that they have addressed with equal fervor, three aspects of teaching: 1) What am I learning about the students and how they learn? 2) What am I learning about teaching and the choices I make to form my practice? and 3) What am I learning about the profession of teaching and the culture of schooling? Our students learn that self-study is one ongoing part of teaching.

Many of our students also become acquainted with collaborative action research. When teachers see their classrooms as laboratories for teacher, as well as student, learning, their are great opportunities for growth. There is a vital link between the growth and development of teachers and the growth and development of their students. To be a learner first is the purpose of this dimension of our teacher education program. Ongoing study of oneself, of the learners whom one serves, and of the profession are emphasized goals of our program. Democratic learning requires continuous self-study that generates information for ongoing renewal.

Teacher as Counselor

We believe that the facilitation of significant learning in teaching and counseling are based on the same factors: creating a relationship in which students can experience empathic listening, unconditional positive regard, and the freedom to pursue questions that really matter to them (Rogers, 1990). Basic counseling skills of active and reflective listening, keen observation of non-verbal as well as verbal behavior, the ability to understand a student's world from the student's perspective, and the ability to facilitate positive and respectful relationships among students, are all needed by teachers if they are to be able to create this sort of learning climate. Beginning teachers should therefore include in their teacher preparation work-studies in listening and observation skills, in basic counseling techniques, in the dynamics of human relationships, and in conflict resolution and mediation.

In the wake of the recent rash of school shootings, Secretary of Education Richard Riley has called for every child to be known well by at least one adult in each school. The isolating and overbearing emphasis on the teaching of content has often outweighed the more affective purposes of schooling. To have a trusted adult advisor for each and every student seems to be the least that we can do. Teachers, following that prescribed focus on content, have often resisted the call to become counselors, stating their lack of preparation for that role. Within this resistance lies the notion that perhaps it was easier to teach in a former time—that the home, church, and community used to do a better job at this part of a child's rearing.

Goddard's program does not discount this complaint, but prefers to acknowledge the realities of current life that demand that teachers pay more personal attention to parts of students' lives beyond the academic realm. Our teacher candidates are encouraged to see students in their familial and community contexts—to get to know them as real people with real lives. To do this, teachers must have the skills to "negotiate the personal," to invite students to bring all of their realities into the classroom. Teachers cannot and should not be expected to fix everything in a student's life, but just being able to offer some genuine empathy is often enough to help. Active listening and genuine positive regard are essential skills in teaching today.

Our students' journal entries are filled with accounts of how they learned to "negotiate the personal" with their students. Shaun, who was working in a third grade classroom, considered a new way to deal with a sullen, angry, uncooperative boy in her class. She asked and received permission to readdress a punishment that had been handed down to this youngster because she sensed an opportunity to reach this child in another way. Using the contract form in Kreidler's book *Creative Conflict Resolution* (1984) she and the child jointly developed an alternative agreement that released him from the punishment in exchange for his future cooperation. This was the beginning of an empowering relationship and a transformation for this child. Shaun's ability to recognize an opportunity for affective development and to apply the skills to take advantage of it provided a chance to sustain a child's academic and emotional growth.

Teaching, after all, is a helping profession. Teachers must know the fundamentals of counseling, conflict resolution, and crisis management because our current culture demands it. Basic physical needs, as well as safety and belonging needs, must be met before we can reasonably expect children to learn. It is not enough to feel empathic (although this is a good beginning) to understand the context for our students' lives. Democracy is about acting compassionately on that understanding when problems arise, or, when possible, before they arise.

Teacher as Guide

In order to be an effective guide for students, a teacher must know the travelers and the territory. This means that educators must have an understanding of human development, of the subject matter or problems to be studied, and of the curriculum, which emerges as the intermediary between the two (Dewey, 1938).

To understand how a child develops, how a child grows and learns, and to understand that this development depends upon the child's own activity, calls for a study of developmental psychology (Piaget, 1954). By studying the range of normal development, sexual, physical, cognitive, emotional, social, moral (Kohlberg & Lickona, 1986) and spiritual (Kessler, 1990), the teacher can gain a comprehensive understanding of each child both alone and in relation to others. The teacher can also recognize what is outside of that range of normal development, and be able to provide specific help to meet the special needs of every child.

Teachers must also understand students within the context of their families and communities. This requires a sensitivity to the variety of economic (Kozol, 1991) and cultural (Banks, 1988; Grant & Sleeter, 1989; Sleeter, 1990; Nieto, 1992) influences which affect each students' life. Teachers should use sensitivity to foster collaborative relationships between the school, home, and community and to guide responsible curriculum development.

These understandings of student growth and context should give the teacher a clear sense of the difference between integrative learning, which is based on continuity and connection, and training or habit learning (Holt, 1995). Training can help children acquire practical skills to support other learning goals, but should be recognized as tools, subordinate to integrative learning, which in a real sense, is development itself. The ability to design integrated curriculum depends on these developmental and contextual underpinnings and rest primarily with the teacher (Connelly & Clandinin, 1988), not textbooks.

The teacher as guide must also be very familiar with the territory to be explored, and must therefore have broad and deep knowledge in the liberal arts and sciences, understand how knowledge is constructed within each field, how to conduct appropriate investigations and inquiries, and also how the various disciplines are connected. The teacher as guide must also be aware of key resources within their field(s) of expertise and how to help students find and use those resources.

At a recent teacher conference, the presenter asked how many in the audience had ever had a course in curriculum in their undergraduate teacher preparation. The low number of hands that were raised was astounding. A few more hands were raised when the presenter asked the audience how many of them had sought their preparation at the graduate level, but not many. We have a history in education of assuming that knowledge of curriculum is much too important to put it in the hands of teachers. It is better left to those who know better: the professors of education and the school administrators. At Goddard we believe that teachers—those closest to the learners—need to be well versed in curriculum theory.

At Goddard, we try to show the reality that no one has a firm grasp on the elusive concept of curriculum, and by doing so, we expose the politics of curriculum theory, i.e. who decides what the curriculum will be. We ask our students to become intimately involved with the learning process of the students they will teach through countless hours of observation and follow-up interviews with students. What do students see as the curriculum in their lives? What seems to be worth learning through, the eyes of a six-year-old? How can teachers build upon these students' perceptions of curriculum?

And as our students come to see learning through children's eyes, they begin to unravel the political layering of curricular concerns. The focus on learning over teaching helps them to develop a critical view of textbooks, prepackaged and published curricular materials, and their own teacher-developed lessons. Our prospective teachers learn that they will scrutinize educational materials differently depending upon the group of children they will serve. They look to see how the questions of their students might be served by someone else's conception of important material. They also seek the appropriate fit between the ever-increasing demands of standards-based curriculum and the concerns of their own students. To successfully negotiate the external curricular demands imposed upon teachers, they must be able to understand them with their students' minds.

Many of the culminating projects of Goddard students' endeavors meet the formal curriculum through student-responsive work. Susan, a Spanish teacher, was seeking to develop a curriculum for her Spanish IV class that would facilitate the learning of the Spanish-speaking culture. Through extensive reading on curriculum negotiation and action research, she and her students developed a project-based format that allowed for learner choice and the responsibility to share these projects, in an accessible form of the language, with other Spanish classes. Coming to understand learners as producers, not just consumers, of knowledge is a very empowering shift of mind for all involved.

This leads our students naturally to other epistemological concerns and to a propensity to develop a more integrative view of learning. When teachers understand students within their context, study how they learn best, realize the questions they have about themselves and their world, they see curricular concepts as more organic and less reducible to a list of knowledge and skills. Integrative learning requires teachers to share control of the curriculum with their students, to watch for the questions that emerge regardless of the disciplinary boundaries that may be in place, and to stay open to the possibility of that learning taking on a life of its own.

We do not show our students how to write lesson or unit plans because an emergent curriculum of this sort is hard to prescribe. We do ask our students to offer a rationale for their lesson planning that accounts for this organic nature, to suggest a way to track the process of the study at hand, and to reflect daily on the issues that arise for students. One of our teacher candidates even developed a process for her middle grade students to map the progress of their integrated unit on "relationships." To plan as well as any teacher is a fundamental goal, but only so that the planning can free one up to the possibilities of what might happen through the learning process. When a teacher always ends up teaching to the plan, there is a lack of responsiveness and integration to that mode of teaching.

Democratic forms of curriculum are responsive, contextual, integrative, and organic. Teacher as guide helps students develop this understanding.

Teacher as Facilitator

Equipped with a clear sense of purpose, an understanding of how children learn and grow, and the context in which they live, teachers must seek answers to the various pedagogical questions—the "how tos" of teaching. Teachers are no longer the source of information as much as they are facilitators of learning.

Skilled teachers design and refine responsive instruction. They understand how to tailor learning tasks to students' learning styles and preferences (Gardner, 1983; Lazear, 1991; Dunn & Dunn, 1992; Campbell, 1994). They make learning whole by showing and allowing students to make connections beyond subject boundaries (Hopkins, 1937) and welcome opportunities to negotiate study with their students (Boomer et al., 1992) because they understand that empowered learners are responsible learners (Wigginton, 1986). They make keen use of resources including the students themselves by creating opportunities for cooperative learning (Johnson & Johnson, 1975) and by fostering communities for learning (Short & Burke, 1991). And they know that creative assessment is an ongoing part of the learning process; they help their students critique, evaluate, and respond to their learning (Carini, 1987; Wiggins, 1995).

The teacher facilitator domain is the one most practiced by more traditional teacher education programs, sometimes at the expense of some of the more foundational concerns that we emphasize at Goddard. What are the strategies and techniques to be used in actual practice? We do not reject the notion of teacher as technician, because certainly teachers do use techniques. But if a teacher does so blindly without a more thorough knowledge of why a certain practice is chosen for a particular situation, then technical teaching can be dangerous. Certainly skills are not the only part of a good teacher's practice, but without them one will never be a good teacher.

Goddard's program is sometimes justifiably criticized for its emphasis on philosophical, political, and social foundations over its focus on pedagogical skill. In a program of limited duration, we make this choice knowing that our students, well-grounded in those foundations, can walk into any classroom, observe with no knowledge of a technique a teacher may be using, and decide why that approach is being used, what philosophical proclivities that teacher has, and whether or not this is a worthy technique to adopt or adapt in one's own practice.

For example, it is important for a teacher to have some idea of what approach to use in issues of classroom management. (My colleague, reluctant to use a control metaphor, coined the phrase "classroom choreography.") We expect our students to know the entire array of disciplinary approaches. One's preferred style as a teacher may simply not be what a student needs at any given moment. We expect our students to know the assumptions behind each approach and to be flexible and thoughtful enough to apply what is needed at the proper time.

Likewise, we encourage our prospective teachers to explore pedagogy that empowers their students. This is one of the fundamental tenets of democracy— to empower others to self-govern. Our pedagogical emphases lie in learning styles, multiple intelligences, curriculum negotiation, cooperative learning, the creation of learning communities, and authentic assessment. When students become knowledgeable about how they learn, they can become confident in their abilities—finding their own voice. This voice can then be used to exercise curricular choices in a negotiation process with the teacher and with other learners. When they exercise their voice and hear others exercise theirs, students become aware of the diversity of learning approaches and aptitudes within one setting. It is in this realization, and in the subsequent cooperation and negotiation that follows, that students build a learning community whose members can think together and debate respectfully. They begin a genuine search to accommodate those learning differences and support one another to find real learning opportunities. Performance assessment is a reality in our public schools, but teachers who have developed an empowering pedagogy look for ways to make that learning even more real—to find ways to apply it in real life. Instead of a simulation on how to run a business, the class initiates a real business and works to make a profit for a worthy cause they have collectively selected.

There is a significant difference between the image evoked by the word "grade" (from Latin *gradus* meaning step) and the word "assess" (from Latin *assistere* meaning to sit beside). Our teachers learn how to assess because they have experienced advisors who do not grade but who "sit beside" and discuss the value of one's learning. Advisors do not write an evaluation until the student has done so. Through this modeling our students learn the importance of self-evaluation; they take that practice into the classroom with them. These teachers encourage their students, through thoughtful consideration of their learning documentation, to make judgments about their learning with feedback from parents, peers, and others, and to set renewable learning goals.

One can learn the technical aspects of teaching much more readily than the moral dimensions of this profession. Although it is unacceptable to send beginning teachers with underdeveloped skills into the classroom to facilitate and guide student learning, it is even more abhorrent to have teachers engage in practices about which they have little depth of understanding. Each strategy a teacher adopts needs to be examined for its assumptions and questioned about its consequences. To do less would be unwise and unhealthy. Teachers must not acquire practice as a collection of tools that are passed from the teacher educator to the student. Rather, prospective teachers need to selectively embrace those strategies (or parts of them) that are consistent with their beliefs about learning and their call to teach. We, as teacher educators, need to invite students to discover techniques that are congruent with who they are.

Teacher as Colleague

As schools change and the roles of educators change, it becomes increasingly important for teachers to learn to build a collaborative culture (Saphier & King, 1985; Lieberman & Miller, 1991). Collegiality is more than getting along; it means joining with other teachers to talk about practice, observe one another, work on curriculum, and teach each other (Barth, 1990; Little, 1982). This contradicts the traditional "egg-crate" model of teacher isolation, which supported fragmented individualism, balkanization, and contrived forms of collegiality (Hargreaves).

Learning to work in teams (Thousand & Villa, 1996) and developing excellent group skills (Johnson & Johnson, 1987) are now essential requirements for teachers. To create a sense of community in schools teachers must be willing and able to extend beyond the classroom to work cooperatively not only with other teachers, but also with administrators, parents, community members, and students (Fullan & Hargreaves, 1991).

Learning to teach as we were not taught means rejecting the old egg-crate model of schooling by which each cell operated independently of another. This was not only unhealthy for students who often were left with a fragmented and disconnected experience as they moved from class to class, but it also left teachers alone to reflect on their individual struggles.

At Goddard we use group advising to illustrate to students how helpful the clarifying comments and questions from peers might be. Our students learn how to carefully and sensitively critique each other's work and to positively apply that feedback to the construction of their own learning goals and products. It has been our experience over the years that teacher candidates should seek out a classroom for their practicum whose teacher has a good philosophical match to the tenets of progressive education that we espouse at Goddard. But it has become equally important that there be a good personal match as well, not just for the sake of congeniality, but because collegiality demands a certain level of honesty in a relationship. This is much easier to do with someone who is liked and respected on a personal level than with someone who might only share a philosophy.

Our students are also encouraged to consider who ought to be the teacher's colleague and what one might expect from such collegial relationships. When possible, students are placed in team-teaching situations, so that they can not only observe firsthand the dynamics of collaborative teaching, but also so that they might benefit from the team expectations that foster collaboration. We look for resources that build bridges between parents and their teachers, so that our students understand the powerful dynamic when parents and teachers work together in an equal relationship. We even ask that our teacher candidates consider students as colleagues—as a source of worthy, insightful feedback on their teaching practice. Finally, there is a need for teachers who understand their role beyond the classroom to work to advocate for their charges and their families in community settings. Democratic teaching reaches out to involve everyone as an equal partner in the education of the community's children.

Teacher as Citizen

Today's teacher must prepare students for a rapidly changing, complex, and increasingly interdependent world. The notion of citizenship must expand to encompass local, nationa,l and global concerns. A teacher, as a citizen, must have a broad understanding of how social, economic, and political structures affect educational policy (Apple, 1990; Grundy, 1987; Giroux, 1991; Stanley, 1992), as well as the ability to educate students to think critically about these and other issues (Goodman, 1992). Teachers need to understand and be able to communicate clearly about problems connected with social class differences and their effects on the classroom (Anyon, 1980; Coclough & Beck, 1986; Weis & Fine, 1993), about gender inequalities (Gilligan, 1982; Ellsworth, 1980; Belenky et al., 1986; Weiler, 1987; Weis & Fine, 1993), about poverty and economic deprivation (Edelman, 1991; Kozol, 1991), about racism (Ogbu, 1978, Grant & Sleeter, 1989; Nieto, 1992; Weis & Fine, 1993), about social injustice (Giroux, 1991; Friere, 1985; Bastian, 1986; Brameld, 1970). Closely aligned to these concerns are issues of freedom and authority in schools, the uses and abuses of testing and evaluation, and the problems inherent in tracking and labeling.

The understanding of these pressing social issues requires the study of philosophy (through which a teacher learns to ask significant questions), some knowledge of social theory, and the study of the history of educational ideas. The teachers must also understand the complex relationship of the school to the community and of schooling to society (Selakovich, 1973). It is important for teachers to develop a moral vision of the educational endeavor (Purpel, 1988), and to become active supporters of children's rights and active agents in improving the quality of life in schools for the young people whom schools serve.

In addition, teachers must understand the importance of modeling responsible civic behavior—demonstrating ecological awareness and appropriate environmental attitudes and behavior (Bowers, 1990,1992), active participation in civic life (Aronowitz & Giroux, 1985), respect and value for human diversity, a cooperative approach to problem-solving and service to the community.

The teacher as citizen must have a clear sense of his or her own purposes, informed by the study of the history and philosophy of education, contextualized by an understanding of the dynamics of human development and the processes through which children learn, and tempered by one's interpretation of the appropriate relationship of schooling to society.

Teacher as citizen is the second pillar of Goddard's teacher education program. This teaching dimension, counterbalanced by the focus on personal integration, seeks to develop social responsibility in one's practice. We have little evidence that education, as a social institution, does much more than reflect and perpetuate society's current values. But we at Goddard are engaged in teacher education because we believe that education should make the world a better place.

We insist that our students know the historical roots of progressive and holistic education and become aware of the inherent advantages as well as the weaknesses and past failures of this approach. We ask our students to become aware of reform initiatives on a national and local level and to become involved in these efforts as community members, prospective teachers, parents, or in other roles. The best way to distinguish between change and progress is to get involved in an educational effort and to study the dynamics of that endeavor. To bring one's personal morality to bear on school-wide reform efforts is to exercise one's democratic responsibility. Many of our students participate actively in school reform initiatives beyond the scope of classroom practice, including community projects, parent programs, and school-wide programs.

Responsibility is literally the ability to respond. Another way to respond is to use one's curricular authority to teach democratic content such as peace, justice, equality, ecological sustainability, and cultural diversity. Now, in a system of public schooling, which seems to strive more for perceived stability and pretends to perpetuate a moral neutrality, this is no smooth path to follow. And some of our students are so busy learning the way things are that they have little time to enact a vision of what could be. But being responsible means stepping up—calling on one's personal integrity—to find ways to effectively challenge some of the evils of institutionalized learning and the poisonous pedagogy that sometimes passes for teaching in the halls of our public schools.

To do this our students need the support of an ongoing community of radical educators who are thoughtfully and sensitively discussing such issues as: How do we teach potentially controversial material? When and how is personal disclosure a useful teaching technique? How can we help our students raise critical issues in ways that also teach? And how we can help our students find their own voices and become informed critics and reshapers of the school system in which they participate?

Tom, a secondary social studies teacher, developed a unit to teach the nature and history of oppression through the musical traditions of African Americans, Native Americans, and the American labor movement. His students wrote modern day versions of these songs and performed them for classmates and parents. Kelly's middle grade students directly took up the question of what democratic education might actually look like in practice. They created lists of qualities that they used to evaluate their own classroom structure and practice. Other students have developed and taught topics such as media literacy, waste management, and human rights.

These are not easy tasks for new teachers to tackle. We prepare our students for this endeavor by modeling critical analysis in our studies with them. By posing probing questions about how things are currently done and seeking the underlying reasons for this mode of operation, we help our students learn to see the political realities of teaching. This realization allows them to build what practical form their social responsibility will take inside and outside of the classroom. We expect that because they become socially responsible educators with knowledge of the history and philosophy of progressive education, our students might be so bold as to consciously make their own historically significant footprints. Thus, democratic education has the ability to recreate itself in self-renewing forms.

Afterthoughts

Our program, always under construction, is not without its dilemmas and problems. Let me note a few of these that flow from the previous discussion. First, most students seem to be attracted to Goddard for the opportunity to construct their own program of study—to meet the required competencies in flexible meaningful ways. The chance to develop one's individuality through independent study initially takes precedence over the need to build community. Teacher as person is more readily addressed than teacher as citizen. It takes time for some students to see the synergistic relationship between personal integrity and social responsibility. Also, related to this problem, we often find it difficult to help students situate themselves in truly collegial settings for their internships. Teacher as colleague is not an established norm of the profession and a neophyte hardly has the influence to change this reality. How do we teach the benefits of collegiality when it is not readily available within our school culture?

Another problem we face as we send our teachers into schools is how to help them rearrange the often bland, pablum-like content so prevalent in schools. The attempts to neutralize any potential for spirited discourse usually reign. But democracy demands a free and open moral debate on issues of concern to people. How we encourage this level of moral and political discourse in schools by our prospective teachers continues as a focus of our preparation.

Finally, as an alternative program, we have chosen to counterbalance the technical form of teacher education with a contextual one that is grounded in the philosophical and social foundations of education. We continue to search for effective ways to help our students realize their own pedagogical approach within a system that often prefers a "teacher-proof" curriculum. How we lead prospective students to discover and apply the necessary skills in ways that are consistent with a larger understanding of what education might become within a democracy remains our most compelling challenge.

These domains of one's teaching persona constitute the organization of our teacher education program. They set forth the values that we believe a teacher needs to cultivate to be a caring, inspired leader in a democratic society. They guide our students in their choice of resources through which they will develop these domains. They organize the expectations for student documentation of teaching competence. But most of all, they serve as a platform for our ongoing conversation about what democratic teaching must be for a society that must get on with its mission to renew its commitment to compassionate possibilities.

Figure 1
LEARNING AND TEACHING THROUGH INQUIRY, ACTION, AND REFLECTION
Education for Personal Development, Interpersonal Competence, and Social Responsibility

	DOMAIN	KNOWLEDGE (Knowing)	SKILLS (Doing)	QUALITIES
S E L F	Teacher as Person	Self-knowledge Strengths and weaknesses Awareness of own biases Clarity of personal identity, values and moral commitments Awareness of personal needs being filled through teaching personal philosophy of teaching	Demonstrates authenticity and congruence in the classroom Models commitment to morals and values Maintains clarity about boundaries between teacher needs and student needs	Authentic Congruent
	Teacher as Inquirer	Liberal Arts Content and process of learning Awareness of how knowledge is constructed Understanding of the connection between disciplines	Asks and answers questions in various academic disciplines Conducts classroom research Reflects on experience Learns through inquiry and discovery Integrates disciplines and subjects	Curious
O T H E R S	Teacher as Counselor	Principles of counseling, active listening, and effective communication Organization and structure for teacher advisory programs Knowledge of issues in child and/or adolescent mental health, and family as a context for child development Understanding of principles of conflict resolution and mediation Awareness of group process	Uses counseling skills: active listening, crisis intervention, conflict resolution Creates safe and supportive group climate Communicates own ideas and feelings in an assertive, nonjudgmental way Communicate effectively with parents and community Fosters student awareness of and responsibility for personal health	Empathetic Caring Assertive
	Teacher as Facilitator	Human development and learning Learning Styles Age and Content appropriate methods and materials Principles of integrated curriculum, authentic assessment (including portfolios) Classroom organization, structure and dynamics Multicultural education Special needs Cooperative learning Technology in the classroom	Facilitates active, inquiry-based learning poses problems Structures learning environment Builds community in the classroom Plans and assesses curriculum units and daily learning experiences Helps students set own goals and self-evaluate Designs and structures developmentally appropriate learning experiences Assesses equity issues in the classroom	Dynamic Organized Facilitative Creative Flexible

			Selects and uses appropriate technology	
	Teacher as Guide	Knowledge and skill in specific academic content Awareness of resources	Shares information and understandings Leads students to appropriate resources	Confident Challenging Supportive Patient
	Teacher as Colleague	Principles of team-building, group process, and group support	Works with colleagues in collaborative planning, teaching, and assessment	Cooperative Collaborative
S O C I E T Y	Teacher as Citizen	Current Trends in educational change, and the dynamics of school restructuring How community and social contexts affect children and their families Critical analysis of the functions of schooling and its relations to our social system Social, historical, legal and ecological context of schooling Philosophy and goals of education Impact of social inequities on schooling process Awareness of social problems	Works for school improvements Advocates for students and families Relates teaching techniques to goals, philosophies, and social issues Works for equity and justice in school and society	Active Aware

References

Apple, M. W. 1990. *Ideology and the Curriculum.* London: Routledge.

Aronowitz, S. and H. Giroux. 1985. Education Under Siege: The Conservative, Liberal and Radical Debate Over Schooling. Boston: Bergin & Garvey.

Banks, J.A. 1988. *Multiethnic Education: Theory and Practice.* 2d. ed. Boston: Allyn & Bacon.

Barth, R.S. 1990. *Improving Schools from Within.* San Francisco: Jossey-Bass.

Bastian, A. 1986. *Choosing Equality: The Case for Democratic Schooling.* Philadelphia: Temple University Press.

Belenky, M., B.M. Clinchy, N.R. Goldberger, J.M. Tarule. 1986. *Women's Ways of Knowing: The Development of Self, Voice and Mind.* New York: Basic Books.

Anyon, J. 1980. "Social Class and the Hidden Curriculum of Work." *Journal of Education* 162 (1): 67-92.

Boomer, G., N. Lester, C. Onore, and J. Cook. 1992. *Negotiating the Curriculum: Educating for the 21st Century.* Washington, D.C.: Falmer.

Bowers, C.A. 1992. *Education, Cultural Myths and the Ecological Crisis.* New York: Teachers College Press.

———. 1990. *Responsive Teaching: An Ecological Approach to Classroom Patterns of Language, Culture, and Thought.* New York: Teachers College Press.

Brameld, T. 1970. *The Climactic Decades.* New York: Praeger.

Campbell, B. 1994. *The Multiple Intelligences Handbook: Lesson Plans and More.* Seattle: Campbell and Associates.

Carini, P.F. 1987. *On Value in Education.* Occasional paper, City College Workshop Center, New York.

Carkhuff, R.R. 1983. *The Art of Helping.* Amherst, Massachusetts: Human Resources Development Press.

———.1983. *Interpersonal Skills & Human Productivity.* Amherst, Massachusetts: Human Resources Development Press.

Clift, R. and M. Pugach. 1990. *Encouraging Reflective Practice in Education.* New York: Teachers College Press.

Colclough, G. and E.M. Beck. 1986. "The American Educational Structure and the Reproduction of Social Class." *Sociological Inquiry* 56 (4): 371-386.

Connelly, F.M. and D.J. Clandinin. 1988. *Teachers as Curriculum Planners: Narratives of Experience.* New York: Teachers College Press.

Dewey, J. 1938. *Experience and Education.* New York: Collier.

Dunn, R. and K. Dunn. 1992. *Bringing Out the Giftedness in Your Child: Nurturing Every Child's Unique Strengths, Talents, and Potential.* New York: John Wiley and Sons.

Edelman, P. 1991. *Adolescence and Poverty:Challenges for the 1990s.* Washington, D.C.: Center for National Policy Press.

Elliot, J. and D. Ebbut. eds. 1986. *Case Studies in Teaching for Understanding.* Cambridge, England: Cambridge Institute of Education.

Ellsworth, L. 1989. "Why Doesn't This Feel Empowering? Working through the Oppressive Myths of Critical Pedagogy. *Harvard Educational Review* 59 (3): 297-324.

Friere, P. 1985. *The Politics of Education.* Boston: Bergin & Garvey.

Fullan, M.G. and A. Hargreaves. 1991. *What's Worth Fighting For? Working Together for Your School.* Andover, Massachusetts: Regional Laboratory for Educational Improvement of the Northeast and Islands.

Gardner, H. 1983. *Frames of Mind: The Theory of Multiple Intelligences.* New York: Basic Books.

Gilligan, C. 1982. *In a Different Voice.* Cambridge: Harvard University Press.

Ginott, H.G. 1976. *Between Parent and Child.* New York: Avon Books.

———. 1993. *Teacher and Child.* New York: Macmillan.

Giroux, H.A.. and P. McClaren, P. eds. 1989. *Critical Pedagogy, the State, and Cultural Struggle.* Albany, New York: SUNY Press.

Giroux, H.A. Ed. 1991. *Postmodernism, Feminism and Cultural Politics: Redrawing Educational Boundaries.* Albany, New York: SUNY Press.

Goodman, J. 1992. *Elementary Schooling for Critical Democracy.* Albany, New York: SUNY Press.

Goswami, D. and P.R. Stillman. 1987. *Reclaiming the Classroom: Teacher Research as an Agency for Change.* Portsmouth, New Hampshire: Boynton Cook Publishers.

Grant, C. and C. Sleeter. 1989. *Turning on Learning: Five Approaches for Multicultural Teaching.* Columbus, Ohio: Merrill.

Grundy, S. 1987. *Curriculum: Product or Praxis.* London: Falmer Press.

Hargreaves, A. 1990. "Cultures of Teaching" in *Teachers' Lives* edited by I. Goodson and S. Ball. Boston: Routledge & Kegan Paul.

Holt, J. 1973. *How Children Learn.* New York: Delacorte Press

Hopkins, D. 1985. *A Teacher's Guide to Classroom Research.* Philadelphia: Open University Press.

Hopkins, L.T. 1937. *Integration: Its Meaning and Application.* New York: D. Appleton Century

Hunt, D.E. 1971. *Matching Models in Education: The Coordination of Teaching Methods with Student Characteristics.* Toronto: Ontario Institute for Studies in Education.

———.1987. *Beginning with Ourselves in Practice, Theory, and Human Affairs.* Cambridge, Massachusetts: Brookline Books.

———. 1992. *The Renewal of Personal Energy.* Toronto: The Ontario Institute for Studies in Education.

Jersild, A.T. 1955. When Teachers Face Themselves. New York: Teachers College Press.

Johnson, D. and R. Johnson. 1975. *Learning Together and Alone.* Englewood Cliffs, New Jersey: Prentice Hall.

Johnson, D. and F. Johnson. 1987. *Joining Together: Group Therapy and Group Skills.* Englewood Cliffs, New Jersey: Prentice Hall.

Kessler, S. 1990. "The Mysteries Program: Educating Adolescents for Today's World," *Holistic Education Review* 3.(4): 10-19.

Kliebard, H. 1975. "The Rise of Scientific Curriculum Making and Its Aftermath," *Curriculum Theory Network* 5. (1): 27-38.

Kohlberg, L. and T. Lickona. 1986. *The Stages of Ethical Development: From Childhood hrough Old Age.* San Francisco: Harper.

Kozol, J. 1991. *Savage Inequalities: Children in America's Schools.* New York: Crown Publishers.

Kreidler, W. 1984. *Creative Conflict Resolution.* Glenview, Illinois: Scott Foresman & Co.

Lazear, D. 1991. *Seven Ways of Knowing.* Palantine, Illinois: Skylight Publishing.

Lickona, T. 1992. *Educating for Character: How Our Schools Can Teach Respect and Responsibility.* New York: Bantam Doubleday Dell.

Lieberman, A. 1992. "The Meaning of Scholarly Activity and the Building of Community," *Educational Researcher* 21 (6): 5-12.

Lieberman, A. & Miller, L. eds. 1991. *Staff Development for Education in the 90's: New Demands, New Realities, New Perspectives.* New York: Teachers College Press.

Little, J.W. 1982. "Norms of Collegiality and Experimentation: Workplace Conditions for School Success," *American Educational Research Journal* 5 (19): 325-340.

Nieto, S. 1992. *Affirming Diversity.* New York: Longman.

Nixon, J. ed. 1981. *A Teacher's Guide to Action Research.* London: Grant McIntyre.

Ogbu, J. 1978. *Minority Education and Caste.* New York: Academic Press.

Piaget, J. 1954. *The Construction of Reality in the Child.* New York: Basic Books.

Purpel, D. 1988. *The Moral and Spiritual Crisis in Education: A Curriculum for Justice and Compassion in Education.* Boston: Bergin & Garvey.

Rogers, C.R. 1978. *On Personal Power.* New York: Dell.

———. 1995. *On Becoming a Person: A Therapist's View of Psychotherapy.* Boston: Houghton Mifflin.

Saphier, J. and R. Gower. 1997. *The Skillful Teacher: Building Your Teaching Skills.* Littleton, Massachusetts: Research for Better Teaching.

Saphier, J. and M. King. 1985. "Good Schools Grow in Strong Cultures," *Educational Leadership* 43 (7): 67-73.

Selakovich, D. 1973. *The Schools and American Society.* New York: John Wiley and Sons.

Short, K. and C. Burke. 1991. *Creating Curriculum: Teachers and Students as a Community of Learners.* Portsmouth, New Hampshire: Heinemann.

Sleeter, C. ed. 1990. *Empowerment through Multicultural Education: From Reproduction to Contestation of Social Equity through Schooling.* Albany, NY: SUNY Press.

Stanley, L. 1992. *The Autobiographical I: Theory and Practice in Feminist Autobiography.* Manchester, England: Manchester University Press.

Thousand, J. and R. Villa. 1996. *Creating an Inclusive School.* Alexandria, Virginia: Association for Supervision and Curriculum Development.

Valli, L. ed. 1992. *Reflection in Teacher Education: Cases and Critiques.* Albany, New York: SUNY Press.

Weiler, K. 1987. *Women Teaching for Change: Gender, Class, and Power.* Boston: Bergin & Garvey.

Weis, L. and M. Fine. 1993. *Beyond Silenced Voices: Class, Race & Gender in United States Schools.* Albany, New York: SUNY Press.

Whitman, W. 1982. *Complete Poetry and Collected Prose.* New York: Library of America.

Wigginton, E. 1986. *Sometimes a Shining Moment: The Foxfire Experience.* New York: Anchor Books.

Wiggins, G. 1993. *Assessing Student Performance: Exploring the Purpose and Limits of Testing.* San Francisco: Jossey-Bass.

TEN

Democratic Education:
Judy and the Dance*

Carl D. Glickman

* I wish to thank colleagues—students and faculty—at Goddard College and The University of Georgia for their insights and suggestions in shaping this manuscript.

Goddard College sits off a rural Vermont highway, up on a hill, near the small town of Plainfield. In 1994–1995 I accepted a visiting faculty appointment at the College to teach in the Master's Degree residency program, which involved working with twelve students for one year. This included two ten-day institutes—one in early summer, the other in January—and ongoing communication with each of the twelve students while they completed individual contracts leading to a Master's Degree in Teaching and/or professional certification. The final products of their work were a portfolio, a thesis, and a public exhibit of their learning. I was one of a team of seven faculty members—five in a visiting, part-time positions and two, full-time faculty who taught year-round in both the undergraduate and graduate program.

After twenty years of teaching at a large university, I was eager for this small community experience. I had friends at Goddard, my spouse's family was from Vermont, and for the past thirty years, I had spent every summer at family dwellings in the northern part of the state. Furthermore, I had been raised in New England and began my education career in small towns in Maine and New Hampshire. So returning to a small town and a small college in New England had obvious attractions. However, the greatest reason for me to be at Goddard was the reputation of the college as Deweyan in origin and as an embodiment of progressive education and community life.

That year, I took a partial leave from my own university—the University of Georgia—where I hold a special career appointment as University Professor of Education. Among my duties, I serve as Chair of the University's Program for School Improvement, which operates a nationally recognized collaboration with more than one hundred schools that are involved in the renewal of democratic education, the League of Professional Schools (see Glickman 1993). I took this partial leave to study the historical, political, legal, philosophical, and sociocultural connections between democracy and education. I hoped that teaching at Goddard would help me make concrete connections, provide me with ways of thinking about my own teaching, and suggest ways to improve teacher education programs at my own university. My spouse, Sara, who is an extraordinary public school teacher, took a leave with me and we planned the year to include visits to other universities, public schools, and educational organizations throughout the United States, Canada, Turkey, and Greece. As part of my leave, I returned to Georgia every six weeks for four weeks at a time to continue with collaboration with schools and with state and college policy work, to attend to the development of a new department, to complete essays for a forthcoming new book,[1] and generally to stay in touch with colleagues about other college and university matters.

The University of Georgia (UGA) is the oldest state university in the United States, chartered in 1785. It too is nestled up on a hill. But the similarities stop there. UGA is in the city of Athens, with a student population of about 30,000 students within a total city population of about 100,000. The College of Education is the second largest in the nation, consisting of 220 faculty members and several thousand undergraduate and graduate students. The town and the university are a thriving mix of academics, sports, art, music, and vibrant night life.

There are great differences between Goddard and UGA. Goddard is tiny in size (550 students), private, and has high tuition. Its academic programs provide an array of choices for students and the structure of its programs, core requirements, and grading systems are vastly different from most other colleges and universities. Goddard attracts mainly out-of-state students; the student and faculty bodies tend to be politically moderate to radical left with a sprinkling of a few independent conservatives. On the other hand, the University of Georgia is large, public, has very low or free tuition (state funds pay full scholarships for almost all entering students), and more than ninety percent of undergraduates and approximately fifty percent of graduates are from the state. The student body tends to be moderately conservative to moderately liberal and the faculty is moderately liberal. Athens is often cited as the most progressive town in Georgia with regard to music, art, and politics, and lifestyles. It attracts a substantial group of persons with counterculture ideologies. The majority of citizens voted for Jesse Jackson and the Rainbow Coalition in one of the past presidential elections and it has a two-term female mayor who won as the candidate of a progressive coalition of preservations, artists, and liberals. Because UGA and Athens are in the southern bible belt, they draw a diverse student body from all areas of the state; the UGA community includes a substantial number of conservative and religious persons with fundamentalist beliefs. The university is best characterized as a very good major public university with competitive admission requirements and a loyal following of alumni, friends, and legislators throughout the state. Its undergraduate academic preparation programs are mostly traditional with large introductory classes and a two-year requirement of core liberal arts for all students before they can major in a discipline or a professional field. Most undergraduate academic advising is done by staff members, not by faculty.

While Goddard is a small, private college with faculty who are hired to teach and advise students, UGA is a comprehensive, land grant, sea grant, research university where all education faculty are budgeted one-third time for research. The College of Education at UGA consistently ranks as one of the top national research institutions, measured by publications, research conducted, and grants received (ten to twelve million dollars a year in external grants). Promotion and continuing employment of faculty at Goddard are weighted toward developing excellent courses *with* students, providing personal advisement, and providing service and research to one's local community. Promotion and tenure at the University of Georgia also must include evidence of strong teaching but are weighted toward research, grants, and publications in national and international journals. This is not to say that Goddard faculty and students could not succeed at the University of Georgia or that UGA faculty and students could not succeed at Goddard, but student and faculty expectations are quite different. Goddard students expect and demand that faculty respond to their individual needs. UGA students expect that they will attend large classes, take required courses, and generally will not receive much individual faculty attention.

My Beginnings

Two days before the first residency at Goddard, visiting faculty arrived from different parts of the United States and Canada and we all met together with the two regular faculty for dinner at a local restaurant. Preparatory discussions continued the next day on the campus of Goddard. Because I was the only new visiting faculty member, the rest of the group reviewed for me procedures, requirements, advisement schedules, and short courses. We then finalized details for the upcoming ten days. I immediately felt comfortable in the discussions. The discussions were free of the personal tensions that I often experience in academic department meetings. (I later learned that this absence of tension was due in part to the ad hoc and temporary nature of the faculty group rather than the normal Goddard faculty interactions. The full-time academic faculty at Goddard were in the midst of intense personal and professional conflicts as a result of a controversial and divisive administration.) I was impressed with my Goddard colleagues—their experience, their care in reviewing student work, and their thoughtful dialogue. Any previous snobbery that I may have held that faculty at small, private, and non-highly-selective colleges are not of the same intellectual caliber of faculty at selective, research institutions was discarded immediately. I quickly came to the conclusion that my Goddard colleagues could clearly hold their own academically and intellectually in other institutions and were at Goddard by their own choice.

My own thinking about students, teaching, learning, and programs seemed to fit nicely with theirs. However, I did harbor private fears that I might not be up to the task of the "Goddard Mission" in my own teaching practice. At the University of Georgia, I have received honors for my teaching, yet, I did not know how well I could work with Goddard students who were not coming to learn from me, but were, instead, expecting me to adapt to what they wanted. At Georgia, I was known for using participatory methods and had learned such practices from some of the most acclaimed masters of progressive education.[2] I knew how to involve students in activities and assessments. But Goddard students would be different; they would expect such involvement as their right, not as part of a special situation. Frankly, I wasn't sure how to handle this. I anticipated uncomfortable times with Goddard students because I know, as a teacher, that I want the ultimate authority over student work. At UGA, I remind my students from time to time that what they want to do may not be the same as what they need to do. When UGA students are not taking their assignments, activities, and learning seriously, I have the traditional authority of the academy to back me up. I wasn't sure that in this new situation if "push came to shove" with students that such a student-centered institution as Goddard would provide a supportive climate for me to exert faculty authority. Goddard had few attendance policies, gave no letter grades, and had no required courses. Virtually all aspects of the program were negotiated between students and faculty. Readings, activities, and fulfillment of requirements were open to discussion and negotiation. I was concerned that I either might simply let students have more freedom than I thought desirable or I would restrict their choices more severely than other faculty and be perceived as a tyrant.

The residency commenced. It went nonstop, all days and most nights. Students would have a daily schedule consisting of a group meeting or individual conferences with me, two short courses with me and other faculty, and a selection of college-wide seminars, presentations, or special events given by faculty, students, or special guests. The previous year's graduating students were in attendance at the beginning of the residency to present their theses and everyone attended the graduation ceremony where every graduating student has a chance to speak. In addition to the activities that I have mentioned, a number of other academic, social, or recreational activities were added daily.

I was provided with an office (the graduate residency program occurs on campus when the regular undergraduate program is on break) and a dormitory room. I brought four cardboard file boxes full of books and reference materials from my office at UGA in anticipation of what students might find helpful. (Because I have a bad back and there are no elevators in Goddard's teaching facilities, once the materials were in place, they stayed!) We—faculty and students—had breakfast, lunch, and dinner together each day in the common dining hall. The last night of each residency was devoted to a talent show that was conducted by willing students and faculty. After nearly twenty years of an academic routine of pre-established times for office hours, set time for classes, and a strict separation of my professional and personal life, I found myself on a very different schedule. For the next ten days, students would become an integral aspect of almost every waking moment. Even when I might find time to be alone, I would be aware of students outside my door or on the same walking paths or waving to me from the garden. The only physically separate time from students would be when I was sleeping, a one-hour faculty meeting each afternoon (devoted to talking about them), and the time I could find before breakfast to prepare for them.

Other faculty warned me that by mid-residency, feelings of exhaustion would set in and I would need to steal away and find more personal time for quiet.

Judy Couldn't Dance

Let me dwell on a few events that symbolized what I learned at Goddard. My group of twelve students was a mix of persons from all over the country (all U.S. citizens): one from Vermont, others from Korea, Minnesota, France, Washington, New York, and California. Nine were working on a Master's Degree and three were working on a postgraduate teaching certificate. Eight were women, four were men, ages ranged from twenty–two to forty–four, and years of formal teaching experiences ranged from none to twenty. We sat in a circle in heavily used chairs in a very warm room. I began the first meeting with our residency group by looking at this casually attired collection of students and explaining how this group would belong to all of us. If it worked well, it would be because we all took responsibilities for the group. Because I was new, I asked students with previous experience at Goddard to help explain the expectations, rules, and forms that I had. I then asked them to develop a list of what they each wished to accomplish in our scheduled time of group meetings over the next ten days. I concluded by asking them to each explain why they had chosen Goddard.

The first responses to my question were predictable and pragmatic. Students cited reasons of career advancement, wanting to learn about something in particular, and needing a flexible program, until we came to Judy. Judy, who was young, tall, and pleasant looking, and had a strong physical presence, was from a community farm in the Midwest. She spoke softly of why she was here. She explained that she had come to Goddard because of what happened to her in grade school. As a very young child, she had loved to dance—out in the fields, at home, and with playmates. In her first year of school—kindergarten—she was asked by her teacher to dance for the entire school in the auditorium. She readily agreed and enjoyed every moment of her performance. After concluding, the principal then went to the podium and announced that another child had won the contest. Judy remembers feeling confused and humiliated. She did not know until that moment that she had been in a contest, and now everyone in the school knew that she couldn't dance. Since that moment, she has not danced in public. The idea of public performance puts a knot in her stomach and she wants to run and hide. But now, as a mother and as an adult, she is at Goddard to become a teacher. Yet being a teacher is a public performance, and thinking about being in front of students continues to trigger deep anxiety. She wishes to learn to be comfortable as a teacher so she can help students develop their own talents without public fear or shame. But she must overcome her own fear first.

Her statement, said at first quietly, slowly, and haltingly, increased in volume, anger, and emotion, and the rest of us were moved to tears. In that moment, our group was born. Individuals thanked Judy for speaking from her heart and then each of them spoke about their own private issues of education including issues of religion, race, faith, gender, abuse, cultural identity, and finding one's way in the world. I spoke of my own private fear of trying to do a job worthy of them and me.

We became a major part of each other's lives from this residency to the next, and beyond. For a year, we were a group. Together we organized learning topics, students counseled each other, socialized together, and offered each other endless support. Students helped plan each other's learning contracts; they selected, facilitated, and, discussed readings; and they built a library for each other. I had been prepared for Goddard students to bring personal issues to the residency, but I was totally unprepared for the sheer, unadorned candor. The last time that I had heard such private expressions made public to new acquaintances was in 1968 when I had participated in a sensitivity training as part of the Teacher Corps Program (one of the national programs to address poverty in schools). In 1968, I remembered being hesitant about the openness and lack of restraint. Now, in 1994, I was excited by the candor but concerned that our group be more than a support group; I wanted us to become a learning group about ideas, practices, issues, and methods, that built upon, but moved beyond, personal experiences. bell hooks (1995) refers to this as moving personal experiences to "theory in action." Experience is essential to, but not synonymous with, learning. I realized that my job would be to facilitate personal expressions *only* as it built toward new intellectual knowledge, application, and reflection.

How Did It Work?

I was most conscious of being a co-learner with students, but not being their social peer. Memories that I hold of a few professors and their relations with students during my own undergraduate days at a small liberal arts college remain distasteful. These faculty members took advantage of their positions by imposing themselves on students in both social and personal situations. Students, no matter what setting or age, are vulnerable to faculty members who use them for personal attention and social belonging. Students will often allow faculty to intrude in their social settings, allow them to dominate social conversations, and often pretend to laugh at a professor's storytelling or humor to placate them. Because of their unequal status with faculty, many students often feel obligated not to offend. This faculty intrusion and student compliance occurs everywhere in educational settings, but it is more apt to occur in a small, intimate community setting. [3]

I observed that faculty members at Goddard had worked out the delicate line of maintaining a professional distance while being personally attentive and supportive. For me, this separation was more difficult because of my unfamiliarity with the gripping emotional disclosures on the part of students and my wishing to be open to them. So I had to work hard to consciously establish my role. I did this by not inviting myself to student social activities and declining many well-intentioned social invitations from them. Through such acts, I let it be known that our mutual work together was to emphasize professional engagement over personal friendships. By doing so, I gained the reputation of perhaps being nice, but hard with students, expecting them to do more than they initially wanted. This does not mean that I didn't become friends with them; some of us still correspond and visit years later, but it did mean that we were fellow travelers, not peers.

According to solicited, anonymous feedback, the two ten-day institutes went extremely well. Students were very busy and so was I; there were endless last minute preparations for advising individual students, organizing group meetings, conducting short courses, and participating in seminars. During the six-month interim between residencies, I was in constant communication with every student, receiving and reading their progress reports and papers and sending them feedback every three weeks. Depending on my travel schedule, I occasionally met with students in their home locations. Students created a partially successful electronic mail network that connected them with each other and every six weeks I would write and disseminate a common newsletter to them about what I was studying, what I was hearing from each of them, and to notify them of approaching deadlines.

In one case, a most able student stopped sending in her assignments. I called her one Sunday morning to find out what was happening. She told me that teaching and family responsibilities were overwhelming and she couldn't keep up with graduate work. She had been feeling depressed and had decided to quit the program. Knowing her as an exceptional student with great insight into issues of postmodernism and education, I told her that I understood, but if she decided to reconsider, I would work with her to get back into sequence. I told her what I thought of her abilities and how much I had learned from her. She called me back a week later to tell me that she had reconsidered, wanted to continue, and we worked out a new schedule. She graduated a semester later than normal with an outstanding thesis. During the last occasion I attended at Goddard, she came over to me, gave me a hug, and thanked me. She told me that it was that one quiet Sunday call that had given her the encouragement to continue.

When I think about the overall experience with these twelve students and what resulted, I am quite satisfied and proud of their work. There were four high quality master theses as good as some doctoral dissertations that I have guided. All students, except one, secured or advanced in their professional jobs, three took new leadership positions, and two went on to doctoral studies at Union College and Teachers College of Columbia University. The Goddard experience seemed to work for me.

Comparisons

The experience gave me specific applications to try upon my full-time return to the University of Georgia as well as thoughts about what Goddard could learn from UGA. I found that both institutions—in their operations and academic programs—could learn from each other. What I found most significant in comparison were (1) faculty discussion about students, (2) personal relations as part of—not separate from—academic learning, (3) diversity in field experiences, and (4) diversity in intellectual perspectives. Finally, my greatest overall learning as a teacher was my reconceptualization of the old content/process dichotomy through a balancing of three dimensions of teaching to guide student learning for democratic education.

(1) Discussions
I found at Goddard that faculty talk about students constantly. They talk about how individual students are progressing, they ask each other to review student work, they advise each other on how to work with a particular student or group of students, and they review with each other their own teaching and student assessments. In their interactions with each other, Goddard faculty are like faculty at excellent public or private primary and secondary schools. With the exception of a small, regional university that I taught at early in my higher education career, I have not experienced such depth and comprehensiveness of discussions about learning and students. Faculty in most academic departments at large universities that I am acquainted with rarely talk with each other about progress or concerns with individual students (unless it is to complain about students) nor do they talk about their own teaching and the assessment of student learning. There are notable exceptions in particular departments or programs, but most department meetings are about procedural matters, academic program components, internal politics, enrollments, and budgets. The nature and quality of the learning experience for students is rarely discussed. Most other professional discussions among faculty are usually about their research, their papers, their publications, and their presentations to professional organizations.

At Goddard it is nearly impossible for a student to become lost. Each faculty member knows their own students extremely well and furthermore they know by name and interest most of the students other than their own. Knowing students well is a very high priority for almost everything Goddard faculty do. These ongoing discussions about students and ways to improve teaching and learning for them is—as I previously stated—characteristic of successful K–12 schools that colleagues and I have studied (Glickman, Gordon, and Ross-Gordon, 1998). For example, when I am at home I constantly hear my spouse, Sara, talking at night with her middle school colleagues about students, teaching activities, and curriculum plans for the next day. Goddard reminded me of Sara's ongoing and endless conversations with her team members. In order to have such discussions at large research institutions, they often must be galvanized in special forums that are connected to research agendas, or with special invitations to like-minded people to work together. Such conversations simply don't come with the territory of everyday normal responsibilities at large universities. [4]

At Goddard, a focus on students and teaching is the culture of the institution. New faculty are assimilated into it. If you don't participate in these conversations, you are regarded as atypical. At large universities, the culture is more one of independence, allegiance to one's discipline, and individual academic freedom. If a faculty member does participate in discussions about students and teaching, it is usually due to special initiatives that attempt to modify the institutional culture.

(2) Personalization

Another striking difference is personalization of learning as integral to education. At Goddard, students know faculty as people living the same everyday lives as themselves. At UGA, students know faculty as professionals who teach classes and hold set office hours. With the exception of advanced graduate students and undergraduates who are fortunate enough to be in experimental teacher education programs, Georgia faculty typically do not know or remember by name most of the students they teach. This is due to the greater numbers of students, expectations of faculty work, and the very distinct separation of faculty from personal life.

(3) Diversity of field experiences

A major state research university such as UGA has a much richer environment of diversity than an institution such as Goddard. In Goddard short-residency program, student field work, internships, and student teaching are done off campus most often in the area where the student lives. The selection of site, supervisor, and cooperating teacher is usually left to the student to initiate and then is approved by Goddard faculty. With limited faculty and with students spread across the country and the world, such a process of selection by students is understandable, but control over the diversity of settings is lost. UGA has developed ongoing relationships with a number of public schools as Professional Development Schools, sites where the university and the school work together to plan optimal experiences with student teachers. In addition, there are large numbers of individual teachers, K–12, in hundreds of schools who have been screened as good teacher models and mentors for practicums and student teaching. If a UGA student does not have a good working site, the University intercedes and makes corrections. Over a student's time at Georgia, most students have experiences with many teachers and several schools and have a diversity of classrooms and work with different populations of students who vary by socioeconomic class, race, and ethnicity. At Goddard, due to the reliance on the student in the residency program to seek his/her placement, there are no such assurances of quality and diversity of placements. For example, while I was at Goddard a few students did their student teaching in affluent, private school settings, yet later took teaching assignments in public schools. They were simply not prepared to handle such a different setting. This matter of placement is not a major issue for mature graduate students who are already teaching and working toward a master's degree, but it is for those working on initial licensure. [5]

(4) Intellectual diversity

Another difference between the two institutions is the degree to which students are exposed to a variety of perspectives, experiences, and ways of thinking. Students at the University of Georgia have a major research library to draw from and they receive instruction from highly specialized researchers who have mastered a specific field and hold definite points of view, often different from each other. Students thus learn of differing ideologies about education from faculty and other students who are confident explainers of their positions. A state university such as Georgia by virtue of its affordable (and most often free) tuition and its more inclusive reach to attract students from all regions of the state also contains a greater plurality of thinking among faculty and students than a college such as Goddard. Students and faculty tend to think more alike at Goddard than students and faculty at a place such as the University of Georgia.

It is hard for those who argue for conservative and/or fundamentalist positions to be of significant numbers and to have influence at Goddard—this is not so at Georgia. At UGA, often you will see students sitting side by side, one with a clean, pressed suit and tie and the other with body hanging garments and pierced body adornments. In these settings, in my opinion, students can more readily understand different expressions of truth and make public judgments about what decision or course of action should be taken. To do so at Goddard, faculty need to be extremely deliberate about bringing oppositional ideas, different from their own, to students. This is not meant to imply that Goddard faculty are closed to the range of ideas, but it is more difficult for Goddard students to hear from the oppositional believers themselves. To bring a greater range of academic ideas into a respectful, thoughtful discourse for students, Goddard faculty, with students, might need to do more selections of oppositional books, readings, speakers, and settings.

Discussion and Applications

Since my Goddard experience, I have found that it is not simply the scale of an institution that creates participatory learning environments, rather it is the mission and purpose of faculty within an institution. For example, there are larger research institutions that have small teams of cohorts of students, faculty, and public school educators that capture some of the features of the Goddard experience. Of course, there are small colleges across America the size of Goddard that can be more highly structured, more impersonal, and engaging students less than do large institutions. Large numbers of students and faculty usually create more bureaucratic rules, regulations, centralization, and standardization of programs, but it doesn't necessarily have to be an absolute limitation.

Some departments of teacher education at UGA have developed undergraduate and graduate degree programs based on small-scale interactions and negotiated curriculum. Not to the extent of Goddard's student-centered approach, in that grades and some required courses still exist. But students and teachers are part of a learning community and work together intensely in field settings and ongoing problem-solving and reflective seminars (Hudson-Ross, et al. 1999). Our new Ph.D. program in Social Foundations was developed with aspects of the Goddard experience in mind; cohort groups, a shared curriculum among students and faculty, community learning and action research teams, and individual contracts. Goddard, in turn, might further improve its small residency programs with the borrowed features of a large university by purposefully supplementing the program with other types of speakers, settings, readings, and ideas.

But before leaving this section on application, let me describe how Goddard personally affected me as a teacher upon my return to Georgia.

In my department at UGA, we gave ourselves the freedom to recon-ceptualize the large introductory course that we teach to all education majors. Some of my experiences at Goddard helped me to rethink how I would do it. I accepted that I could not possibly know most of the 240 Georgia students, who would take the course as well as I knew every one of my twelve Goddard students. However, I realized that I *could know Georgia students better* by making simple changes. For example, now I arrive at my UGA classes at least a half an hour before starting time and mill outside with waiting students. They know that I will be there; they can ask me quick questions; and I can talk to them informally about the latest news on campus. I also remain after class so the same type of interaction can take place and they can ask me questions about the day's class or the upcoming assignment. Also, I followed up on the Goddard experience of calling students at home and even in my largest classes, I will call five or six of my Georgia students on Sundays to find out how they are doing, how the course is going, and if they need help with any questions. After my first Sunday of such calls at Georgia, word spread throughout my entire large class that I call students, not because they are in trouble, but just to check on them. Most students were both amazed and most appreciative. Such calls have resulted in decisions with students that would not have occurred if I had waited for them to initiate a conversation. Based on these Sunday calls, one student changed her major, another learned about a particular graduate program that she was later accepted into, and another decided that education, as a career was simply not what she wanted to pursue.

The reality at Georgia is that I could not have students as involved and making as many choices as Goddard students, but again I saw that I could have Georgia students *more involved and making more choices than ever before.* By seeking help from experienced UGA colleagues who had the reputation for working well with large classes, I was able to make a traditionally passive lecture course into a highly interactive ones that included community learning, provocative discussions, fast-paced technology that included videos and music, team projects, student-led forums, and student-initiated introductions, questions, and critics of guest speakers.

After my experience at Goddard, I wanted to see if participatory-oriented teaching, although most easily done in small groups and community settings, could still be done in large group settings. The final anonymous and confidential evaluations of my first attempt to do a required and large undergraduate UGA course found that over ninety percent of students found the course to be intellectually challenging, provocative, open, and demanding. The success was due to reorienting my thinking as a teacher about the capacity of students, regardless of the size of the class. Of course, I had to spend a full five weeks of my summer to plan the learning environment and activities. I and colleagues had carefully chosen teaching assistants who could manage small group discussions and student contracts, and I had the benefit of a number of faculty colleagues to call upon for help. When the first class of this large course began with an amplified version of Pink Floyd singing "we don't need no education," students knew they were in for a different large class experience.

Balance and Tensions of Democratic Education

I think public universities such as UGA and specific private institutions such as Goddard have a public purpose for why they educate. What I mean is that these institutions—in their standards, expectations, and educational programs for students—have a responsibility to prepare teachers who will teach their students as equals who deserve dignity and respect and to provide an education that will accord each and every student life, liberty, and the pursuit of happiness (Glickman 1998). The goal is to educate students to think independently as they learn to contribute to a more just and better democratic society. Public purpose education must work to create a generation of citizens who are more intelligent, caring, and committed than the generation before. To achieve such purpose, schools and programs need to employ a pedagogy of learning that demonstrates to students in day-to-day interactions the power of democracy as the most powerful way to learn and live together.

Schools and colleges with democratic aims use the process of governance to implement learning that will result in wiser and more participatory students. John Dewey knew this point well; his colleague, William Kilpatrick, knew it much less so. Democratic education in the classroom does not translate into moment by moment egalitarianism where students and teachers have the same authority. Dewey held that the teacher has the moral duty—due to experience, knowledge, and commitment—to establish the educational conditions to guide such student learning. Dewey found no contradiction in advocating that teachers assert control in the classroom to ensure that learning occurred from the interaction between current knowledge and the natural interest of students. He differed forcefully with William Kilpatrick and others who advocated that a teacher's role was to facilitate the interest of students through projects (see Dewey 1938).

Democratic education is achieved when faculty use authority to help students gain authority. This is done through a set of intentional activities. Eventually, such a democratic education enables students to question, synthesize knowledge, and make new applications. It results in citizens who can make private and public judgements (Massaro 1993, 70).

So what I learned in contrasting, applying, and synthesizing my experiences at Goddard and the University of Georgia is that democratic education can be done in multiple settings—small and large, public and private. Democratic education is conditioned on attending to three realms and keeping them in constant balance and tension. The dimensions most helpful to me are *knowledge*, *relations*, and *participation*.

By *knowledge*, I am referring to content, understanding, and skills within and across disciplines that equips students to gain mastery of "cultural capital," that knowledge that allows one to access and critique one's life in relation to society and choose how to live. (I believe that writers as different as E. D. Hirsch and Lisa Delpit are correct in saying that there is a cultural literacy of those in power in America and students who are not privy to it will be limited in their ability to gain, resist, or change existing conditions.)

By *relations*, I am referring to the dignity and respect accorded to and among students and teachers, their commitment to listen and learn from each other, and the high degree of confidence, care, and expectations that teachers and students have for each other.

By *participation*, I am referring to the interaction between knowledge and the learner that defines a learning experience. This involves student choice, activity, application, demonstration, and contribution of what is learned from, to, and with others. Through participation, students move from knowledge to wisdom and find new paths of interest and talent to pursue.

If teaching focuses on one or two realms to the exclusion of the others, potential learning is obstructed. For example, if I, as a teacher, focus on participatory methods and personal relations and neglect knowledge, then students may be more interested and involved, but they will acquire little outside information. If I focus on knowledge and relations, and disregard participation, then the student will not be able to make applications beyond what has been immediately learned. If I emphasize participation and knowledge and fail to attend to personal relations, then students will not be open emotionally, spiritually, or personally, to learn with and from others. Keeping these three dimensions in tension and integration allows for democratic education; students gain the authority to determine what is correct; they have the ability to understand a range of perspectives, consider various actions, and examine reasons for their decisions.[6]

Conclusion

My last memory of Goddard was our group's final time together. We walked together through a half a foot of fresh snow to the community hall for the culminating and celebratory talent show. We sat together, took numerous pictures of each other, and reminisced about our past events. As the show began, a few members excused themselves. The lights went down and the master of ceremonies announced that we were about to hear a recently formed band. When we looked up, there were four members of our group on stage, instruments in hand, ready to play. As they launched into their opening number, a dancer entered from the side stage with tambourine in hand. She was exuberant, graceful, and radiant. It was Judy, and she was dancing!

Judy's journey was a metaphor for the learning journey we took together. We learned about what is possible when education and democracy are treated inseparably from each other. Democratic education is a dance with both structure and improvisation, performed on different stages and in different halls, where performers, observers and directors are all part of the performance. It is quite exhilarating to dance!

Endnotes

1. The book was published in 1998, Revolutionizing America's Schools. Jossey-Bass Publishers.
2. I had participated with Jon Bremer of the Parkway Program, had been a principal of an open education school in New Hampshire that Jean Piaget and Barbara Inhelder had visited, had been an assistant professor at Ohio State University and was greatly influenced by the faculty of the laboratory school and, more recently, I had worked as a colleague at Georgia with Eliot Wigginton of Foxfire acclaim.
3. Faculty at all institutions, traditional or progressive, have influence over students in both obvious and subtle ways. Faculty have power to negotiate away certain requirements for students, to give official approval of student work, or to make a student's progress more difficult.
4. At UGA I have been heartened by the focused attempts to galvanize such discussions recently in (a) collaborations between the faculty of the College of Education and the College of Arts and Sciences in extended retreats, (b) new teacher education programs by invitations to faculty to form cohorts with students and selected public schools, and (c) priority funding of college grants to faculty wishing to study their own teaching.
5. One must remember that I am referring to criteria for the placement of students in the part time residency program. I am not referring to the full-time undergraduate program at Goddard, with which I am not familiar.
6. Reasons can be communicated from multiple ways of knowing and not only from the use of scientific positivist logic (Barber 1992, chapter 4).

References

Barber, B. R. 1992. *An Aristocracy of Everyone*. New York: Ballantine.

Dewey, J. 1938. *Experience and Education*. New York: Collier Books.

Glickman, C.D. 1993. *Renewing America's Schools*. San Francisco: Jossey-Bass Publishers.

———.1998. *Revolutionizing America's Schools*. San Francisco: Jossey-Bass Publishers.

Glickman, C. D., Gordon, S. P., and Ross-Gordon, J. M. 1998. *Supervision of Instruction: A Developmental Approach*. 4th ed. Needham Heights, Massachusetts: Allyn and Bacon.

hooks, b. 1995. *Teaching to Transgress*. New York: Routledge.

Massaro, T. *Constitutional Literacy*. Durham, North Carolina: Duke University Press.

ELEVEN

Extending Democracy from Classroom to Schoolhouse:
Studying Democratic Governance at Goddard College[1]

Richard Schramm

Goddard College, a small, progressive democratic institution in central Vermont seeks a risk-taker committed to participatory democracy as a way to make decisions in an egalitarian manner. Pedagogy at Goddard is also progressive and democratic. Since its inception in the 1930s, Goddard College has been at the forefront of experimentation in higher education. Part of our innovation in teaching places the student at the center of the educational experience, and emphasizes social change and justice.
—Start of advertisement for Goddard College president (early 1997)

Introduction

In theory, Goddard College strives to educate its students through all of their experiences at the college and to extend their say in their education to include everything from the nature of their independent studies to how the college is run. Consequently there is talk of a "twenty-four-hour curriculum" and of Goddard as a "democratic institution." Students not only participate in a variety of classroom and tutorial studies but also in a college work program and a myriad of student life and community meetings. Students are given considerable say in the design and conduct of their studies and have representatives on the college's Executive Committee and its Board of Trustees which allows them some influence in the conduct of the college as well. All of this is seen as a part of democratic education and of the education of students for active and informed participation in a democratic society. In practice, however, this process at Goddard may stray from this democratic education ideal.

This chapter reports on a group study (Goddard's form of "class" or "course") in the fall of 1995 that looked at one element in this set of beliefs about Goddard and, along the way, learned some things about other elements. In particular we asked to what extent is Goddard truly a democratic college and, where it falls short, what can be done to make it more democratic? At the same time we learned more about how a democratic college can contribute to student education and how democracy can be enhanced at the classroom level. We report all of these findings here.

To keep the task of this chapter manageable, we do not dwell on distinctions between democratic education and education for democracy but treat the two as essentially the same. We also do not emphasize the substantial educational contributions of democracy at the classroom level, but search out the contributions that arise from placing the classroom in a larger democratic context. And finally, we acknowledge the importance of culture, commitment, knowledge, and skills in democratic organizations, but we focus most of our investigation on the question of democratic governance and the organizational structures that support such governance. This latter focus grew out of our initial assessment of where Goddard College was most challenged as it strove to become a democratic college.

We proceed as follows:

- We review some of the literature on the educational value of democracy and how this extends to the institutional setting in which students are learning.
- We then turn to the setting in which our group study took place and the purposes and participants of the group study itself. This was a time of considerable tension at the college between the forces for more "top-down" hierarchical decision-making and the forces for more "bottom-up" participatory decision-making. This tension played a large role in the design, goals, and conduct of the group study.
- Next we address the group study process that transpired and what we learned from it about implementing democracy at the classroom level, and where this might be enhanced by placing the classroom in a more fully democratic organizational setting.
- We then turn to the main question of the group study — the extent to which Goddard provides this democratic organizational setting and what might be done to move it toward being more fully democratic.
- Finally we report on how this all worked out at Goddard and provide some general principles and examples for other colleges that seek to become more democratic.

The Rationale

Because Goddard's stated mission is to undertake "new experiments based on the ideals of democracy and the principles of progressive education asserted by John Dewey," when we turned to the question of the educational benefits of a democratic college, we turned first to the writings of John Dewey.

According to biographer Robert Westbrook, Dewey's conception of democracy was almost synonymous with education. A true democracy, according to Dewey, would be "a society in which there would be opportunities for free communication of feeling, knowing and thinking. The foundation of such a society would be free participation by each member of the society in setting its goals and purposes, full and willing contribution by each person toward the fulfillment of these goals" (Westbrook 1991, 249).

Dewey firmly believed that only through "associated life" could one achieve one's full human potential. "Regarded as an idea," he said, "democracy is not an alternative to other principles of associated life. It is the idea of community itself." Thus, only through active democratic participation could one become whole (Westbrook 1991, 229).

In *John Dewey: Rethinking Our Time*, Raymond Boisvert argues that for Dewey, "the ideal of 'do your own thing' can be recognized . . . [as] precisely what democracy is not. Democracy is 'primarily a mode of associated living.' It is a way of living together characterized by 'conjoint communicated experience.' This means that the primary responsibility of democratic citizens is concern with the development of shared interests that lead to sensitivity about repercussions of actions on others" (Boisvert 1998, 57).

Dewey not only recognized the need for all concerned parties to be involved in the goal-setting for the society; he also insisted that power extend into the realm of implementing these goals, into the realm of management as well. "All those who are affected by social institutions should have a share in producing and managing them," he claimed. "The two facts that each one is influenced in what he does and enjoys and in what he becomes by the institutions under which he lives, and therefore he shall have, in a democracy, a voice in shaping them, are the passive and active sides of the same fact" (Westbrook, 433).

We found strong support for extending democracy to the organizational level as an educational goal in other writings as well. Ordway Tead argued in his book *Democratic Administration (1945)* that democratic management is educational by its very nature.

> Democracy has high in its constituent elements the aim of conserving and enhancing the personality of all individuals — the idea of respect for the integrity of the person and the primary value of developing persons as worthy and worthful ends in themselves. . . .
>
> [T]he word "personality". . . includes the discovery and use of unique talents, the fullest possible expression of creative powers, the responsible assumption of a share in shaping the conditions which are found to make growth in the quality of personal living possible. . . . [It] includes also the acquiring of sufficient knowledge and understanding, the sense of enough status with one's peers, the sentiment of friendly attachment with one's fellows, the possession of enough voice and power in one's society, so that one feels that he is in fact helping to shape the conditions which make possible the achievement of individual, creative release. It has to do also with a continuing reexamination of self and society to assure that the dignity of the person is being maintained under

changing conditions. . . (58–59).

And, according to some, the more democracy the better. Democracy, especially participatory democracy, is good education. In *Power and Empowerment: A Radical Theory of Participatory Democracy,* Peter Bachrach and Aryeh Botwinick write that

> The underlying premise of participatory democracy—in contrast to liberal representative democracy—is that participatory democratic politics encompasses self-exploration and self-development by the citizenry. In sharp contrast, liberal doctrine conceives of democracy as merely facilitating the expression of *perceived* interests, not in helping citizens discover what their real interests are" (Bachrach 1992, 10–11).

On the specific question of education for democratic living, Philip Slater believes:

> All the education in the world cannot teach democracy, any more than books will teach a child how to swim. Democracy is learned through practice — through personal involvement in issues of personal concern. People are "ready for democracy" when they say they are. Since democracy is a process, being ready means being ready to learn that process. Democracy is on-the-job training. There is no preparation, no way to avoid mistakes. Democracy requires that we make mistakes. *Democracy is the process of learning through trial and error how to engage in the process of learning democracy* (Slater 1991, 179).

And, as the late founder of Summerhill in England, A. S. Neill, put it, "As education, self-government is of infinite value" (quoted in Chapman 1995, 46).

Thus the experience of participating in a class, school or society in which one truly shares in the formulation of goals, development of policy, implementation of decisions, and the assessment of progress in association with others is a critical element in the development of human potential. The more one can expand the sphere of associational life and decision-making, the more opportunities for learning open up for those participants. Conversely, as we argue below, as the domain of democratic education shrinks, the more the power of undemocratic decision-making can limit the efficacy of the educational process.

The Setting

With this rationale for the educational value of this expansion of democracy to the college itself, and with Goddard's view of itself as a "democratic institution," we turn to our group study's efforts to study democracy at Goddard. We look first at the context in which the study was carried out.

This group study was conducted in the fall of 1995, after the first year in office of the college's president. When the president arrived in August, 1994:

- the College was operating under a newly documented governance system, put on paper after many years of controversy and confusion about the College's governance system and the role of different groups in Goddard's major decisions and policies

- the college's board of trustees was largely self-selected, consisting of a maximum membership of twenty-five, twenty of whom were at-large members elected by the board itself and who served five-year terms. The other members were two students (elected by students to one-year terms), one staff member (elected by staff to a three-year term), one faculty member (elected by faculty to a three-year term) and the elected head of the alumni/ae association (one-year term)

- the governance system also included a College Executive Committee (CEC) consisting of two faculty, two staff, two students, and five upper-level managers (including the president) that played an important role in the budgeting, planning, and policy coordination process of the College

- students, faculty and staff participated in a range of college functions (beyond the CEC) that included many of the standing committees of the college and community-wide meetings which are also part of the governance system

- participation in these activities, and in the democratic educational processes of the college, supported an organizational culture that thought of the school as participatory if not fully democratic, and which expected faculty, staff and students to play a role in college decisions, although this role might vary depending on the type of decisions

- the president of the college was ultimately accountable to the board, but was also expected to operate according to the dictates of a governance document that emphasized shared governance and participation, and was subject to the pressures of a democratic organizational culture. The governance document was silent about how this contradiction was to be resolved.

By fall 1995, when the group study began its work, the president of the college had just completed a highly contentious first year in office. This year included a reorganization of the college (the CEC did not play a substantial role in this reorganization), which involved the laying off of several highly respected staff; the resignation of the academic dean over disagreements with the president about his actions and future plans in regard to faculty reappointment and management style; a confrontation between faculty, staff, and student representatives and the board of trustees at their June meeting about these actions and how they had been carried out; a slowdown in the growth in college revenues with a substantial redirection of moneys from instruction to administrative overhead; and increased secrecy about the college's finances.

Although the board continued to support the president, at that June meeting they did request that the president set up a governance task force in the fall to review the governance document and system and make recommendations back to them. This request grew out of two concerns. The governance document was viewed as a draft description of how the college was governed, so it was felt that it needed to be "cleaned up" to eliminate internal inconsistencies and increase clarity about the roles and responsibilities of different groups and officials in governance. The second concern was the growing differences between the president and the faculty, students, and some staff about their roles in governance, and the hope that this review would straighten out those differences or at least cool them off for a while.

The Group Study

A "group study" at Goddard is similar to a traditional class in that it brings together faculty and students around a common interest or topic and provides academic credit to students who satisfactorily complete their work. It differs from most classes, however, in that students play a large role in the organization, design, and carrying out of the group learning activity. The faculty member is often referred to as a "facilitator," and students and faculty complete narrative evaluations (there are no grades). For the purposes of this chapter we will use the terms "group study" and "class" interchangeably.

This group study was entitled "Business and Democracy at Goddard College" and initially sought to address the following questions:

1. What does it take to operate a college successfully as a business? How well is Goddard College doing in this regard? What are its strengths and weaknesses as a business?

2. What does it take to operate a college as a "democratic organization"? What do we mean by a "democratic organization" and how do existing democratic organizations operate effectively (or do they)? To what extent is Goddard operated democratically, and how well is it doing in this regard?

3. Can a college operate well both as a business and a democracy? Can governance, administration, and operations be conducted both democratically and efficiently? What types of structures, processes, and education are needed for individuals at Goddard to participate responsibly and effectively in democratic management of the College?

Ultimately, however, the events around us led the group study to focus most of its attention on the second question about democracy at Goddard.

The group study consisted of six core members who stayed with the study throughout the semester:

- one faculty member who was the group facilitator and a member of the newly formed governance task force
- one faculty member who was a member of the College Executive Committee
- one staff member who was the coordinator for the campus program, worked with the academic dean, and also served on the governance task force
- one staff member who directed the college/community radio station and was

the staff member of the Board of Trustees
- one student who was in her next to last semester and who was a student member of the Board of Trustees and
- one student who was in his first semester at the college

Other faculty, staff, and students joined the group study from time to time as interested participants and resource people about specific topics.

The group study composition was clearly not like that of the typical group study at Goddard (one faculty member and ten or twelve students), but it did have an educational agenda typical of most group studies. The group was assembled to learn more about the nature and development of democratic organizations, using Goddard College as a case study, and spent considerable time at this task. Everyone in the group shared a common interest in understanding more about the educational value of a democratic college, what constituted a "democratic college," how Goddard stacked up compared to such a college, and what might be done to make the college more democratic.

The Democratic Classroom

Although it was not our principal interest, organizing the group study and carrying out our study of democracy at Goddard led us early on to the question of democracy within our group. It also raised for us the associated question about how democratic we could be if the college itself was not democratic, and to what extent we found our learning diminished by the possibility that our group study class did not occur in a democratic college. We discussed these questions as we started and reflected on them throughout the semester.

At Goddard we think of our educational process as "democratic." Students, either individually or in groups, determine what they want to study and what they hope to learn over the semester. Working with faculty, students refine their educational goals, develop a process by which they will achieve these goals, and participate in an evaluation process by which they document their learning and judge to what extent they have achieved their goals. This process gives students considerable control over their learning.

In this process the faculty sees itself playing a significant role in assuring that this learning is successful. We think of ourselves as advisors, counselors, coaches, and/or partners and not as traditional teachers who determine what will be studied, what questions will be asked, how learning will occur, etc. We think of ourselves as involved in a highly participative process with students, in which the students have very clear "rights" in terms of the definition, conduct, and evaluation of the study.

We felt that our group study advanced this democratic education process somewhat and that we made progress with two dilemmas often encountered in group studies: how to balance individual and group learning, and how to balance faculty support and faculty direction of student work. This progress resulted from our almost unconscious use of what might be termed a "task force" model of group learning.

The Task Force Model

Once formed, our group study began to operate in a fashion that might best be described as a task force. We had a common vision of what we wanted to learn (our "charge"); we shared a sense of accountability to the college which we felt needed our study (other faculty, staff, and students and several board members had expressed interest in our work); we had a "chair" in the form of the faculty facilitator; we regularly agreed on the work that each member would do for the next meeting and reported back on our findings; and we saw the need to provide written products at various points over the semester (and also envisioned a final report). In these ways it felt like a very intense and conscientious task force. This form of operating had several important educational results.

First, the learning needs of the group became very important — we had to educate one another about what we were learning outside of class in order to do our work — which provided a counterbalance to the emphasis in highly student-centered education on the learning needs of individuals. Sometimes the emphasis on individual learning creates a dynamic in groups where individuals may not see why they have to help others in the group learn or even, in some cases, why they have any responsibility to the group at all or why they even need to be in the group. However, the task force model, because it addresses a complex, multidimensional problem that is too big for any one person and inherently requires different perspectives, provides a clear reason why a group is needed, why everyone has to help everyone else keep "up to speed," and why an individual member's learning, and learning agenda needs to be in balance with the group's learning agenda. In some ways, the task force model forced us into the "associational living" that Dewey felt was the heart of democracy as opposed to the "do your own thing" conception. And our learning was enhanced by this necessity.

Second, in the classroom the relationship between the faculty and the student in the task force model tends to make the faculty member more of a "partner" with the student (in a kind of partnership in learning) than either a "director" or a "supporter" of student learning. In student-centered learning, the faculty member may play the role of a resource person to the student, perhaps even going as far as playing solely an "I'm here to help; let me know what you need" kind of role. In an effort to avoid being too directive, the faculty member may become a passive, silent partner, almost "potted plant" figure in the learning process.[2]

In the task force model, the direction of a student's learning comes from his or her interests ("I'd like to look at the role of community meetings in a democratic college") and the group's needs ("we have to study various organizational structures at the college"), and not from the faculty member in charge of the group study. This partnership with the group carries over to the relationship between individual students and the faculty facilitator. Every member of the group, including the group study faculty facilitator, needs to contribute actively to the group's learning. Potted plants are of no help. This leads to a more authentic (less restrained) sharing of knowledge and ideas in the group, and ultimately between faculty and student. At the same time the faculty facilitator meets regularly with individual students outside of the group to be sure that their individual learning needs are being met.

From our experience, this task force/partnership model of learning worked well for all faculty and staff participants and for the student who had more experience with the Goddard approach to education. It was less successful, however, for the student who had just entered the college. He expressed to me at the end of the class that he felt he had been intensely involved in this process, but came away with some confusion about his learning and a wish that he had more time during the semester to process what he was learning from this experience.

Limitations on Democracy and Learning

Although our task force approach extended the democratic education model in several important ways, it did little to change the structural realities that limited the extent to which the class was truly democratic.

Although students in this and other group studies at Goddard have considerable say in their education, they are required to develop and carry out their study plans according to a set of college policies, rules, and procedures. Furthermore, once an agreed-upon study plan has been developed, faculty are expected to see that the study plan is followed (or that changes in the plan are agreed to by both parties and then followed), and ultimately report on how well the student has performed, whether or not the student has achieved his/her educational goals, and whether or not academic credit should be granted. Thus, in addition to their role as advisors or coaches or resource people, faculty members also serve as enforcers, evaluators, and standard bearers for the College.

This raises the obvious question of whether student-centered education (student developed study plan, self evaluation, etc.) can be truly democratic *if* the advisor has the ultimate power to approve or disapprove the student's plan and to decide if the semester's work is, or is not, satisfactory.[3]

These requirements and procedures are essentially a "given" in the environment in which the group study operates, and the task force model did not change this reality. To the extent that students do not have their fair share of control over this regulatory environment and over the faculty members who serve as their advisors, evaluators, and enforcers, the group study is not democratic. To the extent that these requirements and the evaluator/enforcer role of the faculty constrain or limit students' feeling of safety to learn what they want to learn in ways that they prefer, the group study is not fully serving its purpose of supporting and promoting student learning.

In practice, this group study created considerable safety and approached a fully democratic class. But this depended a lot on the particular personalities involved, and perhaps on the fact that there were faculty and staff participants in the group, not just the usual one faculty facilitator.

The classroom becomes more democratic the more that students are able to change the educational procedures and policies under which they operate and hold faculty accountable for their actions as advisors and evaluators. At Goddard, students can participate in student life and community meetings that provide a forum for expressing their concerns; they elect two members (out of ten) to the College Executive Committee, which is designed to have a say in budgetary, planning, and policy matters; and they elect two representatives (out of twenty-five) to the Board of Trustees. They also complete evaluations of their group study faculty facilitators (as well as of their advisors and independent study facilitators), which are "inputs" that are submitted to the academic dean, who conducts evaluations of faculty every year.

Although these college structures and processes provide some ways for students to exercise power over the procedures and faculty they engage with in their learning, in general student power is quite limited. Furthermore, the amount of individual influence students can have may vary widely. For our group study, student influence outside of the classroom varied from one student who was a board member and had previously been on the CEC to a first-semester student who was just learning the ropes.

We concluded from this experience that for democratic education to be fully effective, the power imbalances in the classroom needed to be offset by some political structure and process that enabled the student to have a greater say in educational policy and procedures and in faculty evaluation and personnel decisions. The ability of students to have a genuine say in the choice of board members and the president and a role in faculty search and evaluation committees seemed necessary to provide some basis for faculty advisors to feel truly accountable to students, not only the other way around.

Participation in such college-level decision-making not only would enhance democratic learning in the classroom, but would also extend that learning more fully to students' experiences outside of the classroom.

The Democratic College

Once persuaded of the importance of placing the democratic classroom in a democratic school, the group study turned to the question of what elements of democracy needed to be in place in a democratic college and how close Goddard came to meeting that ideal. We looked first at democracy, then at governance structures in democratic organizations, and finally at Goddard College.

Defining Democracy

Inquiring about democracy at Goddard College led us to the larger question, "What is a democracy or democratic society?" We posited that a democratic organization is like a small democratic society—a different basis for membership perhaps, and a different set of decisions covered — but still like a democracy.

So we began with that broader question about democracy and a democratic society, hoping that a look at democracy in general would provide us with an awareness of the ingredients or dimensions of democracy that could guide our study of democratic organizations. Democracy is difficult to define fully and easily but here are the key elements that played a role in our study of democracy at Goddard.

First, democracy is about governance — how a society is organized to make decisions about its goals and priorities, how it carries out these decisions, how it weighs individual concerns versus societal concerns, how it resolves conflicts that arise around these matters, and how it maintains and changes this system of governance. Governance is a system of "ruling," of exercising authority over a nation, state, city, institution, or organization.

Second, democracy is a particular form of governance, a system by which, according to standard dictionary definitions, "government is by the people . . . government in which the sovereign power resides in the people as a whole, and is exercised either directly by them . . . or by officers elected by them."

Third, a democratic governance system, especially a system that governs many people, requires definitions, rules, organizational bodies, regulations, procedures, etc. to spell out the terms and arrangements that make up the governance contract. These formal agreements define the democratic governance system and provide the structure of democracy, the framework within which democracy operates.

Fourth, democracy, however, requires more than a governing structure. It requires a democratic or participatory culture — a set of values, attitudes, rituals —in order for the system to work. Frances Moore Lappé and Paul Martin DuBois stress that democracy is not so much what we have but what we do. "Democracy — whether it works or not — depends on how each of us lives our public life. . . . [It] is not just about changing the rules; it's about changing the culture — our attitudes, values and expectations" (Lappé 1994, 229). Or, as Jean Bethke Elshtain puts it, "[D]emocracy is not simply a set of procedures or a constitution, but an ethos, a spirit, a way of responding, and a way of conducting oneself" (Elshtain 1995, 80).

A democratic culture values the sharing of power, rights, and responsibilities; broad and active participation; wide access to information; the importance of education and learning; an open and inclusive environment; and accountability to all members of the society. Democracy values differences, the working out of conflicts, the seeking of common ground and sharing.[4]

Finally, in addition to a democratic structure and supportive culture, successful democratic governance requires that members of the society have the knowledge and skills, and access to information, to be effective participants in the governance system. Effective participants in democracy need knowledge of their role and responsibilities in a democratic society as well as specific skills, such as leadership, organizing, conflict resolution, mediation, facilitation, and conducting meetings, that make them more effective in democratic settings.

Governance Structures in Democratic Organizations

These elements of effective democracy—democratic governance structures, culture, skills and knowledge—provided a starting point for our study of democracy at Goddard. They also constituted an agenda that we soon discovered would quickly exhaust the limited time and resources of our small group. Consequently we decided to focus our efforts on the area where Goddard seemed the furthest from being a democratic organization — its governance structure.

The hierarchical board to president to management decision-making structure and the participatory faculty-student-staff democratic classroom, community meeting, and College Executive Committee decision structure presented so clear a contradiction that we ended up giving this most of our attention. Issues of culture, skills, and knowledge were addressed to the extent that they supported or muted this structural contradiction.

In order to understand governance structures in democratic organizations we began by clarifying organizational membership and decisions, then asked how decisions needed to be made in a democratic organization, and finally examined organizational structures that supported democratic decision-making. We turned to books and articles on governance in business organizations (Adams 1992, Ackoff 1994, Bernstein 1976, McLagan 1995, Semler 1989, Tead 1945) and in educational organizations (Chapman 1995, Glickman 1993,1998, Schuster 1989, and Shor 1996) to help us in this task.

Members as Stakeholders. Who are the "members" of an organization? Although our first guess might be those who show up for work each day, or those who own the organization, or both, when we think about membership in the context of democracy, organizational "membership" needs to be expanded to all of those who are directly affected by the organization's decisions and operations. As Russell Ackoff writes in his book *The Democratic Corporation*, "The societal view of enterprises as social systems focuses on those they affect *directly*, their stakeholders, and the ways they are affected. This concern is reflected in what has come to be known as the 'stakeholder theory of the firm'" (Ackoff 1994, 37).[5]

Ackoff argues that organizations may have many and different types of stakeholders — those groups that are directly impacted by what the organization does, such as managers, workers, stockholders, suppliers, vendors, investors, creditors, government and the public. We added students, faculty, alumni/ae, etc.

If the organization's objective is "to give each [stakeholder] a measure of satisfaction," than it is a logical next step to argue that these stakeholders should have some role in defining how the organization provides that "satisfaction." This approach suggests, therefore, that stakeholders can be seen as the organization's "members."

Decisions.[6] Decisions made by and within organizations can be grouped into four categories: ownership or governance, management or administrative, operations, and individual/constituency decisions. These different decision-making spheres are shown in Figure 1.

Figure 1: Types of Organizational Decisions

Ownership/Governance Decisions:

    establishing the mission
    strategic planning
    major resource development and use
    operating and capital budget approval
    policy setting
    selection, direction, and evaluation of senior management

Management/Administrative Decisions:

    organizational structure and staffing
    coordination and planning of operations, policies, and budget

Operational Decisions:

    operational planning, policies, and procedures
    work-related decision-making

Individual/Constituency Decisions:

    prices/costs/policies that affect individuals and constituencies
    personnel policies, benefits, compensation to employees
    products, services, prices, impacts on consumers, suppliers, others (if considered members of the organization)
    civil rights of individual members
    grievance process for individuals, groups, constituencies

---

Within a college setting, examples of decisions that fit into each category of this table are:
- ownership or governance: final agreement on mission, major policies and budget agreements

- management or administrative: developing the organizational structure, hiring and firing, coordinating educational programs, formulating major policies and budgets
- operational: setting educational policy, developing the curriculum, creating new educational programs
- individual or constituency-oriented: wage and tuition decisions, handling violations of civil rights, responding to student concerns

Individual members of an organization may be involved in different types of decisions at different times. For example, a student may be on the board that makes governing decisions, on the College Executive Committee that reviews reorganization or budgeting choices, on the curriculum committee that makes operating decisions, and part of a student group that is pressing the college for lower tuition.

Structure and Decision Making. As our next step, we asked what role does the organization's membership play in decision-making in a *democratic* organization? Russell Ackoff answers this question by identifying the stakeholders for a particular decision and then applying what he calls the "participative principle" that "Either all those who are directly affected by a decision, the decision's stakeholders, or representatives they select, should be involved in making that decision" (Ackoff 1994, 57).[7]

For an organization to be democratic, this principle needs to be incorporated in the organization's charter, constitution, and by-laws, and spelled out more fully by the organizational structure that defines positions, departments, committees, job responsibilities, etc. These documents, organizational entities, roles, and responsibilities represent the structure of the organization.

But what does it mean "to be involved" in a decision that has direct impacts on you? Is it enough to have "input" or "informal influence"? Or does it require having your own "vote"? Because democracy is a system where those being governed have power over those doing the governing, in a democratic organization those affected by a decision need to make that decision themselves, or have power over those who do make the decision. This form of power represents a share of *control*, a vote on that decision, not just being able to let the decision-maker(s) know your feelings or "input" or having other forms of *influence* on the decision.

In a democratic organization members must have control over the organization's decisions. This control need not always be direct, by which the members make the decision as a joint body, but may be indirect through representatives who are elected by the membership who make the actual decision or who oversee those who do. There may also be combinations of direct and indirect control that reach into all spheres of decision-making.

Furthermore, control of certain decisions need not always be in the hands of the entire membership. Membership groups that are not affected significantly by some decisions may not have a role in making those decisions. For example college alumni/ae may not be affected by their college's current curriculum decisions, so they may not need to play a role in those decisions; they may, however, be affected by the college's long-range educational strategy so that a role in those decisions would be appropriate.

Because members of particular organizations may exert control in some areas, have influence in others, and have no say in other areas, the group study tried to identify where member control was essential for an organization to be democratic. We concluded that an organization can not be democratically structured without member control of *governance decisions* (see Figure 1). Unless the members control ownership or governance decisions that ultimately determine budget, structure, policies, personnel, grievance, and decisions in all the other spheres, an organization cannot be democratic. Without control of the larger, more systemic ownership/governance decisions, "control" in any other arena is really not control. This led us to focus our attention on an organization's key governance body, its Board of Trustees.

The Role of the Board. The composition and powers of the board play a critical role in determining whether or not an organization has a democratic structure. To learn more about the role of boards, especially in nonprofit organizations, we drew on the book *Boards That Make a Difference*, by John Carver.

According to Carver, "[E]ffective boards concentrate on the real business of governance: making policy, articulating the mission of the organization, and sustaining the organization's vision. Key to performing this role well is the concept of the board as 'owner.'

Carver uses "the concept of 'moral ownership' to isolate the various stakeholders to whom the board owes it primary allegiance. . . . A board cannot carry out its responsibilities without determining exactly whom the ownership includes and how they can be heard" (Carver 1990, 17).

"Stakeholders for a nonprofit or public organization may be clients, students, patients, staff, taxpayers, donors, neighbors, general citizenry, peer agencies, suppliers, and others." Among these stakeholders, "the special class [Carver] calls owners are those *on whose behalf* the board is accountable to others" (131). This allows the nonprofit organization to identify those particular ownership groups that have a significant stake in the organization and have the board represent those groups in its deliberations.

Carver goes on:

[T]he board's first direct product is the organization's *linkage to the ownership*. . . . The identity of ownership and perhaps the favored channels for connecting with it are deliberated and then set forth in . . . board policies. . . . Linkage with the ownership can be viewed as attitudinal, statistical, and personal. The first . . . is [that] board members behave in the belief that they are moral trustees for the owners. . . . At a second level, the board gathers statistical evidence of the owners' concerns, needs, demands, and fears [surveys, interviews by third parties, statistical data]. . . . [T]he third level . . . engages board members in direct contact with owners and owners' representatives [interviews, focus groups, public forums, invited presentations at board meetings, dialogue with other boards]"(140, 144–46).

Following Carver's line of argument, a democratic organization needs to be clear about its membership and ensure that its membership and their values are fully represented by the board of the organization.[8] To ensure that such representation occurs, at least formally, we argued that at least a majority of the board of a democratic organization should be elected by its membership; either by different membership constituencies, the whole membership, or some combination of the two. At-large members would be selected from other stakeholder groups, such as progressive educators or local residents, for whom elections might be very difficult and/or costly.

Authority and Accountability.[9] Figure 2 illustrates that when the board is elected

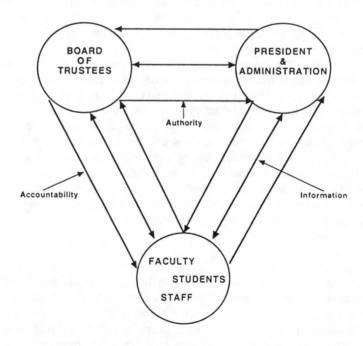

DEMOCRATIC GOVERNANCE
STRUCTURE

Figure 2

by the members or stakeholders of the organization (or the board is implementing effective moral ownership), this creates an important circularity of authority and accountability: authority becomes circular, from organization members to board to management to members. Accountability also becomes circular but operates in the other direction, from members to management to board to members. This circularity provides clarity about roles while providing more equality in relationships. Members are still accountable to management but the management is also accountable to them through the board.

The structure of authority and accountability affects the flow of information as well. The circularity encourages information flows in both directions, among members, board, and management.

Without a democratically elected board, authority, accountability and information become largely one-way flows in a hierarchical structure. For example, members are accountable to management, management to the board, the board to the owners (in for-profit organizations) or to no one in particular (in many nonprofits). We discuss this further below, when we look at Goddard's governance structure.

Characteristics of Democratic Organizations:
How Well Did Goddard Do?

This is a summary of what our group study learned about characteristics to look for in democratic organizations[10] and an overall assessment of the extent to which Goddard embodied these characteristics in the fall of 1995. We also provide some more specific observations on its governance structure.

There are many dimensions of democracy in organizations and Goddard had some democratic and some nondemocratic elements.

1. Democracy reveals itself in widely held *organizational values* such as shared power, rights, and responsibilities; a commitment to broad and active participation; wide access to information; the importance of education and learning; an open and inclusive environment; and accountability to all stakeholders of the college.

We found that many at Goddard held democratic values, and that many outside the College believed that these values found expression in Goddard's governance, management, and operations more than at most other colleges.

2. Democracy reveals itself in *organizational structures* that are used to ensure that the interests of organizational stakeholders are taken into account in decisions made in organizations.

Goddard had a variety of structures that made governance, management, and operational decisions, some of which involve a highly democratic process (community meetings, search committees, group studies, student life). The college, however, lacked many appropriately designed organizational structures that place governance fully in the hands of the college community (e.g., the structure of the board of trustees and the college executive committee were inadequate in this respect; also there were no committees to provide governance oversight and resolve disputes about governance). We discuss governance structures further below.

3. Democracy reveals itself in *organizational processes and systems* that support informed decision-making and participation in organizational structures. For example, systems that make information available to all those in the college who need it or allow and support active participation of stakeholders in budgeting are an essential part of a democratic organization.

Goddard College lacked many organizational processes and systems needed to ensure and carry out effective democratic management of the college (e.g., for policy clarification and development, resolution of conflicts, participatory budgeting).

There also was no open information policy or the information systems necessary to ensure that broad, decentralized decision-making could occur in an efficient fashion.

4. Democracy reveals itself in the *skills and knowledge* of members of the college community that help them to be more effective in carrying out their responsibilities in a democratic setting. This includes knowledge of one's role and responsibilities in a democratic society as well as specific skills, such as leadership, organizing, conflict resolution, mediation, facilitation, and conducting meetings, that make one more effective in those settings.

At Goddard we found that many individuals throughout the organization — administration, staff, faculty, students alike — needed better skills for more efficient democratic management, including the skills of participatory and collaborative leadership, and there was no explicit commitment at the college to support these forms of human development. Furthermore, neither the board nor the president provided the kind of collaborative, participatory leadership necessary to support increased and effective involvement of Goddard stakeholders in college operations, management, and governance.

In sum, Goddard College appeared democratic in its educational processes but in spite of its mission, educational philosophy, and long-standing democratic values, it was not democratic in its management and overall governance. This lack of democratic governance, as discussed earlier, detracts from the democratic nature of its educational processes.

The Board Is Key

"Authoritarian colleges which issue rules formulated by trustees, presidents and faculties are not equipped to educate for democratic living," said Royce (Tim) Pitkin, founder of Goddard College.

The group study felt that the board composition and selection process in 1995 was a major reason that the college was so far from its democratic ideal.

Figure 3 illustrates a hierarchical governance system typical of most organizations, with authority flowing down from the board, and accountability and information flowing up to the board. Although Goddard's governance may involve more sharing of authority, accountability, and information than many

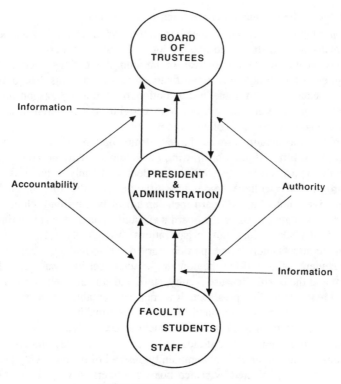

HIERARCHICAL GOVERNANCE STRUCTURE

Figure 3

organizations, the group study felt that its structure came much closer to a hierarchical model than it did to the democratic model shown in Figure 2 above.

Figure 3 illustrates how the composition and selection process of the board operated to inhibit the growth of democracy and effective participatory decision-making at the college. Goddard was organized hierarchically. At the top was the board and its executive committee, in the middle the president and his "management team" (which is also a majority of the college executive committee), and at the bottom the staff, students, and faculty. Unlike the circular flows shown earlier in Figure 2, at Goddard authority flowed from the board to the president, and from there to the rest of the organization. The source of the board's authority was unclear although there were some very general state regulations of nonprofit organizations in Vermont that might be construed as providing this authority. We found almost no oversight of nonprofit organizations by the state, and virtually nothing in Goddard's file at the Secretary of State's office that was charged with this oversight.

Accountability flowed in the opposite direction. Faculty and staff were accountable to the president, the president was accountable to the board, and the board, with eighty percent of its members self-selected (elected by the board),[11] was formally accountable to no one except to the State of Vermont, which had over sixty years shown no interest in holding the college accountable for anything, even for filling out required financial condition forms. Board members may feel accountable to some vague notion of "fiduciary responsibility" or perhaps "progressive education," but were certainly not required in any direct way to be accountable to the college community.

Finally, information flowed largely from bottom to top through the president, with little information flowing down and virtually no communication between the board and faculty, staff, and students. The only formal link between the board and the college community was through the four elected board representatives (out of a full board membership of twenty-five). None of these college representatives was on the board's executive committee at that time.

Goddard College, like most organizations, was clearly not structured in a very democratic fashion. Some participatory decision-making went on among faculty, students, and staff but the domain for such decisions was defined by the president and the board. Because faculty, staff, and students were accountable to the president while the president was not accountable to them, a power difference was created that inhibited shared decision-making.

The group study argued that this structural contradiction with democratic governance would be remedied if the board were more directly and contractually accountable to the larger college community, instead of having eighty percent of its at-large members elected by seated board members. A majority of members who would be elected by major constituencies for similar length terms was seen as an important step toward a democratic Goddard. We also discussed matters such as weighted voting and different ownership classes as methods to pair up stakeholder groups more appropriately with the specific decisions being made by the board. We felt, however, that the more important next step in extending democracy at the College was gaining the circularity of Figure 2 through more elected members of the board.

Conclusions

This summary of the findings of the group study on "Business and Democracy at Goddard" illustrates learning from the process of the study as well as from the object of the study.

Our experimentation with a task force approach to learning helped us discover an effective way to increase group as well as individual learning, and to support the process of everyone teaching everyone else in order for the group to meet its goals. This model also provided some useful ideas about how to develop a clearer faculty-student partnership relationship in learning, as opposed to a more directive "teacher" role or a more passive "resource person" role.

The group study experience, furthermore, helped us identify ways in which the democratic nature of the learning process might be compromised by the very limited power available to students in the group study to modify the college policies and regulations that govern the group study process and to hold the faculty facilitator accountable for his or her role in determining the quality of their educational experience.

We learned a considerable amount, too, about the object of our study: the ways in which the college did or did not provide equitable and effective democratic means for students and other stakeholders to participate in the governance of the college. Although we discovered that there were clearly a variety of factors that contributed to how democratic the College was— organizational structures and processes, culture, skills and knowledge—we ultimately focused our attention on the existence and nature of organizational structures to support democratic governance.

This emphasis grew out of what may be an inevitable contradiction in democratic education in traditional hierarchical organizations. The more the educational process is democratized and interest in participation in school decisions that affect the classroom bubbles up from below, the more pressure is put on an organizational system that is designed to control from the top and to have everyone ultimately accountable to the president and board. This contradiction can be handled by heavy-handed administration or charismatic leadership or the development of some form of faculty/staff/student union, but it won't go away unless there is a change to a more democratic governance structure.

The principal solution argued for here is to develop more circularity in authority and accountability, so that everyone in the system, in some sense, has authority over and is accountable to those both above and below them in the organization. At Goddard, the starting point for this was the Board of Trustees, which was self-selected and largely unaccountable to anyone, not even to owners, as for-profit boards are likely to be. When the percentage of board members who are elected by faculty, students, staff, and alumni/ae is increased, the accountability of the board becomes much clearer. Under this system, even the president, by reporting to a board that is controlled to a greater extent by faculty, students, and staff, becomes accountable to those above and below, and more likely to listen to both and to involve both in the conduct of college affairs.

Postscript: What Happened Next at Goddard?

Because our group study had an action agenda as well as a study agenda, it seems appropriate to report a few of the events that have transpired at Goddard through early 1998, some of which were due to efforts of the group study or its members.

First, the group study made a report to the board that argued for a change in the composition and selection process of board members. This was followed in the next year by a similar recommendation from the faculty representative to the board. No action was taken by the board.

Second, group study members on the governance task force (which consisted of two faculty, two students, two staff, two board members, and two upper level managers) contributed to a final report (June 1996) that made the CEC more representative and developed open information and meeting policies (informed governance). However, a recommendation for a change in the board composition and selection process was never acted upon by the task force.

Third, the president resigned in the summer of 1996.

Fourth, the advertisement in early 1997 for a new president (in the *Chronicle of Higher Education* and other publications) that was quoted at the beginning of this chapter also included the following statement:

> In the past, presidents at Goddard have resigned, due in part to conflicts with a community committed to complete participation in all important decisions affecting the college. Goddard needs a leader who is sensitive to a politically radical conception of education and governance. We need someone who is prepared to lead us through a process that questions the necessity of a President in the first place, and can, if necessary, conceptualize alternative governing methods.

Finally, a fall 1997 Future Search© exercise generated unanimous agreement among seventy representatives of the College's stakeholders (board, staff, management, faculty, students, alumni/ae, local residents, Vermont legislators, progressive education supporters, and scholars) that a major theme for Goddard's future was *Governance to Increase Participation and Accountability*.

This theme was adopted unanimously by the full group in response to goals that emerged from smaller group agreements, which included continuous growth toward becoming a democratic learning organization, shared leadership, clarification of what it means to have grassroots democracy as a principle, innovative democratic governance, self-governing community, re-examination of administrative power, and effective grassroots democracy at the college.

The forces for democratic governance, consistent with the college's commitment to democratic education, are still alive and well at Goddard College.

Endnotes

1. This paper builds on the research, discussions, and findings of a fall 1995 group study at Goddard College, entitled "Business and Democracy at Goddard College" which included Catherine Weidner, Stuart Bautz, Tokiko Nobusawa, Chandra Napora, Quayum Johnson, and me. Although I have continued to research this and related topics since that study was completed, many parts of this paper draw on discussions in that group. I am indebted to all of the members of the group but want to especially acknowledge the paper written for the class by Chandra Napora on John Dewey and democratic education. I also thank Jack Stock and Steve Schapiro for their helpful comments on earlier drafts of this paper.

2. See Freire and Macedo (1995, 377–402) for a discussion of the teacher/facilitator role in the context of democratic education.

3. Ira Shor, *When Students Have Power* (1996), provides a very rich discussion of the issues encountered, and some ways to deal with them, when one tries to democratize a college class in a traditional college setting.

4. Elshtain (1995, 80) writes:

    Democracy requires laws, constitutions, and authoritative institutions, yes, but it also depends on what might be called democratic dispositions. These include a preparedness to work with others different from oneself toward shared ends; a combination of strong convictions with a readiness to compromise in the recognition that one can't always get everything one wants; and a sense of individuality and a commitment to civic goods that are not the possession of one person or of one small group alone . . . Democracy is precisely an institutional, cultural, habitual way of acknowledging the pervasiveness of conflict and the fact that our loyalties are not one; our wills are not single; our opinions are not uniform; our ideals are not cut from the same cloth.

5. According to Igor Ansoff, quoted in Ackoff (1994, 37):

    This [stakeholder] theory maintains that the objectives of the firm should be derived from balancing the conflicting claims of the various "stakeholders" in the firm: managers, workers, stockholders, suppliers, vendors. The firm has a responsibility to all of these and must configure its objectives so as to give each a measure of satisfaction. Profit which is a return on investment to the stockholder is one of such satisfactions, but it does not receive special predominance in the objective structure.

6. Dakota Butterfield, a consultant on democratic organizations from Cambridge, MA who met with our group study, was very helpful in our understanding of organizational decisions and democratic organizations.

7. John Dewey takes this a step further. For him the role of individuals and

groups in a democracy must meet the following conditions:
> From the standpoint of the individual, it consists in having a responsible share according to capacity in forming and directing the activities of the groups to which one belongs and in participating according to need in the values which the groups sustain. From the standpoint of the groups, it demands liberation of the potentialities of members of a group in harmony with the interests and goods which are common. Since every individual is a member of many groups, this specification cannot be fulfilled except when different groups interact flexibly and fully in connection with other groups. (quoted in Boisvert 1998, 55–56)

8. In determining who should be on the board, Carver says that
> only responsible stewardship can justify a board's considerable authority. Board members who do not choose to accept this breadth of responsibility should resign. . . . Being warm, being willing to attend meetings, being inclined to donate money, and being interested in the organizational subject matter do not constitute responsible board membership. These characteristics are desirable but far from sufficient." (Carver 1990, 133–4).

In the *Chronicle of Higher Education* (December 8, 1995, B1–2), Roberto Haro, reporting on interviews with more than 100 college and university trustees from 1992 through 1994, wrote that
> At private institutions, trustees are often selected because they have the same educational, business, or social background as other members of the board — and because they are wealthy or have access to affluent potential donors. In such cases, board members tend to "clone" themselves and set policies that limit the number of women and members of minority groups on the boards, some frustrated trustees (including white males) told me." He also observed that "most [trustees] had met with students only rarely and felt insulated from them by the institutions's president and senior staff members."

9. Marty Zinn and Pete Hill, consultants on democratic organizations from Glouster, Ohio who taught democratic management in the Goddard Business Institute, were especially helpful in developing this understanding of the role and structure of the board in a democratic organization.

10. For additional discussion of the characteristics of democratic organizations see Ackoff (1994), Bernstein (1976) and McLagan (1995).

11. The full board has 25 members, 20 of whom were elected at large by seated trustees and serve five-year terms. They represent themselves; some are familiar with Goddard because they are former students. Of the remaining five, two were elected from a faculty of 70 and an administrative staff of 50 to serve three-year terms; two students were elected for one-year terms, one

by an on-campus student body of 180 and one by an off-campus student body of 400; and, finally, one representative was elected by an alumni/ae body of 8000 (of which maybe 100 are active) for a one-year term.

References

Ackoff, Russell. 1994. *The Democratic Corporation.* New York: Oxford University Press.

Adams, Frank T. and Gary B. Hansen. 1992. *Putting Democracy to Work.* San Francisco, CA: Berrett-Koehler.

Bachrach, Peter and Aryeh Botwinick. 1992. *Power and Empowerment: A Radical Theory of Participatory Democracy.* Philadelphia: Temple University Press.

Belasco, James and Ralph Stayer. 1993. *Flight of the Buffalo: Soaring to Excellence, Learning to Let Employees Lead.* New York: Warner Books.

Bernstein, Paul. 1976. *Workplace Democratization: Its Internal Dynamics.* Kent, Ohio: Kent State University Press.

Birnbaum, R. 1992. *How Academic Leadership Works: Understanding Success and Failure in the College Presidency.* San Francisco: Jossey-Bass.

Blair, Margaret. 1995. *Ownership and Control: Rethinking Corporate Governance for the 21st Century.* Washington, DC: Brookings Institute.

Block, Peter. 1993. *Stewardship.* San Francisco: Berrett-Koehler.

Boisvert, Raymond. 1998. *John Dewey: Rethinking Our Time.* Albany, New York: State University of New York Press.

Campbell, Clyde M., ed. 1952. *Practical Applications of Democratic Administration.* New York: Harper & Brothers.

Carver, John. 1990. *Boards That Make a Difference.* San Francisco: Jossey-Bass.

Chapman, Judith, Isak Froumin, and David Aspin, eds. 1995. *Creating and Managing the Democratic School.* London: Falmer Press.

Elshtain, Jean Bethke. 1995. *Democracy on Trial.* New York: Basic Books.

Freire, Paulo and Donald Macedo. 1995. "A Dialogue: Culture, Language, and Race," *Harvard Educational Review* 65 (3): 377–402.

Glickman, Carl. 1993. *Renewing America's Schools: A Guide for School-Based Action.* San Francisco: Jossey-Bass.

———. 1998. *Revolutionizing America's Schools.* San Francisco: Jossey-Bass.

Lappé, Frances Moore and Paul Martin DuBois. 1994. *The Quickening of America.* San Francisco, Jossey-Bass.

Manz, Charles C. 1993. *Businesses Without Bosses.* New York: John Wiley.

McLagan, Patricia and Christo Nel. 1995. *The Age of Participation: New Governance for the Workplace and the World.* San Francisco: Berrett-Koehler.

Neill, A. 1968. *Summerhill.* Harmondsworth: Penguin.

Schuster, J.H. and L. H. Miller, eds. 1989. *Governing Tomorrow's Campus.* New York: MacMillan.

Shor, Ira. 1996. *When Students Have Power: Negotiating Authority in a Critical Pedagogy.* Chicago: University of Chicago Press.

Semler, Ricardo. 1989. "Managing Without Managers." *Harvard Business Review* (Sept/Oct, 76–84).

Slater, Phillip. 1991. *A Dream Deferred*. Boston: Beacon Press.
Tead, Ordway. 1945. *Democratic Administration*. New York: Association Press.
Westbrook, R.B. 1991. *John Dewey and American Democracy*. Ithaca, New York: Cornell University Press.

Part Three

Conclusion

TWELVE

The Lessons of Practice:
Education for Democracy Revisited

Steven A. Schapiro

What conclusions and lessons about the practice and theory of higher education for democracy can be drawn from the experiments in progressive pedagogy that have been described in the preceding chapters? What, if any, responses do they offer to the challenges to democratic education today that were posed in this book's introduction, concerning: (a) how to educate for democratic citizenship, (b) how to build learning communities among diverse groups of learners, (c) how to help students to affirm and clarify both their individual identities and their commitment to the common good, (d) how to engage students in a genuine search for new solutions to social, economic, environmental, and political problems, (e) how to affirm new epistemologies and ways of knowing while maintaining consistent and common academic standards? These are not easy questions, and I would not suggest for a moment that the experiments describe here fully answer them, but in trying to resolve the specific and "nuts-and-bolts" questions or problems that each experiment poses for itself, they shed much light on these bigger questions as well. Each chapter contains a wealth of specific strategies, practices, and lessons most relevant to the particular content and process involved, and most helpful to others looking for specific models of practice. I won't be trying to summarize all of that here, but in moving from these concrete educational experiments back to the more general level of principles and theories, we ground our answers in the day-to-day work and day-to-day struggles in which these experiments in democratic education were conducted. Taken together, these experiments and the lessons we can draw from them also provide ample evidence for how the concept of education for democracy can once again bring together those two necessarily interrelated themes within progressive education: individual student-centered development, and education for social justice and social reconstruction. In so doing, they also provide examples of a variety of ways in which the principles and practices of critical, feminist, and multicultural pedagogies and of participatory democracy are being applied to and integrated with the ends and means of the long-standing traditions of progressive education.

A useful way to explore some of the responses to these challenges will be to examine the lessons of practice in terms of four elements of any educational endeavor that were outlined in the introduction: curricular content (what is being studied); instructional process (the intentional process of teaching and learning); interpersonal dynamics (the relations among participants in the learning process); and organizational structure and policies (how decisions are made and who makes them).

Not surprisingly, since this is a book written by faculty who are reflecting on their experiences in the classroom and in mentoring individual students, most of the "lessons" learned focus on content and process and not on relations and organizational structures. However, I think it would be a mistake to therefore discount the importance for democratic education of those latter two dimensions. Rather, they serve as a foundation or backdrop within which particular experiments in teaching for democracy can be conducted. The nature of that foundation has a significant impact on how successful those experiments can be.

Curricular Content

Several lessons can be drawn in regard to curricular content. In his discussion of the key elements of teacher education for democratic teachers, Bergstrom presents the expanded notion of the roles of the teacher upon which Goddard's teacher education is based, roles that include that of citizen and colleague. This puts the content of education for *democratic citizenship at the core of the curriculum.* In modeling for our students *how to be engaged and active participants in our communities,* in working collaboratively and democratically with our school colleagues, and in asking future teachers to explore how they can integrate these roles into their own lives, both personally and professionally, and how they can learn *the skills needed for active listening, democratic decision-making and constructive conflict resolution,* Goddard's teacher education program clearly addresses the challenge of education for democratic citizenship. That education must clearly begin with our teacher educators, who can model and teach these skills and attitudes to our future teachers, who can in turn pass these on to their students. In other words, we must, at all levels of the educational process, practice what we preach. Students learn from what we do, not from what we say. Democratic citizenship is not a spectator sport and students need to see it in action if they are to learn how to practice it themselves. The skills and knowledge needed for democratic citizenship should therefore be included in any teacher education curriculum.

Jelly makes clear, in both theory and practice, the importance of *helping students to explore, from both directions, the connections between their individual problems and concerns and the social context in which they are engaged,* be it a small study group, a school, a family, or a society in general. In a democratic society, we need to learn how to take the needs of our fellow citizens into account and also to recognize how our fate is so intertwined with others, how our self-development depends on the context in which we live. Therefore, whether the educational focus is on the personal and individual level, or the social/institutional/political level, the democratic educator needs to make sure that the content that is studied examines the relationship between those two dimensions. An inquiry may begin with student questions and concerns in either of those dimensions, but it is our responsibility as democratic educators to raise questions and problems that can help students to explore those connections. In my own discussion of anti-sexist education for men, I explain how I dealt with this issue in helping men to see the connections between the limits they may experience in regard to male gender roles and personality stereotypes and the institutional and cultural dynamics of sexism and heterosexism in which those roles and stereotypes are embedded. Similarly, Vermilya explains that in order for such writing to be as empowering and liberating as it can be, it must go "from catharsis to universality." It must help students to see their own personal stories in historical and social context, so that they can come to understand (and potentially overcome) both their internalized oppression and the externalized structures that enforce that oppression. So, to borrow an old slogan from the women's liberation movement, democratic education must help people to see how the personal is political, and how the political is personal. Helping students to see their own experience in social context can also help them to recognize the relationship between their own individual identity and the common good, a society that can support and affirm the diversity of all of its members.

Vermilya also provides a powerful argument for including in the curriculum *students' stories about their lives*, demonstrating the use of *memoir and autobiography* in helping those from marginalized social groups (those whose experiences are usually not included in the curriculum) to find voice, identity and empowerment. This "identity pedagogy" as she calls it, can give such students a firm and secure place from which to enter into dialogue with others on an equal level. Because students themselves are the "experts" in regard to this content, the use of autobiography turns upside down notions of authority and expertise in the classroom, and helps students to develop trust and confidence in their own perceptions and insights. The role of the teacher in this process, however, is not only to help students to express themselves, but also to help those students to place their personal stories in the broader historical, social, and political context.

Several other chapters provide examples and rationales for *making students' current experience (in their classrooms, schools, dormitories, relationships, families, etc.) the content of the curriculum, as the object of critical analysis, reflection, and problem-solving.* The Lyn-Pilusos, for example, describe how they make their own interactions between their students and themselves as teacher-authorities, the educational policies and structures that provide the context for their teaching, and the group dynamics in their classes all objects of critical analysis and reflection, thus helping students to question and deconstruct the structures, assumptions, and beliefs that underlie these interactions. This process can help students to problematize all of these situations and in the process to recognize that all such structures and forms of interaction are not givens, but social-historical creations that people made and that people can change. Similarly, both Schramm and Jelly describe, respectively, how their group studies took on some of the structures and processes of Goddard College, as an organization and as a progressive educational institution, critically analyzing the match between the college's professed ideals and its current realities, and developing proposals for how it could move from here to there. In my piece on anti-sexist education with men, I also describe how to make the interpersonal and group dynamics within a study, and one's relationships with women, men, fathers, mothers, etc. outside the group the objects of study and reflection. Kesson does the same in regard to students' spiritual practices, and Aquino in regard to their creative process. In *building content around students' current experiences, concerns and needs*, all of these examples provide evidence of how to find within those experiences the generative themes that can engage students in meaningful study about things that they care about, and in the process help them to develop their critical consciousness in regard to such issues. These approaches make education much more than a charade or a simulation game, but a real process of solving real problems in living.

The last two chapters mentioned (those by Kesson and Aquino) also provide examples of how we need to *reconceptualize our notions about appropriate boundaries of disciplinary knowledge, of appropriate subject matter for the college classroom, and therefore about how knowledge is created or discovered.* Kesson's discussion of spirituality and education describes how, in this postmodern era, we can incorporate nonrational, nonlinear, spiritual aims into the educational process by helping students to study their own spiritual practices and experiences, while Aquino's description of Goddard's new program in interdisciplinary art is responding to the need to provide frameworks and structures for art education that fit the ways of thinking and creating of students and artists, rather than forcing them to fit themselves into predetermined and outmoded disciplines and categories. This argument can and should be made in regard to all areas of study, not just the arts.

In making room within the curriculum for spiritual experience that may stand outside of organized religions and for new ways of thinking about art and creativity that go beyond the traditional institutional constraints, these exciting new practices are responding to students' search for meaning, for transcendent experiences in their education and in their lives, and for ways of experiencing and understanding the world that lie outside of the mass-media global consumerist society that so dominates our mass culture and our mass educational institutions. By bringing such ways of thinking and knowing into the academy, we can help to bring back the democratization of art-making and of meaning-making, create room for values that are removed from consumerist materialism, begin to open some cracks in the hegemony of our dominant cultural forms and ways of knowing, and allow some fresh, subversive, and potentially revolutionary thinking, learning, and creating to go on.

As we help students learn to critique and potentially reconstruct our social, political, and educational institutions, we also need, in the service of democracy, to be careful to *expose students to a variety of points of view in regard to the issues at hand, and not just the current or most popular critique and perspective.* As Glickman reminds us in his chapter, democracy requires that students learn how to choose their beliefs from a variety of alternatives and to engage with others in civil discourse about those beliefs. Progressive educators with particular social change goals in mind, like traditional educators with strong views of their own, have a special responsibility to include in the curriculum content and critical perspectives from a wide variety of points of view. To do otherwise is to risk turning students into parrots of the latest politically correct ideology, not critical thinkers with minds of their own.

Instructional Processes

One of the precepts underlying a progressive approach to education is that students learn as much, if not more, from the how—the process of learning, the hidden curriculum of classrooms and schools—as they do from the what—the explicit curricular content. The learning process is therefore of importance not only for how well it does or doesn't help students to learn a particular content, but for the lessons it imparts in and of itself along the way. Within the experiments described above are a number of instructional processes of particular relevance to the purposes and challenges of education for democracy that we have been discussing.

Within the process of *negotiating the curriculum* of a group study, as described in most detail above by Jelly and Schramm, as students and teachers express their own questions about the issues at hand and their preferred ways of studying, they are able to *learn and practice many of the skills needed for democratic group living and citizenship.* As they learn to assert their own needs, listen carefully to others, find common ground, compromise, and build consensus, students learn invaluable lessons about how to live and work collaboratively and democratically with others, and about the never-ending challenge of finding the best balance of individual and communal desires. When the curriculum negotiation process works well it can provide a way to build learning communities out of diverse groups of individuals by making sure that each individual voice is heard and honored and the common ground among those individuals is identified and cultivated.

In Mitchell's description of her work in engaging students with the study of literature, in Kesson's work on spirituality in education, in Vermilya's work on memoir and autobiography, in mine on men and masculinity, and in Glickman's piece on "Judy and the Dance" we see the importance placed, as an instructional process, on *student learning that starts from their own immediate, primary and unmediated experience of the world*—be it the sounds and rhythms of a poem, visceral memories of abuse, the pain of a wounded relationship with one's father, early experiences in school, or the sense of connection to the universe that is derived from one's spiritual practices. Through this democratic approach to the grounding learning in each student's unique individual experience, we can then help students to become active learners and constructors of knowledge, not passive receivers of knowledge who are waiting to be entertained or put to sleep. From that basis, students can move on to find common ground with others' experiences and then *make sense of that experience through the study of the relevant theoretical, historical, or literary analyses.* As Glickman cautions us, however, one of the challenges here is in how to help apply that experience to the intellectual and academic goals of the curriculum. And as Dewey himself pointed out time and again, all experience is not equally educative; it is in the reflection on and reconstruction of experience that our learning comes. Or as Kolb more recently put it, "knowledge is the result of the transaction between social knowledge and personal knowledge" (1984, 36) a concept that Mitchell explains in these words in her chapter in this volume:

> Social knowledge is here defined as a socially and culturally transmitted network of comprehensions, and personal knowledge as our apprehensions and socially acquired means of explaining and interpreting those apprehensions. Social knowledge makes personal knowledge possible. At the same time, personal knowledge, based in our powers of apprehension, enables us to maintain our individuality. (144)

Another instructional practice common to several of the experiments that are described is what, following Freire, we have called *problem-posing or problematizing* education. This approach involves *posing back to students as problems to be solved—not as given and unchangeable facets of social reality—concerns and limits that they are experiencing,* be it the constraints of the male gender role, the hesitation of some women to speak out in a large group, the lack of democracy within a supposedly democratic organization, or the oppressive realities of heterosexist culture as experienced by lesbians and gay men. By helping people to envision and articulate a more ideal reality in which those limits could be overcome, in analyzing the gaps between the current reality and that vision, and in thinking about steps to take to begin to move from here to there, problematizing is an essential instructional practice for a pedagogy aimed at helping people learn how to engage in democratic social reconstruction. And if those problems lie within the dynamics of a group itself, or draw people into collaborative social action within the wider community, this process can help students gain direct experience in a democratic and collaborative process of social reconstruction.

This problem-posing process is based in an *inquiry-directed approach* to learning in which we don't assume that we as teachers and professors have the answers already figured out, but we instead engage with our students in a collaborative search for new knowledge and new meaning. Jelly's, Schramm's, the Lyn-Pilusos', Kesson's, and my own descriptions of our group studies provide examples of this group inquiry approach in action, exploring in real and genuine ways questions about, for example, the nature of human relationships, the meaning of democracy in education, the roots of classroom interactions, and the nature of our spiritual experiences. This sort of inquiry, where we don't know where we will end up, also requires a process of assessment and evaluation that is not based on standardized examinations, but on students' own reflections on and construction of their most significant learnings. As explained earlier, students must also demonstrate through portfolios and public performances their mastery of the general degree criteria, but there can be no standardization in regard to what students get out of each learning experience. It is through this sort of inquiry-directed learning process and reflective self-assessment that students learn how to take charge of their own learning process and how to be self-directed lifelong learners.

Although some approaches stop with problem analysis and a clearer understanding of the social realities in which we are submerged, others move on to the next step of *praxis—action to solve those problems, followed by reflection, followed by more action in response.* The experiments described above by me, Vermilya, and Jelly all take that next step, which can result not only in constructive change but also in a deeper understanding of the issues with which we are dealing, be it men's violence against women, Goddard's educational structures, or the dynamics of our own interpersonal relationships. At times, it is only in trying to change something that we can come to a deeper understanding of it. Or as Freire puts it, it is in the process of acting collaboratively to analyze and transform our social reality that we are fulfilling our "vocation of becoming more fully human." (1970, 28) The "identity peda-gogy" described by Vermilya, which uses memoir and autobiography to help marginalized students find voice and power, can itself be characterized as a form of praxis, as people rename and reclaim their own experience. For those who have internalized the negative images that the dominant society holds of them, those who have been silenced and rendered invisible, the very process of telling their stories in their own authentic voices is itself an act of liberation and transformation, an act that can in turn create an environment in which others feel freer to speak out, an environment in which those from more privileged groups can learn from the pain of those who have been oppressed. In such a context, we can begin to create learning communities in which the full diversity of its membership can participate as full and equal members.

The broader framework for anti-oppression education that I describe in the context of my work on anti-sexist pedagogy for men can provide a way of thinking about the sorts of learning environments we need to create in order to make such transformative learning possible for all learners. By providing learning environments that are, in turn, confirming, contradicting, creating, and continuing, we can provide support for the developmental change process that includes the phases of unfreezing, changing, and refreezing. And in being part of a learning environment that is at once supportive and challenging and is built on collaborative learning and on norms of honest and genuine communication, students can gain direct experience of the kinds of learning communities that they can go on to recreate in their own contexts.

Kesson's description of the elements of what she calls a *"postmodern spiritual pedagogy"* demonstrates how we can integrate such nonrationale experiences into the classroom, *honoring students' spiritual quests and their intuitive, subjective ways of knowing, while at the same time helping them to subject their beliefs and practices to critical analysis and deconstruction,* thus bringing them closer to a direct and unmediated experience of these other realms of knowing.

Aquino's discussion of the *pedagogy of reciprocity* is the clearest description in the book of Goddard's student-centered, dialogical approach to teaching and learning within the individualized short-residency programs for adult learners. Although he situates this discussion within the new MFA program in interdisciplinary art, the reciprocal process he describes of *individualized study planning* is at the core of Goddard's approach to working with adult learners. As Aquino describes it, this process puts the student at the center, not the teacher or any required curricular content. *In dialogue with her or his faculty advisor, students set their own learning goals, the activities and resources they will use in order to meet those goals, and their process for assessment and evaluation.* The process begins with each learner's questions, passions, and needs. Through a process of dialogue, faculty mentors help students to connect those questions and issues to wider theoretical, political, and practical concerns, and ultimately to meeting the college's degree criteria in their own unique ways. Underlying this process is once again an inquiry-directed and problem-focused approach to learning that is by nature interdisciplinary or transdisciplinary. The focus is not on mastering a particular set of materials or on learning the tools of a particular discipline (although both of those objectives may come into play), but on answering questions and solving problems, for which many disciplines and all kinds of content may be relevant. As the faculty advisor helps students to discover and articulate their questions and needs and to find their own answers and meanings, the advisor serves not as an expert or leader (although their expertise and their leadership may sometimes be called for), but primarily as a helpmate who walks beside the student on his or her learning journey.

Interpersonal Dynamics

This sort of reciprocal democratic relationship between teachers and students, in which each is learning from and with the other, is fundamental to both the individual and the group study instructional processes described above. It is within the safety and the challenge of such relationships that students can learn to become self-directed and collaborative learners. Within such relationships, teacher/advisors can serve as both mirrors and windows, reflecting back to students their own questions, concerns, and emerging knowledge, while also opening windows on new perspectives and new resources. These teacher-student relationships develop within an overall context of democratic egalitarian social relations, in which everyone—teachers, students, staff, and administrators alike—is addressed on a first-name basis, with no titles used, and it is assumed that everyone has something to learn from everyone else.

Faculty-student and student-student relationships are ideally conducted not on the basis of transmission of information or of argument and debate, but rather on the basis of dialogue, which, in Freire's words, "As a democratic relationship...is the opportunity available to me to open up to the thinking of others, and thereby not wither away in isolation. (1994, 119). This can sometimes be a challenging and unsettling role for teachers to take on, for in entering such a dialogue, we open ourselves to the possibility of being changed through those interactions. As bell hooks has put it,

> When education is the practice of freedom, students are not the only ones who are asked to share, to confess. Engaged pedagogy does not seek simply to empower students. Any classroom that employs a holistic model of learning will also be a place where teachers grow, and are empowered in the process. That empowerment cannot happen if we refuse to be vulnerable while asking students to take risks. (1994, 21).

However, the personal and democratic nature of this sort of teacher-student interaction brings a special responsibility to remember that these relationships exist for the students' learning and growth, not for our own. We still hold some power and authority in these relationships (however much we may try to share it and give it away) and we must be careful not to misuse it. As Glickman points out in his chapter above, the personal relations of the learning process must not take a back seat to the learning and knowledge goals for which the relationship exists. Although a close teacher-student relationship is one of the elements that can help make for powerful and transformative student-centered learning, this ethos also brings with it the responsibility to be careful about keeping clear boundaries between our personal and professional roles, our needs and those of our students.

Organizational Structures and Processes

Because it focuses more on pedagogy and the process of learning and teaching than on governance and the process of organizational decision-making, this book does not deal in much depth with structural dynamics beyond the level of the classroom and the student-teacher relationship. Schramm, in his chapter, however, makes a powerful argument (drawing on a wide body of literature on this issue, including work by Lappé and Dubois, Elshtain, Glickman, Tead, Block, and Bachrach) that education for democracy needs to include the structural and organizational context as well; that the presence or lack of democracy within the organization of a school or college can have a deep impact on the efficacy of efforts to educate for democracy. The quotes he includes from Lappé and DuBois and Elshtain stress that democracy is not so much what we have but what we do; it is a culture and a spirit, not just a set of rules for how to make decisions. "Democracy—whether it works or not—depends on how each of us lives our public life...[It] is not just about changing the rules; it's about changing the culture--our attitudes, values and expectations" (Lappé 1994, 229). Or, as Elshtain puts it, "democracy is not simply a set of procedures or a constitution, but an ethos, a spirit, a way of responding, and a way of conducting oneself" (1995, 80).

If that spirit does not pervade all areas of a school or college, then the potential of education for democracy is limited. If faculty are accountable only to their superiors and not in any sense to their students, the ideal of a reciprocal relationship between teachers and students can be poisoned and undermined. If students have no real say over college policies and college leadership and few opportunities for genuine participation in college decision-making beyond their own classrooms and residence halls (except for limited representation on the board of trustees and on some committees), then their opportunities for learning through the process of real democratic participation are severely limited. If a college administration is accountable not to the staff, students, and faculty whom it serves but to a predominantly self-selecting board of trustees, then a college is not a democratic organization and the danger exists that a small group of people can lead it in a direction that its primary stakeholders oppose. If faculty, staff, and administrators do not carry out their own internal relationships and decision-making on the basis of democratic values, principles, and practices, can their work with students fully embody that spirit? Schramm explains the extent to which Goddard may suffer from all of these limitations, offers suggestions for how to move Goddard and other colleges in a more democratic direction (including some far-reaching and innovative suggestions for how to restructure the board of trustees), and explains some small proposals that have been made in order to move in that direction.

Although his argument leaves unanswered many questions about the appropriate balance of power and authority among a board, administration, faculty, staff, and students (questions beyond the scope of the group study project that he describes), it also raises many important questions about the relationship between a pedagogy for democracy and the context in which it is carried out. One thing that seems quite clear, however, is that the more opportunity students have to participate in genuine democratic decision-making, the more they will learn how to be constructive democratic citizens. The more that students are able to live democracy, and to see it lived by those around them, the more they will be able to learn how to create more democratic communities and institutions. If Goddard and other schools interested in educating for democracy are to be as effective as possible in working toward that end, they need to continue to find new and innovative ways of democratically balancing the needs of their various stakeholder groups, and of carrying their missions forward while also finding ways to survive, both financially and politically. If, in order to survive, they have to sacrifice those principles upon which they were founded, then survival may not be worth its price.

These lessons of practice, as summarized here, do not do justice to the complexity, detail, and subtlety of the experiments and practices from which they are drawn, and they reflect only a small sample of the kinds of experiments in progressive pedagogy going on today at this college and in other institutions of higher education. Not included, for instance, were any examples of the community-action and community-change projects based in local communities that are fundamental to any education for democratic citizenship (perhaps because those doing such work were too busy to stop and write about it). These lessons, then, are not meant as an exhaustive set of guidelines for democratic education, but as a source of ideas and inspiration for those who would like to reclaim higher education's mission of education for democracy and to do more to make that mission a reality. And as limited in scope as these lessons are, if such practices became more widely used, then our colleges and universities will be doing much more to meet the challenges to democracy that our society is facing.

The experiments in progressive pedagogy that are described in this volume draw on many of the basic and long-standing precepts of progressive education, such as problem-focused, student-centered, and inquiry-directed learning, and apply those approaches to new contexts and new issues, such as oppression, diversity, and alternative ways of knowing. In so doing, they demonstrate new ways of integrating those two sometimes diverging strands of the progressive education movement—student-centered personal development and problem-centered social reconstruction—and show us how liberation from oppression, social reconstruction, and the development of new ways of knowing all involve processes that are both individual and social, both personal and political.

It is educators like those represented in this volume who continue to experiment with and develop new forms of education for democracy and in the process make possible transformative and liberatory learning experiences for their students. Those forms of learning must continue to evolve in response to the new and changing challenges that we will face in the future. Like democracy itself, progressive education for democracy is an unfinished project that needs to continually reinvent itself in response to the needs of those it serves. Our society needs places such as Goddard where this sort of experimentation can go on. To once again quote Boyd Bode's statement some forty years ago marking the demise of the Progressive Education Association: "If democracy is here to stay, then the spirit of progressive education can never become obsolete. We may discard the name but we can never surrender the vision upon which it is based" (in Graham, 1967, 145). Thus far, Goddard College has helped to keep that vision and that spirit alive, as I think the essays collected in this volume can attest. If our society is to fulfill its democratic promise, then this work of education for democracy must become much more widespread.

References

Bachrach, Peter and Aryeh Botwinick. 1992. *Power and Empowerment: A Radical Theory of Participatory Democracy.* Philadelphia: Temple University Press.

Block, Peter. 1993. *Stewardship.* San Francisco: Berrett-Koehler.

Elshtain, Jean Bethke. 1995. *Democracy on Trial.* New York: Basic Books.

Freire, P. 1970 *Pedagogy of the Oppressed.* New York: Continuum.

————.1994 *Pedagogy of Hope.* New York: Continuum.

Glickman, Carl. (1993). *Renewing America's Schools: A Guide for School-Based Action.* San Francisco: Jossey-Bass.

————.1998. *Revolutionizing America's Schools.* San Francisco: Jossey-Bass.

Graham, P.A. 1967. *Progressive Education From Arcady to Academe: A History of the Progressive Education Association, 1919–1955.* New York: Teachers College Press.

hooks, b. (1994). *Teaching to Transgress: Education as the Practice of Freedom.* New York: Routledge.

Kolb, David. 1984. *Experiential Learning: Experience as the Source of Learning and Development.* Englewood Cliffs, New Jersey: Prentice-Hall.

Lappé, Frances Moore and Paul Martin DuBois. 1994. *The Quickening of America.* San Francisco: Jossey-Bass.

Tead, Ordway. 1945. *Democratic Administration.* New York: Association Press.

NOTES ON THE EDITOR AND THE CONTRIBUTORS

The editor:
Steven A. Schapiro is a faculty member in education and psychology at Goddard, where he has previously held positions of Dean for Academic Affairs and Director of Teacher Education, and where he founded and directed the Goddard Institute on Teaching and Learning. Previously, he was a high school teacher and counselor. He is interested in the integration of humanistic, critical, and democratic approaches to teaching and leadership, especially in regard to issues of equity and diversity. He is a contributing author to *Teaching for Diversity and Social Justice: A Trainer's Guide* (1997), and is a member of the board of directors of the Folk and People's Education Association of America.

The contributors:
Eduardo Aquino is presently teaching interdisciplinary arts at Goddard College and environmental design at the University of Manitoba's School of Architecture in Winnipeg. As an artist he has realized several installations of ephemeral character in Brazil, Europe, the United States and Canada that question the viewer's perception through the use of mirrors, projections, computerized systems, and elements commonly found in the urban environment.

Kenneth L Bergstrom is a faculty member in teacher education at Goddard College. Previously, he was a teacher in Vermont's classrooms at the elementary, middle, and secondary levels. His interests include the philosophy of education, the moral dimensions of teaching, middle level education, mentoring of beginning teachers, teacher lore, and gender issues. He is a contributing author to *Integrated Studies in the Middle Grades: Dancing Through Walls* and *Whole Learning in the Middle School: Evolution and Transition.*

Carl D. Glickman holds the career University Professorship of Education at the University of Georgia. He has established several long-term school renewal collaborations, including the League of Professional Schools. His area of interest is the relationships among education, democracy, and school renewal. Books he has published include *Renewing America's Schools: A Blueprint for School-Based Action* (1994) and *Revolutionizing America's Schools* (1998).

Katherine L. Jelly, who is now Director of the Master of Education Program at Vermont College of Norwich University, taught for eight years in education and related areas at Goddard College. She has also taught English in both alternative and traditional high schools and has been involved in local school improvement efforts. Her research interests and teaching specialities include the areas of school reform, the art of teaching, professional development, moral education, human relations, and social and political issues in education.

Kathleen Kesson is on the education faculty at Goddard and is also a Research Associate Professor at the University of Vermont, where she directs the John Dewey Project on Progressive Education, a policy institute. Her book (co-edited with Jim Henderson) entitled *Curriculum Leadership for a Strong Democracy* will be published this year. She has published several journal articles and book chapters on the connections between spirituality and education.

Geraldine and Gus Lyn-Piluso are both on the education faculty at Goddard, in the Off-Campus Program in Education and Teaching, and they also teach early childhood education at Seneca College in Toronto. They are interested in the political implications of teaching and parenting and the roles communities, families, and domestic values play in education. Their article "Challenging Popular Wisdom: What Families Can Do," was published in a recent book called *Deschooling our Lives*, edited by Matt Hern.

Nora Mitchell has taught at Goddard since 1991, and has directed the Master of Fine Arts in Writing Program there from 1993 to 1998. She has published two collections of poetry, *Your Skin is a Country* (1988) and *Proofreading the Histories* (1996). Her poems have appeared in a range of journals, including *Calyx, College English, Hawaii Review, Hurricane Alice, Ploughshares, Radical America,* and *Sojourner,* among others.

Richard Schramm has taught economics, finance, and community and business development for over thirty years at Columbia, Cornell, Tufts, MIT, the University of Vermont and, since 1991, at Goddard College. His field of work is community economic development with a special interest in businesses, such as cooperative enterprises, that have a social as well as financial mission, and their role in community development. He has worked with dozens of worker and consumer cooperatives and community development organizations.

Shelley Vermilya is a faculty member in the Off-Campus Individualized BA and MA Programs at Goddard, where she previously held the position of director of Community Life and also teaches courses in women's studies and queer studies in the campus undergraduate program. She is working on a memoir titled, *Baby, Are You a Little Queer?*.

Back row: (left to right): Kathleen   Kesson, Gus Lyn-Piluso, Steven Schapiro,
Ken Bergstrom, Richard Schramm, Katherine Jelly

Front row: (left to right): Geraldine Lyn-Piluso, Shelley Vermilya (with Dashell
Vermilya Tredeau), Eduardo Aquino, Nora Mitchell.

(Missing: Carl Glickman)

Questions about the
Purpose(s) of Colleges
and Universities

Norm Denzin,

Josef Progler,

Joe L. Kincheloe,

Shirley R. Steinberg,

General Editors

What are the purposes of higher education? When undergraduates 'declare their majors,' they agree to enter into a world defined by the parameters of a particular academic discourse—a discipline. But who decides those parameters? How do they come about? What are the discussions and proposed outcomes of disciplined inquiry? What should an undergraduate know to be considered educated in a discipline? How does the disciplinary knowledge base inform its pedagogy? Why are there different disciplines? When has a discipline 'run its course'? Where do new disciplines come from? Where do old ones go? How does a discipline produce its knowledge? What are the meanings and purposes of disciplinary research and teaching? What are the key questions of disciplined inquiry? What questions are taboo within a discipline? What can the disciplines learn from one another? What might they not want to learn and why?

Once we begin asking these kinds of questions, positionality becomes a key issue. One reason why there aren't many books on the meaning and purpose of higher education is that once such questions are opened for discussion, one's subjectivity becomes an issue with respect to the presumed objective stances of Western higher education. Academics don't have positions because positions are 'biased,' 'subjective,' 'slanted,' and therefore somehow invalid. So the first thing to do is to provide a sense—however broad and general—of what kinds of positionalities will inform the books and chapters on the above questions. Certainly the questions themselves, and any others we might ask, are already suggesting a particular 'bent,' but as the series takes shape, the authors we engage will no doubt have positions on these questions.

From the stance of interdisciplinary, multidisciplinary, or transdisciplinary practitioners, will the chapters and books we solicit solidify disciplinary discourses, or liquefy them? Depending on who is asked, interdisciplinary inquiry is either a polite collaboration among scholars firmly situated in their own particular discourses, or it is a blurring of the restrictive parameters that define the very notion of disciplinary discourse. So will the series have a stance on the meaning and purpose of interdisciplinary inquiry and teaching? This can possibly be finessed by attracted thinkers from disciplines that are already multicisciplinary, e.g., the various kinds of 'studies' programs (Women's, Islamic, American, Cultural, etc.), or the hybrid disciplines like Ethnomusicology (Musicology, Folklore, Anthropology). But by including people from these fields (areas? disciplines?) in our series, we are already taking a stand on disciplined inquiry. A question on the comprehensive exam for the Columbia University Ethnomusicology Program was to defend Ethnomusicology as a 'field' or a 'discipline.' One's answer determined one's future, at least to the extent that the gatekeepers had a say in such matters. So, in the end, what we are proposing will no doubt involve political struggles.

For additional information about this series or for the submission of manuscripts, please contact Joe L. Kincheloe, 637 West Foster Avenue, State College, PA, 16801. To order other books in this series, please contact our Customer Service Department at: (800) 770-LANG (within the U.S.), (212) 647-7706 (outside the U.S.), (212) 647-7707 FAX, or browse online by series at: www.peterlang.com.